How the
Mass
Media
Really
Work

OTHER BOOKS OF INTEREST FROM MARQUETTE BOOKS

Mitchell Land and Bill W. Hornaday, *Contemporary Media Ethics: A Practical Guide for Students, Scholars and Professionals in a Global World* (2014). ISBN: 978-0-9833476-2-0 (paperback)

Ralph D. Berenger (ed.), *Social Media Go to War: Rage, Rebellion and Revolution in the Age of Twitter* (2013). ISBN: 978-0-9833476-7-5 (paperback)

Ann Bomberger and Vesta Silva, *Raise Your Voice: Composing Written and Spoken Arguments* (2012). ISBN: 978-0-9833476-6-8 (paperback)

John C. Merrill, *Farewell to Freedom: Impact of Communitarianism on Individual Rights in the 21st Century* (2011). ISBN: 978-0-9826597-5-5 (paperback)

John Markert, *The Social Impact of Sexual Harassment: A Resource Manual for Organizations and Scholars* (2010). ISBN 978-0-9826597-4-8 (paperback)

John W. Cones, *Introduction to the Motion Picture Industry: A Guide for Students, Filmmakers and Scholars* (2009). ISBN: 978-0-922993-90-1 (paperback)

John Schulz, *Please Don't Do That! The Pocket Guide to Good Writing* (2008). ISBN: 978-0-922993-87-1 (booklet)

Héctor Luis Díaz, Johnny Ramírez-Johnson, Randall Basham and Vijayan K. Pillai, *Strengthening Democracy Through Community Capacity Building* (2008). ISBN: 978-0-922993-95-6 (paper)

John W. Cones, *Dictionary of Film Finance and Distribution: A Guide for Independent Filmmakers* (2008). ISBN: 978-0-922993-93-2 (cloth); 978-0-922993-94-9 (paper)

Hazel Dicken-Garcia and Giovanna Dell'Orto, *Hated Ideas and the American Civil War Press* (2008). ISBN: 978-0-922993-88-8 (paper); 978-0-922993-89-5 (cloth)

Stephen D. Cooper, *Watching the Watchdog: Bloggers as the Fifth Estate* (2006). ISBN: 0-922993-46-7 (cloth); 0-922993-47-5 (paperback)

David Demers, *Dictionary of Mass Communication: A Guide for Students, Scholars and Professionals* (2005). ISBN: 0-922993-35-1 (cloth); 0-922993-25-4 (paperback)

How the MASS MEDIA Really Work

An Introduction to Their Role as Institutions of Control and Change

Taehyun Kim
Dan Erickson
David Demers

MARQUETTE BOOKS
Spokane, Washington

Library of Congress Cataloging Number
2013955628

ISBN for this edition:
978-0-9833476-9-9

Background cover photo
Copyright © Africa Studio
Used with permission
fotolio.com

All pictures and illustrations in this book
are in the public domain except where noted.

Marquette Books LLC
3107 East 62nd Avenue
Spokane, Washington 99223
509-290-9240 (voice) / 509-448-2191 (fax)
books@marquettebooks.com / www.MarquetteBooks.com

Contents

Preface

More than two decades ago Professor Pamela J. Shoemaker reviewed 15 introduction to mass communication/media textbooks and concluded that "their self-described purpose is to provide a global view of mass communication to neophytes, and their approach is largely descriptive."[1]

Professor Shoemaker also found that the textbooks took "what might be called an insider's approach to socializing new communication professionals." The mass media, especially news media, are portrayed as "adversaries of government," as "watchdogs" of the public, and as "a mirror of reality."[2]

The textbooks contained little information about how media content (1) helps people, government and business leaders achieve their personal and professional goals and (2) reinforces dominant values and institutions. In other words, the textbooks have ignored or underplayed what sociologists call the *social control function* of the mass media.

Today, an increasing number of introductory textbooks focus on the social control role of media. These "pop cultural studies" textbooks, as they sometimes are called, begin with the assumption that mass media are first and foremost concerned about profits and secondarily concerned about people and society. Some draw heavily on Marxist theories and, hence, are very critical of the mass media and free-market economics.

Although these books are a welcomed addition to the literature, many of them fail to understand that mass media, even corporate media, can and often produce content that helps legitimize or facilitate *social change* — change that has at times helps disadvantaged groups and individuals.

Drawing on decades of mass communication research as well as our own research,[3] this book attempts to correct for these shortcomings. It shows that, contrary to popular wisdom, mass media and the content they produce play a crucial role in maintaining dominant values and social institutions. Mainstream mass media create and reproduce a reality that largely supports and maintains the existing power structure, often to detriment of the poor and disadvantaged groups. In similizing terminology, media produce the thread that helps hold the fabric of modern society together.

But the social control function does not mean mass media are simply lap dogs of powerful elites. Media produce, from time to time, content that is critical of dominant values and elites. That content can legitimize and promote ideas that benefit nonelite or disadvantaged groups and individuals; that is, it can stimulate *social change*.

Historically, there are some good examples of mass media as agents of social change. They include the colonial press during the American Revolution; the muckrakers at the turn of the 20th century; and Watergate during the early 1970s. Social change can cool down dissidents and, paradoxically, lead to greater social control.

In analyzing the role and function of the media, this book advocates neither a radical left nor a radical right perspective. But it does assume there is much more that mass media could do to eliminate injustice and inequity in the world. Social control and social change can result in both good and evil, and that determination often depends on who benefits and who does not from media coverage (see Chapter 1).

Thus, one of the goals of this book is to give students of mass media — society's future media professionals — the knowledge to see who benefits from media coverage and who do not. Our hope is that readers will use the knowledge to make the world a better place for themselves, for disadvantaged groups and for society at large.

This book was written to appeal to undergraduate and entry-level graduate students in the United States. This book does NOT include extensive description information about the contemporary structure of mass media markets. The focus is interpretive — it seeks to explain the "why" rather than the "what."

The first five chapters are intended for readers at all levels of college. The Appendix, which provides a formal presentation of the theory upon which the content of this book is grounded, is intended for graduate

How the Mass Media Really Work

students and for undergraduate students who like to dig deeper into the theories of mass media.

Finally, we've tried to make this book more fun and easier to read than other textbooks by using shorter sentences and paragraphs and more narratives and examples. Each chapter begins with a story or narrative designed to "draw" the reader into the topic. Anecdotes and personality profiles also are liberally used throughout the text.

ACKNOWLEDGMENTS

We owe a debt of gratitude to a number of people who assisted in this project. They include C. Brandon Chapman, Purba Das, Krista Della-Piana, Alex J. Henley, Nate Hutchinson, Professor John Irby, Rob Keenan, Professor Igor Klyukanov, Professor Tien-tsung Lee, the late Professor emeritus Val Limburg, Brian McLean, Maria Ortega, Professor Bruce Pinkleton, Professor emeritus Neal Robison, James Sanderville, Professor Alex Tan, Professor emeritus Phillip J. Tichenor, Yungyin Xiang, Ming Wang, Lu Wei, Jessi Wells and numerous "Introduction to Mass Communication" students who, through the years, have provided feedback about the book and the course.

Chapter 1
A TITANIC MEDIA EVENT

Forty-eight-year-old *New York Times* managing editor Carr Vattel Van Anda was working the graveyard shift when he received a wireless telegraph message that the ocean liner *Titanic* had struck an iceberg and was sinking. Few other details were available.[4]

Was the news accurate? Could the *Titanic* — the largest and most luxurious ship of its day and allegedly "unsinkable" — actually be foundering on its maiden voyage? Should the *Times* run the report?

Editors at other newspapers didn't believe the report. But Van Anda deduced that the ship had sunk, because its wireless radio had fallen silent about a half-hour after the first call for help. Within two hours, by 3:30 a.m., Van Anda and his staff had produced nearly two full pages of copy.[5]

On the morning of Monday, April 15, 1912, *The New York Times* became the first newspaper in the world to report the disaster, summing it up with the following headline:

New Liner Titanic *Hits an Iceberg;*
Sinking by the Bow at Midnight;
Women Put Off in Life Boats;
Last Wireless at 12:27 a.m. Blurred

Later that morning, other wireless messages picked up from ships near the disaster scene suggested that the *Titanic* was not sinking but was being towed by another ship and that all of its passengers were safe. "All saved from *Titanic* after collision," the *New York Evening Sun*'s headline declared. Other newspapers ran similar stories, and people began complaining about

"Untergang der Titanic" by Willy Stöwer, 1912 (artist's conception of the sinking)

The New York Times. But those complaints were short-lived. All of the passengers were not safe. Someone apparently had mixed up two unrelated wireless messages.

The *New York Times* report was indeed accurate. And in its afternoon edition, the newspaper scooped competitors again when it reported the loss of more than 1,200 lives. (The final toll was 1,529.) The newspaper also reported that another ship in the area, the *Carpathia,* had picked up nearly 900 survivors (later adjusted to 705) and was rushing to New York City.

QUESTIONING THE MEDIA

Few events in the history of the world have attracted as much media attention as has the sinking of the *Titanic.* At the time of the disaster, hundreds of newspapers and magazines around the world covered the event. But that was just the beginning.

Since then, the sinking has been immortalized in thousands of sermons, poems, books, songs, newspaper stories, magazine articles, television programs, movies, documentaries, and even several Broadway plays.[6] In June 2004, an Internet search using Google produced 1.6 million Web pages for the term, *Titanic;* in 2005, the number of Web sites had doubled, to 3.4 million; in 2006 the number jumped ten-fold to more than 40 million; four years later, in 2010, the number reached 115 million; and in 2012 — the 100-year anniversary of the sinking — the number was 157 million.

The substance of these writings and the electronic productions and content varies. But there are some common themes. Many preach about the evils of wealth, luxury and social status; the limits of science and technology; and the ability of the human spirit to overcome great tragedy.

The first theme, for example, is exemplified in rural African-American story-songs, called "toasts," which tell of a black man named *Shine* who managed to escape and swim to New York, leaving the wealthy whites to die with their luxuries. This toast inspired songwriter Bob Dylan to write "Desolation Row," which uses the *Titanic* as a metaphor for the cruelness of a highly industrialized and policed society.

In 1997, the blockbuster movie "Titanic" also contained several subthemes that were critical of class and gender discrimination. The movie, which starred Leonardo DiCaprio and Kate Winslet and was directed by James Cameron, grossed $2.2 billion in box office receipts worldwide, making it one of the most financially successful film production in history. The movie also earned 11 Academy Awards.

There is little question that the world will continue to be captivated by the *Titanic* disaster long into the 21st century.

To casual observers, the extensive media coverage of the Titanic disaster may appear to be nothing more than a good story, or perhaps an easy way to make a buck. But to mass communication researchers, this coverage raises a number of interesting questions about mass media and their role in society.

What function does media coverage of the *Titanic* disaster (as well as other disasters) serve for individuals, groups and society? Who benefits from such coverage? And why do urban, industrialized societies even have mass media? What roles or functions do various forms of mass

A lifeboat carrying passengers from the Titanic.

media — newspapers, books, magazines, film, television, radio and Internet — perform for individuals, groups and societies? And whose interests do mass media serve, anyway?

This book answers these and many other questions about the mass media and mass communications. To start the process, let's go back in time again and look more closely at how newspapers and magazines covered the sinking of the greatest ocean-going vessel of its time.

COVERAGE OF THE TITANIC DISASTER

On Tuesday, April 16, 1912, the day after the Titanic sunk, newspaper stories began reporting not only the details of the disaster but also its causes and who might be responsible.

The *New York Evening Journal* ran a front-page story blaming White Star Line, the operator of the *Titanic*. The editorial correctly pointed out that the *Titanic* set sail with only enough lifeboats to hold about 1,000 of the 2,200 passengers and crew. The editorial called upon "federal authorities" to "impose new regulations upon British ships and all other ships entering

How the Mass Media Really Work

An artist's drawing of the arrival of Titanic passengers in New York City after the sinking.

American ports — regulations that would make the life-saving equipment of every ship suit the numbers of the passengers and crew."[7]

On Wednesday morning, April 17, President William Howard Taft appointed U.S. Sen. William Alden Smith of Michigan to head a Senate committee to investigate the disaster.

On Thursday, as the *Carpathia* arrived at New York's harbor, a *New York Times* reporter rushed on board to meet with Harold Bride, 22, one of the *Titanic*'s surviving wireless radio operators. Van Anda had arranged in advance to pay $1,000 for the exclusive interview.

On Friday, *The New York Times* once again scooped competitors when it published "Thrilling Story by *Titanic*'s Surviving Wireless Man." The story praised Bride's coworker, Senior Wireless Operator Jack Phillips, who continued sending messages as the ship was going down. Bride said:

> Then came the captain's voice: "Men, you have done your full duty. You can do no more. Abandon your cabin. Now it's every man for himself." ... I looked out. The boat deck was awash. Phillips clung on, sending and sending. He clung on for about ten minutes, or maybe fifteen minutes ... . The water then was coming into our cabin.[8]

On deck, Bride said he could hear the ship's orchestra playing a ragtime tune and then the song "Autumn." Bride said Phillips ran aft as he (Bride) joined another group of men trying to lift a collapsible life raft off the deck. A large wave knocked Bride and the boat into the water, where other men pulled him into the raft. They said the "Lord's Prayer."

Later, when the survivors were pulled aboard the *Carpathia,* Bride saw Phillips in the same raft, but he was dead, apparently from exposure. "He was a brave man," Bride told the *Times* reporter.

Heroes and Villains

Over the next week, newspaper stories created several other heroes, as well as a few villains.

Another hero was Arthur H. Rostron, captain of the *Carpathia*, the ship that had picked up the survivors.

The press also idolized Margaret Brown, a passenger on the *Titanic*. After being lowered into a lifeboat, Brown removed some of her clothing to keep other passengers warm and then helped row. She also helped care for survivors on the *Carpathia*. Brown later became "The Unsinkable Molly Brown" in a 1960 Broadway musical.

How the Mass Media Really Work

Mrs. J. J. "Molly" Brown presents a trophy to Arthur H. Rostron, captain of the Carpathia, which picked up survivors.

The press also praised the ship's 35 electrical engineers, who stayed at their posts to keep the electricity going as the ship was sinking. The lights

Captain Edward J. Smith

delayed panic among the passengers and enabled the crew on deck to launch the lifeboats. A memorial to the crew was erected in Southhampton, England, in 1914.

In contrast, the captain of the *Titanic,* Edward J. Smith, was "villainized." He apparently had given orders to run the ship at nearly full speed even though other ships in the area had warned of icebergs. Smith, who was on his last command before retirement, went down with the ship.

Another "villain" was Stanley Lord, captain of the *Californian,* a ship that apparently passed nearest to the *Titanic* and reportedly saw the distress flares but didn't go to its aid. Lord denied the accusations, but he and his family were never able to clear his name.

The American press also made an example of J. Bruce Ismay, a British citizen and director of the White Star Line, who was on board and saved himself in one of the lifeboats. Many people thought he should have given his seat to a woman or child, even though there was no "women-and-children-first" maritime law.

J. Bruce Ismay was criticized for saving himself before women and children.

New Routes

As the days passed, the news coverage began focusing on the causes of the disaster and how another such incident might be avoided in the future.

On April 25, *Engineering News* reported that, because of the *Titanic* disaster, transatlantic ships were adopting new routes, farther to the south, to avoid icebergs. On April 27, *Scientific American* published an article pointing out that the ship was traveling about 21 knots when it struck a glancing blow with the iceberg. Half speed would have saved the ship, the article argued.

The magazine also published an editorial praising the electrical engineers. "In the roll of the saved there is not the name of a single certified engineer. Why this literal silence of the grave? There can be but one answer. Every man of the engineer watch stuck to his post to the very last and went down with the ship."[9]

Senate Committee: "No Negligence"

Despite the shortage of lifeboats and advance warnings regarding iceberg-infested waters, on May 25 — after 17 days of hearings with 82 witnesses — the U.S. Senate committee did not render a finding of negligence against White Star Line. Instead, the committee passed three resolutions that encouraged the full Senate to (1) re-evaluate all maritime legislation; (2) investigate the laws and regulations concerning construction and operation of all ocean-going ships; and (3) give a medal of honor to Captain Rostron for picking up the survivors.

On July 30, three-and-a-half months after the tragedy, the British commission reached its conclusions, saying that the collision with the iceberg was due to excessive speed. The commission also concluded that a proper watch had not been kept and that the ship's boats were properly lowered but insufficiently manned.

Lawsuits with claims worth nearly $17 million were filed in U.S. courts against White Star Line. However, because U.S. law limited compensation to the salvage value of the ship, which consisted of 13 lifeboats, total liability was limited to about $98,000.

IMPACT ON MARITIME LAW

Although *Titanic's* survivors and families of the victims may not have been adequately compensated, the disaster did prompt major changes in maritime regulations.

The United States, Britain and a number of other countries quickly passed laws requiring ships entering their ports to (1) carry enough lifeboats to save all passengers and crew; (2) equip lifeboats with survival gear; (3) ensure lifeboats are adequately manned and the crews properly trained; (4) conduct a lifeboat drill for passengers on every voyage; (5) carry a wireless radio system; and (6) monitor radio signals 24 hours a day.

Since then, these regulations have saved many lives at sea. For instance, in 1916, four years after the *Titanic* disaster, the hospital ship *Britannic* struck a mine in the Aegean Sea and sank in less than an hour. But only 38 people were lost because there were enough lifeboats on board.

The disaster also prompted authorities to hold the first International Convention for Safety of Life at Sea in 1913 in London. The convention drafted rules similar to those passed in the United States and Great Britain. The International Ice Patrol also was established to warn ships in the North Atlantic about icebergs.

Mass Media and Social Control

To understand the role and function of mass media in society, imagine for a moment what might have happened had there been no newspaper coverage of the sinking of the *Titanic*.

At a minimum, there would have been much greater confusion. News of the sinking would have been delayed at least one full day and probably even longer. Many relatives and friends of the passengers no doubt would have become increasingly worried as time passed. At some point, a White Star Line representative likely would have informed them that the ship had sunk, but there probably would have been additional delays, because White Star Line officials refused to believe the first *New York Times'* story of the sinking.

Eventually, news of the sinking would spread by word-of-mouth. But this form of communication is slow and generally less reliable and less accurate than news reports. Research shows, in fact, that a story passed from one person to another can change and become inaccurate very quickly.[10] And the consequences of rumor are often disastrous. In fact, there are many instances in Europe and the Americas before the 19th century in which inaccurate information fueled violent mobs.

Perhaps more importantly, without newspaper coverage of the sinking, the United States and other governments might never have passed laws requiring passenger ships to carry enough lifeboats for all passengers and crew. According to *Titanic* author and researcher Stephen J. Spignesi, the *New York Evening Journal* editorial that criticized White Star Line for failing to equip the ship with enough lifeboats "was the beginning of a loud outcry."[11] Without that editorial and other news coverage about the shortage of lifeboats, White Star Line could have more easily down-played that problem.

Also, without advance news coverage of the sinking, it is highly unlikely the U.S. Senate would have been able to conduct an investigation before most of the passengers and crew left the New York area. In fact, as the *Carpathia* was steaming to New York with the survivors, J. Bruce Ismay (the director of the White Star Line who saved himself in one of the lifeboats) sent a wireless telegraph message urging White Star Line officials to delay

How the Mass Media Really Work

Prisons are institutions of social control. *(Photo by Ori~, used with permission)*

the departure of another ship from New York so that the *Titanic* crew (mostly British) could be sent back to Britain as quickly as possible.

The hypothetical scenario above does not exhaust all of the possible consequences associated with a lack of newspaper coverage. The key point is that even though news media are not always 100 percent accurate, news reports of disasters like the *Titanic* generally help reduce confusion. And this, in turn, contributes to social order.

Another way of putting it is to say that *mass media content is like a thread that holds the fabric of society together.* In fact, modern society could not exist without mass media or other mechanisms of social control.

What Is Social Control?

For our purposes, social control will be defined as attempts, whether intentional or not, by the state or by social institutions — including mass media — to regulate or encourage conformity to a set of values or norms through socialization or through the threat of coercion, or both. Let's examine more closely each of the major components of this definition.

- The state is a political entity legally permitted to use force within a particular territory. The United States of America, Japan and Nigeria are examples.

- A social institution is a group or organization composed of people working to achieve goals that are sanctioned by the larger society. The goals are guided by values, norms and roles. The police, churches, schools, the family and mass media, such as *The New York Times,* are examples.

- A value is an abstract idea that people in a society or group consider desirable, good or bad. A dominant value is one that most people consider desirable. In most cultures around the world, the sanctity of human life is a dominant value, as is devotion to family, friends and work. Events like the *Titanic* disaster and the September 11, 2001, attacks (see discussion later in this chapter) are always viewed as tragic events by the culture in which they happen, and to the extent that mass media transmit information about such events, they help reinforce values about the sanctity of human life. In addition to the sanctity of human life, most societies place a high value on social order (i.e., not using violence to achieve goals), respect for authority, and religion. Western societies also place a high value on romantic love, education, representative democracy, and a free-market (capitalist) economic system.

- Norms are rules that guide behavior. Norms usually reinforce societal values. Norms may be *formal* (written rules or laws) or *informal* (unwritten verbal rules). Codes of ethics are examples of formal norms. They spell out in writing what is and is not appropriate behavior. In 1912, *The New York Times* did not have a formal code of ethics, but Van Anda very clearly expected his reporters to tell the truth. Today, most large news organizations have formal codes of ethics. The *Times'* code is now 56 pages long.

- Socialization may be defined as the process by which people learn to conform to social norm and values. Historically, parents and religious leaders played key roles in teaching (or socializing) children into the dominant norms and values in a community or society. As societies modernize, schools, government and the mass media also play a role. High school history classes, for example, teach children about the *Titanic* disaster, and, as mentioned earlier, many books, articles and movies now examine various aspects of the disaster.

How the Mass Media Really Work

- Roles are social positions with certain rights and obligations. Roles link individuals to organizations. A "journalist" is a role that links a person to a mass media organization. A major obligation of a journalist is to gather the news and write stories for publication or broadcast. In exchange, the journalist is compensated.

- Coercion is a type of social interaction in which the individual or group is compelled to behave in certain ways either by force or threat of force. After the hearings on the *Titanic* disaster, many governments passed rules imposing stiff penalties on shipping lines that did not provide enough life preservers for passengers. Mass media at the time reinforced this "coercive" effort by writing stories about the new rules and the penalties associated with violating them.

- A law is a formal norm that has been approved, sanctioned or implemented by a state or political entity (e.g., legislature or head of state). Of all the mechanisms for controlling people, the law is perhaps the most obvious. Most of the rules that imposed penalties on shipping lines for failing to provide enough life preservers were formal laws. Almost all societies also outlaw murder, robbery and other "violent crimes." To deter such crimes, lawbreakers are punished. And the police and courts are social institutions that enforce the law through coercive means, such as jail time.

Although punishment or the threat of punishment often is effective in controlling individuals and organizations, noncoercive means of control, such as socialization, are often more effective. Most people, in fact, have life preservers in their personal water craft not because they are afraid of being punished, but because they want to protect their family and friends. Similarly, most people do not commit murder because they are afraid of being punished — rather, they believe killing is wrong. In short, they have "internalized" values and norms about the sanctity of human life.

In sum, social control involves attempts by families, schools, police, the mass media and other social institutions to regulate or encourage conformity to a set of values or norms. In fact, these institutions can be thought of as "agents of social control," although the people who work in them rarely think of themselves in this way.

DISSECTING TITANIC COVERAGE

To see more clearly how mass media play a social control function, let's dissect the *Titanic* news coverage in more depth, beginning with the first *New York Times* story. And let's start at the beginning: Why did that newspaper cover the disaster?

Although we can't get into Van Anda's thought processes, we do know that disasters frequently make the news around the world, partly because, as noted above, most societies and peoples place a high value on human life. As a consequence, tragedy makes news.

Recall, for instance, the Boston *Daily Globe* report that the wealthy and poor "were in deep grief" and "the disaster stunned" theater-goers. Behind these statements is the assumption or belief that human life is precious.

Or how about the *New York Evening Journal* editorial that criticized White Star Line for failing to have enough lifeboats: "No sea-going vessel should be permitted to clear from an American port without being provided with life-saving appliances." This statement contains moral outrage. Can you feel it?

These stories are reinforcing basic values about the sanctity of human life. They also help people share and process the grief. In this sense, the role of the news media may be likened to that of a clergyman at a funeral.

Stories of heroism also reinforce fundamental values that regulate behavior. The unstated but obvious theme is that some people are able to rise above the tragedy and provide inspiration for others.

In the *Titanic* disaster, for example, the heroes include the "brave" wireless man who continued sending wireless radio messages even as water filled the cabin; the orchestra playing music to calm the passengers right up to the end; the dedicated members of the electrical engineering crew, who stayed at their posts knowing they would die; the captain of the *Carpathia,* who raced his ship to the scene to pick up survivors; and the "unsinkable" Molly Brown.

At the same time, there are the stories about those who did not act heroically: the *Titanic* captain who used poor judgment; the *California* captain who failed to respond to distress calls; the man who tried to steal the life jacket from the wireless operator; and White Star Line director who saved himself before saving women and children.

"The Margin of Safety Is Too Narrow!" A 1912 cartoon showing a man representing the public with a copy of a newspaper headlined "THE TITANIC" demands action from a man representing "The Companies."

As mentioned earlier, such stories have the subtle effect of reinforcing a society's values about what is and what is not appropriate behavior. And occasionally such stories may expand or contract the boundaries of acceptable behavior.

SOCIAL CONTROL BEYOND NATURAL DISASTERS

The social control function of mass media is not confined to natural disasters. Virtually all news and entertainment content has implications for social control. This is particularly the case when a social system is threatened by war or terrorist acts. In fact, *the greater the perceived threat, the greater the potential for social control.*

September 11, 2001, supports this proposition. That was the day 19 so-called "suicide terrorists" commandeered four U.S. commercial airliners and about 9 a.m. flew two of them into the 110-story twin towers of the World Trade Center in New York City. A short time later, both towers collapsed, killing nearly 3,000 people.

The third plane was flown into the Pentagon, killing 200 more people. The fourth plane crashed in a Pennsylvania field, killing all 45 on board. Passengers on that plane reportedly fought with the hijackers, who apparently were trying to take the plane to Washington D.C., presumably to strike the White House.

Within two minutes of the crashes, CNN was broadcasting live near the World Trade Center. Other television and radio networks quickly followed. Initially, there was confusion. Were the crashes intentional? If so, who was behind them? And why would they commit such horrendous acts?

To get answers to these questions, the journalists turned primarily to politicians, law enforcement officials and military leaders — or what political scientists call governmental elites, or those who have political, social or economic power. These are the people society entrusts with the authority to explain and interpret such events. This is not to say the journalists didn't make personal observations during the tragedy. But journalistic norms stipulate that they must rely on authorities or elites for more detailed information.

President Bush was informed about a half hour after the first attack. Of course, the media were ready and prepared to broadcast his comments. He is the most powerful person in the United States. Bush went on national television at 8:30 p.m. Eastern time, declaring that "we will make no distinction between the terrorists who committed these acts and those who harbor them."

The next day, newspaper headlines reflected outrage and anger:[12]

"Acts of Mass Murder" —*Newsday*
"It's War" —*New York Daily News*
"Acts of War" —*San Jose Mercury News*
"A Day of Infamy" —*Tulsa World*

The south tower of the World Trade Center after being struck by a jetliner on September 11, 2001 (*Photograph used with permission of Robert; http://www.flickr.com/people/themachinestops/*).

"Terror Beyond Belief" —*Newark Star Ledger*
"Day of Evil" —*Orange County Register*
"A Day of Horror" —*Reno Gazette-Journal*
"Evil Acts" —*Southeast Missourian*
"Bring Them to Justice" —*South Bend Tribune*

The authorities eventually placed responsibility for the attacks on Afghanistan-based Osama bin Laden and his al Qaeda terrorist network. For weeks and months afterward, news stories, editorials, commentaries and letters to the editor condemned the attacks and the "terrorists," and praised the actions of the firefighters, police and passengers on the hijacked plane. New York Mayor Rudolph Giuliani also was elevated to the status of hero for his leadership during the crisis.

In short, news media coverage of 9/11 was not "objective" in any absolute sense of the word. It defined who was "good" and who was "evil." The content helped mobilize public opinion against terrorism and the eventual military offensive in Afghanistan that led to the ousting of the Taliban, which had supported bin Laden, from power. Public opinion polls showed Americans strongly supported the U.S. military intervention in Afghanistan.

After that war, the Bush administration also placed part of the blame for the attacks on Iraqi President Saddam Hussein, even though it was later revealed there were no significant connections between the terrorists and Hussein. In fact, none of the terrorists was from Iraq, even though public opinion polls showed nearly half of all Americans believed this.

In early 2003, the Bush administration launched a public relations campaign to drum up support for ousting Hussein from power. The news media played a key role in mobilizing public opinion to support the attack on Iraq, according to researchers and analysts.[13]

When the United States launched a military strike in Iraq in March 2003, the U.S. public was solidly behind the effort. That support began to fade in early 2004, when it became evident that Hussein did not have weapons of mass destruction or direct links to al Qaeda. By the spring of 2006, public opinion had turned against the war effort, as more evidence emerged that the Bush administration had misled the American public about the reasons for invading Iraq.

MEDIA AND DISASTERS

In times of disaster or the threat of it, people often turn to the mass media to get a better sense of what is happening and, in some cases, to take precautionary measures.

More specifically, mass communication researchers Douglas Blanks Hindman and Kathy Coyle studied the role of local radio news during the April 1997 Red River Valley floods in North Dakota and reached three main conclusions: (1) Radio helped define the disaster and describe officials' actions at fighting the threat; (2) Radio helped mobilize volunteers and helped citizens monitor the threat to their own property; and (3) Radio, television, and newspapers helped enhance the sense of primary group solidarity that is often observed during natural disasters.[14]

In addition, when the disaster is over, the media almost always publish or broadcast stories of heroism and write editorials about the tragic loss of life. And when the disaster is big enough — as was the case with the *Titanic*, the 9/11 attack and the destruction of New Orleans after Hurricane Katrina — it becomes a topic of discussion in many forms of media (such as songs, plays, movies and poems) for many decades to come.

Although disasters tend to make news, this doesn't mean that all disasters or tragedies are covered equally. The *Titanic* sinking generated a lot of media coverage because the ship was the largest in the world, was on its maiden voyage, and was believed to be unsinkable. When John F. Kennedy Jr., his wife Carolyn Bessette, and his sister-in-law Lauren Bessette died in a plane crash in July 1999, that event also dominated American media news coverage for more than a week. They were celebrities. But the 400,000 Africans who died of AIDS that week barely made the news. Many factors contribute to these biases in news coverage, and we'll explore them in more depth in later chapters.

MASS MEDIA AND OTHER EVENTS

As 9/11 illustrates, the social control function of the mass media is most evident during times of war. In fact, historical evidence shows that in virtually all wars at all times mainstream mass media produce content that supports the goals of military and political elites and helps maintain morale "back home." In fact, news reports often downplay negative outcomes and overplay positive ones.

But the social control function is not limited to disasters or wars, or to just the news media.

- *News reports and entertainment programming* (such as television programs and movies) about crime play an important role in defining the boundaries of appropriate behavior. They also generate sympathy for most victims and outrage for most law-breakers. One consequence of such outrage, according to communication researcher George Gerbner, is continued support for tough laws (e.g., capital punishment) and for tough policing practices (e.g., excessive force is often overlooked). Although many people are critical of the violence portrayed in television programs and movies, rarely are hard-core criminals and offenders portrayed as heroes. The message in crime shows is very clear: Crime doesn't pay.

- *Music videos and radio music* play an important role in reinforcing the societal value of romantic love. Young people are drawn to music in part because of this, and romantic love as a value helps reinforce values about the importance of marriage and family. Not all programming, to be sure, reinforces traditional values. Popular music and movies often portray sex without consequences. Such music, in fact, may have contributed to a changing of values about sex before marriage. Media may help promote change (a topic to be discussed subsequently). But there is little question that music continues to construct ideal portraits of romantic love, and to the extent that young people are "smitten" by this value, one can expect music will play a significant role in regulating their thoughts and behaviors.

- *Television entertainment programming and movies* play an important role in helping people to relax. For some, they provide a means of escape from the mundane aspects of everyday life. To the extent that watching such programming alleviates loneliness or stress, television and movies may be seen as solving psychological problems. Some critics even argue that such programming can reduce the chances that people will become politically active. A noncritic sees the "escape function" as harmless and healthy. But in either case, the important point is that the potential for social disorder is lessened to the extent that people's needs for relaxation are met.

- *Advertising* encourages people to buy certain products and services, which in turn provides income for businesses. Advertising doesn't

A screen shot from *Le Voyage dans la lune* (A Trip to the Moon, 1902), an early film with a story line.

always lead to higher sales, but it does work under many conditions. And increased sales help those companies stay in business.

- *Magazines* tend to be more specialized in content and function than other forms of media, which means the functions they perform in terms of social control are very specialized. For example, many teenage girls read *Seventeen, Teen Magazine, Teen People* and other popular press magazines to learn about relationships and love, to learn how to dress and use make-up, and to learn about how other teens deal with personal problems.

- *Public relations professionals* play an important role in providing "raw material" (i.e., news and information) to news organizations. In fact, about three-fourths of all the news published in news media originates from government and private public relations people. Of course, public relations personnel often seek positive news accounts of the organizations they represent. This doesn't always happen. A great deal of news content focuses on actions or proposals that violate values, laws or norms. Good examples are the Watergate scandal and President Bill Clinton's "immoral" affair with Monica Lewinsky. However, this coverage reinforces basic values and laws.
- As noted earlier, *business news* plays an important role in helping executives and politicians make decisions affecting businesses or economic policy. People who own stock or have investments also often follow business news to keep abreast of changing economic conditions. Helping people achieve their business goals contributes directly to social order.
- *Television talk shows*, like *Dr. Phil, Oprah Winfrey* and *Jerry Springer*, are often criticized for being too trivial or too sensational. But interviews with movie stars and with ordinary people who have extraordinary problems play an important role in helping define or reinforce the boundaries of acceptable behavior. In fact, when viewed from afar, such programming may be seen as loosely scripted morality plays. Audience applause and boos usually mirror the dominant values in society.

In short, mass media content plays a key role in helping maintain social order in the societies in which they operate. The media provide information and entertainment programming that people and groups need or use to achieve their personal and professionals goals. Each medium, however, plays a unique role in reinforcing dominant values and institutions in society.

Is the Social Control Function a Conspiracy?

The social control function of the mass media is one of the most strongly supported propositions in mass communication research.[15] But it is very important to point out that social control is rarely the product of a grand conspiracy.

Journalists and media workers do not spend their time trying to come up with ways to control people. In fact, most journalists and media workers are unaware of the extent to which their actions and the content they produce helps maintain social order. Many actually believe they produce content that is free of values and moral lessons.

It is true that Western-style journalism does produce a news story that typically contains more points of view than stories in, say, communist newspapers or newspapers controlled by authoritarian governments. However, there is no such thing as value-free content. Indeed, even the process of selecting a topic involves value preferences that have implications for social control.

So if the social control function isn't the result of a conspiracy, then from where does it come?

In the most general terms, it comes from the way media are organized and integrated into society.

Mass media in all societies depend heavily upon political and economic elites and groups for news and, in capitalist countries, for advertising revenues. As noted earlier, an elite is someone who has power, and power is the ability to make others obey.

To attract large audiences and keep up demand for advertising, mass media cannot produce a lot of content that offends a lot of elites or consumers a lot of the time. If it does, elites and consumers will stop buying the publication or will stop watching the programming. News sources would also stop cooperating. Thus, the dependence that mass media have on powerful elites and consumers serves to constrain the media content they produce.

As you can see, the process of social control is two-way. Mass media content supports and maintains dominant values and elite groups, but media themselves are also controlled. They need to make a profit, and they can't do that if they offend people a lot. There is much more to say about this topic, but we'll explore it in much greater depth throughout the book.

Is Social Control Good or Evil?

To many people, the term "social control" often connotes a nefarious force or evil idea. History is, indeed, filled with numerous examples of atrocities committed by various political and religious leaders to maintain control over people or groups (e.g., Adolf Hitler's Nazi Germany).

But it is important to point out that no society or group can exist without some mechanisms for controlling people and subgroups. In fact, even simple communication is not possible without rules governing language (i.e., grammar) — an extremely subtle form of control that people rarely think about when they talk to each other. Thus, the answer to the question of whether social control is good or bad depends at least in part on who benefits from such control.

- Advertisers clearly like social control when a successful advertising campaign leads consumers to buy more of their products. But competitors may not be very pleased if their sales decrease.

- Law enforcement officials generally like crime news, because it reinforces norms and laws that give them their authority. But during the 1960s and 1970s, many citizens who fought for equal rights for women and minorities and for an end to the Vietnam War felt that media coverage did not help them very much. And research showed they were right. News media ignored the concerns of minorities and women until the 1960s, and provided strong support for U.S. military involvement in Vietnam prior to the 1970s.

- The manufacturers of products and goods targeted to young women clearly reap benefits from magazine stories about fashion and make-up. But women's groups who want people to judge women based on the kindness of their hearts rather than on the beauty of their skin do not appreciate such stories.

- Business and industry generally benefit from newspaper and television coverage of business news. But some organizations condemn the emphasis on consumerism and materialism argue that such business news crowds out more important quality of life issues, such as helping the poor and disadvantaged.

How the Mass Media Really Work

In short, the question of whether the social control function of the mass media has good or bad consequences depends partly upon who benefits from such content.

As a rule of thumb, mainstream groups and organizations tend to benefit most from mass media content, while extremists groups and those that push for major change benefit the least.

MASS MEDIA AND SOCIAL CHANGE

Although mass media produce content that generally supports and legitimizes a society's dominant values and institutions, this doesn't mean that content always supports and never challenges the "status quo," or those in power.

From time to time, mass media content does find fault with dominant values, social norms, institutions or elites, and this criticism can, under some conditions, help promote social change that benefits the less privileged, less powerful. In fact, social change is ubiquitous and necessary for people and societies to adapt and survive. In this respect, social change is complementary, not contrary, to social control. Change often brings greater stability and control.

WHAT IS SOCIAL CHANGE?

Social change is the difference between current and antecedent conditions in a *culture* or *social structure*.

Culture is the symbolic and learned aspects of human society, which includes language, custom, beliefs, skills, art, norms and values. This definition needs to be distinguished from the one that refers to "culture" as "refined ways of thinking, talking, and acting" — popularly expressed in the comment, "She's got culture." In other words, the concern here is not with the aesthetics of culture, per se. Rather, the focus is on values, beliefs, norms or customs and how they change.

Social structure is the patterned relationships between individuals and groups. These relationships are guided by role expectations, social norms and values. A newspaper provides a good example of how social structures can change.

In the early 1900s, the typical daily newspaper was small (7,500 circulation). It employed a handful of workers, and was controlled by a single individual who performed many roles, including that of publisher, advertising manager, editor and circulation manager. In those days, most newspapers did not have a code of ethics, or a set of norms to guide behavior.

But now the typical daily is five times larger (35,000 circulation), employs hundreds of workers, has a highly developed management structure, and is controlled and managed by professionals. The owner, who was once involved in nearly every major decision, is now often an absentee stockholder, or a publisher who focuses more on long-term matters and problems than on day-to-day operations.[16] These newspapers usually have a formal code of ethics.

TITANIC COVERAGE AND SOCIAL CHANGE

The *Titanic* disaster is an excellent case study of the media's role not only as an agent of social control, but also as an agent of social change.

Recall that shortly after the disaster occurred, shipping routes were modified so that ships would make the transatlantic voyage farther to the south, to avoid the icebergs. Maritime laws also were changed to require all ships entering U.S. ports to carry enough lifeboats to save everyone on board. Both of these actions changed the social structure. In other words, people and organizations were now required to behave in a manner different than before the changes. At the same time, it can be argued that these changes had the effect of giving people more confidence in society and its ability to solve problems. To the extent that this happens, one can argue that social order has been enhanced.

The role of mass media in affecting social change is rarely simple or direct. In the case of the *Titanic* disaster, for example, newspaper stories did not directly lead to changes in the maritime laws (which are themselves examples of social norms). Rather, they helped draw attention to the lifeboat problem and "frame" or create the public debate. This is an example of

Folk music activists Bob Dylan and Joan Baez perform during the civil rights "March on Washington for Jobs and Freedom," August 28, 1963.

what mass communication researchers call the agenda-setting function of the mass media. In other words, heavy coverage of an issue in the news media can help set the agenda for public policy making. Mass media often help initiate and maintain public debate on an issue.

The changes made to the maritime laws are an obvious example of how the mass media can play a role in helping promote change. But social change does not necessarily end there.

Recall that the *Titanic* disaster has become immortalized in thousands of stories and other mass-mediated content. The African-American "toasts," James Cameron's movie "Titanic," Bob Dylan and other writers and artists have used the disaster to preach about the evils of privilege, wealth, greed, and social inequality. What impact have these accounts had on people and society? Do they make readers or audiences more critical of social inequality and social class differences? Do they increase the probability that individuals or groups will challenge authority and the status quo?

These answers to these questions are not easy. Social change is one of the most difficult topics to study in the social sciences. It is a complex process and generally does not take place very quickly.

CHANGE IN THE 20ᵀᴴ CENTURY

But there is little question that many societies, especially in the West, underwent a number of social changes during the 20th century. And the media have, in many instances, played a role in legitimizing such changes.[17] For example:

- From the 1890s to about the time of World War I, a number of magazines, newspapers and some books in the United States published stories about corruption in government, poor working conditions, unfair business practices and unhealthy conditions in meat-processing plants. The stories produced by the so-called "muckraking journalists" prompted authorities to prosecute law-breakers and, more importantly, stimulated a public debate that led to a number of changes in laws governing political campaigning, anti-trust practices, safer working conditions and food processing.

- During the 1920s, the press played a major role in publicizing the "Teapot Dome" scandal, in which U.S. Secretary of the Interior Albert Fall secretly leased oil reserves on public land to the Sinclair Consolidated Oil Company and obtained kickbacks in return. When news of the scandal broke, top administration officials resigned and Fall was convicted of bribery.

- During the 1950s, the Nashville *Tennessean* and other newspapers published a number of stories drawing attention to the plight of African Americans in the Deep South. Some reporters went undercover, exposing the role of the Ku Klux Klan. Legendary broadcaster Edward R. Murrow also helped silence Sen. Joseph R. McCarthy, who was conducting a "witch hunt" against alleged communists in government and Hollywood. Hollywood film star James Dean also broke barriers for playing characters that challenged authorities and dominant norms and values.

- During the 1960s, many musicians, such as Joan Baez and Bob Dylan, wrote songs critical of U.S. involvement in Vietnam. Many journalists in Vietnam also began sending back stories highly critical of U.S. policy. Public opinion eventually turned against the pro-war forces. Maverick journalist I. F. Stone also published a newsletter that exposed corruption and inefficiency in the U.S. government. In the early 1960s, Rachael Carson wrote a book, titled *Silent Spring,* that helped mobilize the environmental movement (see Chapter 3). And one study showed that *The New York Times* and other major papers in the United States gave favorable coverage to the civil rights movement, including Martin Luther King Jr.'s famous 1963 "I Have a Dream" speech.
- During the 1970s, the *Washington Post* and other newspapers exposed the Watergate scandal, which led to the downfall of President Richard Nixon and prompted changes to a number of laws governing campaign financing (see Chapter 3). One of those laws led to the creation of a special federal prosecutor, who investigated alleged scandals in the presidential administrations of Ronald Reagan, George Bush and Bill Clinton.

Mass media, then, can have a significant impact on changing the social structure, value systems and public policy. But media messages do not always produce change, even when they challenge dominant values or elites.

THE LIMITS OF SOCIAL CHANGE

After the *Titanic* disaster, writer Joseph Conrad lashed out at the wealthy, the British Board of Trade, the U.S. Senate committee, and the builders and owners of the *Titanic.* Playwright George Bernard Shaw also was very critical of the newspapers for publishing accounts that glorified the actions of the passengers and crew, because he thought those stories helped cover up the fact that the disaster was caused by negligence.

But White Star Line was never found to be negligent legally. Shaw's theory may be right: To the extent that media attention is focused on heroes, other stories or issues may be pushed off the public agenda, which in turn may limit or contain social change.

Paintings are not typically conceived of as mass media, but they nonetheless have implications for social control and change. In this 1872 painting of "Manifest Destiny," artist John Gast paints a scene of people moving west and protected by the goddess-like figure of Columbia. Native Americans and bison are depicted as being driving into obscurity, the dark, as the "light" of Columbia moves west.

As a general rule, people who are in positions of power in a society or in an organization resist change. They resist change because they often have something to lose. On the other hand, if they stand to gain from change, they will often support it. That's what social movements often attempt to do: convince people that change will benefit them.

Although mass media can have a significant impact on changing the social structure, the conditions under which change is most likely to occur are still not well understood. To date, mass communication scholars have not devoted much attention to the study of mass media and social change. Most of the research has focused on psychological effects, such as the impact of violent programming on children's attitudes and behavior.

These are important topics to study. But if the goal of social science is to alleviate injustice and inequities and to make the world a better place, then mass communication researchers need to focus more on the role of the mass media as an agent of change.[18]

Is Social Change Good or Evil?

The question of whether social change is good or evil is same as the question posed for social control: The answer depends upon who benefits from the change.

As a general rule, conservative politicians and groups tend to resist change and frequently complain about media content that criticizes authorities and traditional ways of doing things. Conservatives often fear that change will bring disorder or threaten the power of traditional authorities.

Liberal politicians and groups, on the other hand, are often critical of mainstream mass media because they don't do enough to promote changes that alleviate social inequities and injustices.

Not surprisingly, the conservatives tend to see the media as having a liberal bias, while the liberals tend to see the media as having a conservative bias.

Who's right?

Chapter 2
THE MAINSTREAM BIAS

During the final weeks of the 1996 Presidential election race, Republican candidate Bob Dole accused the national news media of having a "liberal bias" that favored Democrat Bill Clinton. If the media could shed this liberal bias, Dole implied, he could beat Clinton.

Many conservatives agreed.

They believed American mass media have a strong liberal bias. In their book, *And That's The Way It Is(n't): A Reference Guide to Media Bias,* L. Brent Bozell III and Brent H. Baker argue that

> America's most influential media outlets report the news through a liberal prism. With reprints, excerpts and summaries of more than 40 studies conducted over the past decade, (this book) provides the most thorough analysis ever compiled proving the liberal political slant in the national press.[19]

Not so, say the liberals.

They accuse the media of having a conservative bias. As media critics Jeff Cohen and Norman Solomon put it:

> One of the most enduring myths about the mainstream news media is that they are "liberal." The myth flourishes to the extent that people don't ask pointed questions: If the new media are liberal, why have national dailies and news weeklies regularly lauded those aspects of President Clinton's program that they view as "centrist" or "moderate," while questioning those viewed as liberal?[20]

Bob Dole   Bill Clinton

And a third perspective comes from the journalists themselves. They maintain that the news is neither liberal nor conservative. It's objective, or neutral.[21] As former ABC News President James Hagerty put it:

> We're trying to be objective ... we are reporters! We get interpretations from other people and present them. If anyone on this network is expressing his own opinion — well, if I catch him [sic] I won't permit it.[22]

So who's right?

The conservatives, the liberals or the journalists?

None of them, we will point out in this chapter.

The news does contain a bias.

But when viewed from a detached perspective, it is neither extremely liberal nor conservative, nor objective in absolute terms.

It is *mainstream*, centrist, or middle of the road.

In fact, that's why mass media in America are often called "mainstream media."

The Ethic of Objectivity

To under the mainstream bias, it is first necessary to examine the ethic of objectivity in journalism.

Origins of Objectivity

The origins of objectivity are often traced to the 1830s and the so-called penny press in the United States, which sold newspapers for a penny apiece and became the first "mass" medium.

Prior to that time, most newspapers in Europe and the Americas were highly partisan, usually siding with and sometimes being financially supported by political parties. Many contemporary critics of journalism wish for that kind of press again — one that allegedly contained a robust debate.

But, as might be expected from a partisan press, the stories and columns in those publications were often vitriolic, inaccurate and self-serving. Not only that, they also excluded the other point of view. You only got one side of the story.

Moreover, most people didn't get more than one side to a story because they just read their own political party's paper. They didn't read the other party's paper, and this, of course, had the effect of limiting the debate.

But the ethic of objectivity changed that.

Increasingly, newspapers became less partisan and restricted opinion and commentary to special pages. News stories now contained not just one point of view, but two or more views.

Of course, to a certain extent, this took some of the bite out of the partisanship. But, at the same time, it improved the accuracy of the news accounts and, more importantly, brought the story to a broader range of people. Now people who were members of different parties could read the same publication and get the views of not only the leaders of their parties but also the opposition.

A formal conception of objectivity in journalism didn't really take root until late 1800s and early 1900s, when the social sciences (political science and sociology) were developing. Like scholars, journalists were encouraged to remain detached when reporting on a story.

OBJECTIVITY UNDER ATTACK

By 1950, the so-called ethic of objectivity had become a firmly established practice in journalism.

The assumption was truth would emerge if journalists (1) kept their personal opinions out of stories, (2) quoted all sides to a story, and (3) gave roughly equal coverage to those sides. Opinions, journalists say, are properly expressed only on the editorial and op-ed pages, or in news analyses.[23]

However, the ethic of objectivity itself became a target of attack during the so-called "McCarthy era," which began in February 1950 when Sen. Joseph R. McCarthy, a Republican from Wisconsin, charged that 205 communists had infiltrated the U.S. State Department. Although he was never able to substantiate these and many other charges, he held many press conferences and the news media quoted him extensively and covered his senatorial hearings because he was a powerful person.

The ethic of objectivity assumes that readers and viewers can sift through the information presented and find the truth.

The New York Times at the time reinforced this idea, declaring that even if McCarthy's charges "are usually proved false," he was still news, because separating innuendo from truth and accusation from guilt "lies with the readers," not the newspaper.[24]

But, critics asked, how can the public discern the truth if sources are lying and journalists are unable to get all of the facts?

This is the fundamental flaw in the ethic of objectivity.

Sen. Joseph R. McCarthy

How the Mass Media Really Work

A massive amount of research in mass communication over the next five decades eventually would clarify the paradox. The ethic of objectivity produces its own bias, but it is neither radical nor aligned with a particular ideology.

The bias is mainstream.

It reinforces the status quo, which usually mean powerful people and their ideas.[25]

McCarthy was eventually censured by the Senate, but not before he had ruined many careers and lives.

The ethic of objectivity came under further assault during the 1960s, when the U.S. military disseminated false information to journalists in order to promote U.S. involvement in Vietnam and Southeast Asia. Some journalists were not easily misled, but editors at home were reluctant to publish content critical of U.S. policy, even if it was true.

The news media also were criticized after race riots erupted in many U.S. cities in the late 1960s. The Kerner Commission issued a report indicting the U.S. media for failing to cover black communities and issues. Heavy reliance on bureaucratic officials (most of whom were white) as sources of news was partly to blame.

THE NEW JOURNALISM MOVEMENT

The ethic of objectivity survived these assaults, but new forms of journalism emerged in the 1960s to challenge it. The "new journalism" movement was highly critical of objectivity and traditional reportorial methods, because they tended to generate a mainstream bias that excluded alternative or unorthodox points of view.[26]

Instead of objectivity, the "new journalists" advocated various forms of subjectivity, which they said was more effective at revealing the truth.

Tom Wolfe, Jimmy Breslin, Gay Talese, Norman Mailer, Truman Capote, Nicholas von Hoffman and others wrote articles and books that reported on real-life events but combined elements of a novel, such as people's motivations and feelings and extensive analysis of events and surroundings. Truman Capote's *In Cold Blood,* which told the story of two men who killed a family, epitomizes this genre.[27]

The new journalism movement — or some people called it "advocacy journalism" — also got a boost from social movements opposed to the Vietnam War and in favor of more rights for women and minorities. They pointed out that traditional methods of reporting historically had marginalized these groups, or failed to give them a voice. Journalism was too dependent on powerful government and corporate elite sources.

The Watergate scandal in the early 1970s also gave alternative journalism a shot in the arm. Investigative reporting, in particular, was seen as a method that could overcome some of the problems associated with the ethic of objectivity and routine news reporting.

What distinguished investigative reporting from routine news reporting was that the burden of proof lay on the journalist, not the sources, per se. The news media (especially the *Washington Post* and *New York Times*) were highly praised for helping to uncover corruption in the Nixon administration.

The new journalism movement began to wane in the late 1970s.

The end of the Vietnam War and new laws and court decisions providing more rights and protections to women and minorities took much of the steam out of the movement.

The ethic of objectivity survived and remains the primary guiding principle in U.S. journalism. Defenders of objectivity pointed out quite correctly that, despite its limitations, the "objective approach" was effective in providing readers with a greater number and variety of alternative points of view.

However, the ethic of objectivity did not then, nor does it today, mean that every person or institution in society gets the same amount of coverage on all issues. Journalism depends more on powerful sources of information and knowledge and, this, in turn, produces what is known as the mainstream bias.

WHAT IS THE MAINSTREAM BIAS?

The mainstream bias means that news media in the United States (and most western countries, too) rarely give positive news coverage to extremist views on either the left or right side of the political continuum. Communists and

News stories about extremists like these fascist protesters, who rallied on the West lawn of the U.S. Capitol in Washington D.C., in 2008, almost always portray them in a negative light. Such coverage helps define the boundaries of acceptable behavior in American society. *(Photo by Utilisateur bootbeardbc de flickr, <http://www.flickr.com/photos/ bootbearwdc>, used with permission)*

others on the "far left" rarely get sympathetic press coverage in daily newspapers or on national television. But the same holds for neo-Fascists and others on the "far right."

For example, some years ago the (Spokane, Washington) *Spokesman-Review* published a story titled, "White Separatists to be Featured at Survivalist Expo."[28] The story outlined how leaders of neo-Nazi, right-wing Christian separatist, anti-black and anti-Semitic groups would be speaking at the Spokane Convention Center.

But the focus of the story was not on what the speakers would say — as it might have been for mainstream Republican and Democratic speakers. Rather, the focus on the straight news story was on how the views of these groups were contrary to the dominant values of the community. None of the extremist leaders was interviewed in the story, but there was a generous sampling of critics' views.

"From a legal standpoint, there's nothing we can do to block this kind of event," one city official is quoted as saying. "Do we condone it? Do we want it to be there? The answer is, 'Hell no!'" Said another city official: "Like civil libertarians, I am concerned with ... (respecting) ... First Amendment freedoms. But as the human rights specialist, I will continue to speak against supremacy and hatred, and I encourage citizens who want to live in a respectful community to do the same."

With this example, we are not trying to defend the position of right-wing groups — in our opinion, their views are repugnant and based on ignorance. However, in terms of analyzing the media coverage, this example illustrates how news media marginalize extremist groups and, by default, provide support for dominant groups and community values. Stories about terrorism do the same thing.

Another front-page story in the same issue of the *Spokesman-Review* — this one written by a reporter for the *Los Angeles Times* — extolled the virtues of a Russian human rights champion who was tormented in prison during the Soviet days of "totalitarian repression."[29] The implicit moral lesson: Communism is bad.

The only notable exception in terms of giving extremist groups positive media coverage is when they are denied freedom of speech. But in these cases the news coverage focuses on the free-speech issue rather than on the ideological goals or ideals of the groups. This happened in Skokie, Illinois, many years ago, a heavily Jewish community where neo-Nazi groups staged a march through the streets. The American Civil Liberties Union defended the free-speech rights of the neo-Nazis. However, mainstream media news stories strongly condemned and criticized the goals of neo-Nazis.

So what is the mainstream ideology?

In the United States, it is embodied in the Democratic and Republican parties. In England, it is the Conservative and Labor parties. And throughout much of Europe, it is the Social Democrats. These are the groups that get preferential coverage in the news and generally the most positive coverage.

To be sure, there is a lot of critical news directed at mainstream political parties. Most of this criticism stems from the parties criticizing each other. Outside groups, if they are not mainstream, are rarely quoted in such stories.

In fact, *the more extreme the group, the less the news media will cover it and the less favorable that coverage will be.* Conversely, as a rule, the more a group's goals fall

President Barack Obama talks with Ron Klain during a mock presidential debate in 2012. Sen. John Kerry, background, played the role of Mitt Romney.

within mainstream values and norms, the more coverage it tends to get and the more favorable that coverage.

THE MAINSTREAM BIAS IN ELECTIONS

The mainstream bias is easiest to see during a presidential election.

All presidential races include more candidates than just those in the Democratic and Republican parties. In 2012, for example, eight people ran for president in Washington state (not all candidate names are on all state ballots).

Now, if journalists sought to be purely objective, they should give each candidate in a presidential election equal coverage — that is, each should receive the same amount of space, same placement and the same balance of views.

This ideal is sometimes possible when there is only one Democratic and one Republican candidate, because both are from the political mainstream. However, because presidential elections also include candidates from nonmainstream parties, the coverage has never, ever come close to the ideal

Green Party presidential candidate Jill Stein was arrested in 2012 when she tried to enter the site of the presidential debate at Hofstra University to protest the exclusion of her and other nonmainstream candidates from the debates. This practice helps ensure the election of mainstream candidates. In this 2011 photo, Stein is talking to Occupy Wall Street protestors. *(Photo by Paul Stein, <www.flickr.com/photos/kapkap/7999998562/sizes/m/in/photostream>, used with permission.*

of objectivity. The mainstream media always give more coverage to the Republican and Democratic candidates.

In 2012, for example, the lion's share of coverage went to Barack Obama and Mitt Romney. Very little coverage went to Green Party candidate Jill Stein, Libertarian candidate Gary Johnson, and Socialist Workers Party candidate James Harris.

Why do "alternative" candidates get so little coverage?

When journalists are asked this question, they say it's (1) because the alternative candidates have no chance of winning, (2) because the public isn't as interested in their views, and (3) because the newspaper has limited space and resources.

The journalists are right.

Most of the alternative candidates have no chance of winning, and the public generally is less interested in the views of non-mainstream candidates. But this doesn't alter the fact that the election coverage is less than objective. The alternative candidates are "marginalized," meaning they are not assumed to be viable candidates.

So, is this mainstream bias a good or bad thing?

That depends on whether you like the mainstream parties.

During the 1992 presidential election, Dr. Lenora B. Fulani, the only black female candidate in the race, asked reporters why they were not covering her campaign. As expected, they said it was because she didn't raise much money and didn't have much of a chance of winning.

Her response: *How can I raise money and win if you don't give coverage to my campaign?*

Catch-22.

MAINSTREAM BIAS IN OTHER NEWS STORIES

The mainstream bias is sometimes more difficult to see in other news stories, especially in those that are not controversial.

But it is there.

For example, in the same *Spokesman-Review* issue that carried the article about the fascist meeting was a story that examined the motives why a deputy sheriff charged with murder may have shot his wife. She allegedly committed adultery. Fidelity (or monogamy) is a value that most mainstream religious groups' cherish. And the story subtly reminded people of the importance of that value.

Still another story in that issue of the newspaper noted that a new diabetic drug could reduce the need for insulin. This story reinforced social norms and values about the importance of scientific research, and it helped the U.S. Food and Drug Administration get the word out to the public (and achieve its goals).

More recently, *The Arizona Republic* published a story on one of its Monday morning front pages about the Arizona Cardinals professional football beating the Tampa Bay Buccaneers.[30] The story implicitly accepts the notion that sports is good for a community. Many people believe local

Stories about the Yarnell Hill Fire near Prescott, AZ, which killed 19 firefighters, reinforce values about the sanctity of human life and provide information that individuals and groups use to avert such disasters in the future.

sports leagues and events reinforce values about the importance of teamwork and, at the same time, help keep young people out of trouble.

Some scholars also see spectator sports as a mechanism for diverting people's attention away from political and economic injustice in society.

How the Mass Media Really Work

Sports "narcotizes" viewers, one sociologist has suggested. That characterization might be strong, but it is clear that sports is a social institution that helps maintain social order in a community.

The front page of the *Republic* also contained a story about a government investigation into a forest fire that killed 19 firefighters.[31]

Aside from reinforcing values about the sanctity of human life, the story provided information that various groups and individuals will use to understand the tragedy and perhaps avert future disasters. The story also points out that some of the families of the victims will also use the information to file lawsuits.

Although many people dislike lawsuits, they are the civil way in modern societies to solve disputes between people and organizations. Sociologists point out that lawsuits reduce the potential that individuals will use violence to solve a dispute.

We authors must emphasize again that we are not passing personal judgment on these stories or the values promoted in them. In fact, we believe many of them are noble and worthy of coverage.

Our point is that the news is not objective in any absolute sense, despite what journalists may claim. At the same time, the news is not nearly so conservative as the liberals would have us believe, nor as liberal as the conservatives would have us believe. Rather, in all cultures, news in the mass media generally promotes the dominant values of that culture and the powerful social institutions. And, at election time, the mainstream bias helps to guarantee that changes in local or national leadership do not come too quickly or too radically.

By the way, if you want to understand why some people believe the news media are too liberal or too conservative, simply ask them for their political orientation. As a rule, the more conservative the orientation, the more likely they are to see the media as liberal; and the more liberal the orientation, the more likely they are to see the media as conservative.

So much for objectivity.[32]

Mainstream Bias in Entertainment Programming

We have spent most of this chapter talking about the mainstream bias in news media reports. And for good reason. News media play a major role in shaping or influencing public policy. Politicians, bureaucrats, corporate executives, special interest groups and many voters depend heavily on news to achieve their professional and personal goals.

But the mainstream bias also exists in entertainment programming, and the impact of entertainment programming should not be underestimated, especially because most people spend much more time with it than with the news.

Finding examples of entertainment programming that support mainstream values and institutions is not difficult. Take, for instance, shows about law and order. Almost all of them reinforce the value that "crime doesn't pay." Sure, those shows have a fair amount of gratuitous violence. But they rarely encourage people to engage in criminal activity. Lawbreakers are almost always caught, killed or punished. And those that get away usually have noble motives or are up against a corrupt system.

Through the latter half of the 20th century, mass communication scholar George Gerbner argued that crime shows and their accompanying tales of morality help define the boundaries of acceptable behavior and, thus, provide implicit support for authoritarian police practices and laws.

Although Gerbner's social control model makes a lot of sense, some critics believe television violence produces anti-social behavior, including criminal behavior. Social science research over the past four decades has shown that violent programming increases the probability of temporary aggressive behavior in small children. But the question of whether violent programming can contribute to adult criminal behavior is still unanswered.[33]

Entertainment programming also reinforces many other values that contribute to social order and mainstream views. For example, television programming and movies frequently extol the virtues of a good education and a successful career, but the self-absorbed "filthy" rich and those who turn their backs on materialism (the ascetics) both tend to be marginalized or are portrayed as kooks. Education is also highly revered, because it is seen as the ticket to success in the capitalist job market.

Most Western mass media do not support a particular religious institution, because their societies and communities have a variety of religious groups. But they all place a great deal of importance on the idea that religion is important for social cohesion and stability. Generally, it's also

Love is a powerful aphrodisiac for social control. *(19ᵗʰ century painting of the famous balcony scene from Romeo and Juliet by Frank Dicksee)*

good to be religious, but both fanatics (members of cult groups) and religion-hating atheists are usually portrayed in a negative light.

Although many television comedies, particularly in the United States, portray characters in nontraditional family situations, the emphasis is almost always on love, friendship, honesty, sincerity and treating others well.

And then there is love, perhaps the most commonly found theme in media next to violence. Western media idealize the notion of romance and love, and who could conceive of a more powerful aphrodisiac for social control?

ORIGINS OF THE MAINSTREAM BIAS

The mainstream bias is not the product of a conspiracy on the part of journalists, film producers or elites in Western countries. Media in all social systems reflect the general concerns and interests of those in positions of power. If they didn't, they would have a difficult time surviving.

Imagine, for instance, what would happen if a news organization published a story that was sympathetic to extremist views, such as those of the neo-Nazis. Community and mainstream political groups would be outraged. Many advertisers would pull their ads, and many readers would drop their subscriptions. In other words, the dependence that media have on profits to survive is one of the mechanisms for keeping media "in line" — and it helps uphold and protect the status quo.

The mainstream bias is the product of a number of complex legal, cultural, social and economic constraints that media face to survive in the marketplace. These forces did not just emerge yesterday. They go back to the origins of mass media themselves.

The first newspapers in England and the United States faced major legal constraints. If they published content that was critical of the authorities, the newspaper could be shut down and the publisher prosecuted. In fact, the first newspaper in the United States was shut down after the publication of its first issue in 1690, because it published stories that angered the colonial governor.[34]

Legal constraints, which include libel law (content that harms a person's reputation) and privacy law, continue to play an important role in regulating what journalists and people can say. However, formal laws are only a small part of the picture. Cultural and social factors also play a key role.

When John Campbell began publishing a newspaper in the American colonies in 1704, he was well aware that he had to stay within certain moral and ethical boundaries — not just to please the British authorities but to please community leaders, too.

At that time, a story about women's rights or sexual relations, for example, would have offended many clergymen and sparked harsh criticism of the newspaper. Most mainstream media, in fact, did not support women's right to vote until after 1916, when President Woodrow Wilson declared his support for the 19th Amendment. And Wilson's change of heart, no doubt, was influenced at least in part by the fact that Australia and New Zealand had already given women the right to vote.

Although times have changed and stories about women's rights and sex are much more common today, media are still bound by cultural values and the interests of those in power. Women and minorities in most Western countries still struggle to achieve equality in the workplace. And the media

How the Mass Media Really Work

President Woodrow Wilson, shown here with his cabinet in 1918, eventually supported passage of the 19th Amendment, which gave women the right to vote.

rely heavily on political and economic elites — not the general public — for news, which means the news tends to legitimize the institutions these elites run.

The dependence that media have on elites for news can be traced in large part to the development of news beats.

Prior to the 1830s, the content of most newspapers was composed of national or international affairs. The accounts were usually lifted from newspapers in other countries or from official government documents. Local news stories, when they appeared, were often gleaned from other local newspapers, private letters, correspondence and, occasionally, personal contacts with governmental officials. Newspapers were directed largely to elite audiences, which included government officials, politicians and business people.

Most newspapers were highly partisan in character, and many were supported by political parties. Although colorful, such papers had limited appeal — generally to members of their political party.

This changed dramatically with the emergence of the penny press in the 1830s. The penny papers focused not just on economic and governmental news but on social news, which included reporting the affairs of the local police, courts and community groups. These papers were very popular because they were cheap (1 cent). Circulation and advertising revenues grew rapidly.

To maintain a continuous flow of news copy, newspapers created "beats." These beats were anchored in the centers of power in a community, which included governmental sources (police, courts, city hall), businesses (Wall Street), community groups (religious, social) and, eventually, lifestyle beats (sports, food, women's pages).

The penny press also helped shape the ethic of objectivity. Gradually, throughout the 19th century, newspapers began to shed their partisanship in favor of a more neutral stance. This appealed to more readers, which in turn boosted advertising sales and revenues.

Whereas the ethic of objectivity did mean that newspapers were now printing more than one opinion when covering a controversial issue, it did not mean that newspapers were objective in some absolute sense. They still obtained news and information from the powerful elites, and those outside the mainstream power groups were still marginalized, meaning they were perceived to be less credible and newsworthy.

In sum, the mainstreaming effects of the news media are not a product of a conspiracy; rather, they stem from organizational routines and constraints on the news operation. Through a unique set of historical circumstances, media linked themselves to the centers of power, which created a symbiotic, or mutually beneficial, relationship. By cooperating with the media, elites helped to legitimate the role of the media in covering news. And the news coverage generally helps elites achieve their goals.

MAINSTREAM VALUES IN THE MEDIA

News coverage of presidential elections highlights one of the major mainstream values promoted in the news — moderatism. In other words, excess or extremism in politics should be avoided.

Sociologist Herbert J. Gans has identified seven other enduring values in the news: ethnocentrism, altruistic democracy, responsible capitalism, small-town pastoralism, individualism, (social) order and national leadership.[35] Although he was writing about U.S. media, these values actually can be applied to news media in most Western and many other nations around the world, and to most forms of entertainment programming on television, at the movies and on radio.

By ethnocentrism, Gans means that the news media value their own nation above all others. This ethnocentrism is most explicit, he says, in foreign news, "which judges other countries by the extent to which they live up to or imitate American practices and values." War news and humanitarian efforts provide the clearest expression of this principle. Recent examples include coverage of the ethnic conflict in Yugoslavia, the 1991 Gulf War, and the 2003 wars in Iraq and Afghanistan. In all of these conflicts, Western news media coverage helped legitimate intervention by NATO, the United States and other Western countries.

The value of altruistic democracy is highlighted in stories about corruption, conflict, protest and bureaucratic malfunctioning. The news implies that politics should be based on the public interest.

The value of responsible capitalism means that the news has an optimistic faith in capitalism, the good life and competition, and that unreasonable profits and gross exploitation of workers is wrong. Stories about corporate investors who violate federal laws reinforce this value.

Small-town pastoralism refers to the love affair that most Americans and Westerners have with the idea of small-town life, and to the problems posed by industrialization: urban crime, increasing social conflict and urban decay. British author Peter Mayle's books about rural French life, such as *A Year in Provence*, strongly support this value.

Individualism promotes the idea of freedom of the individual both within and against the system. People are expected to participate in society and act in the public interest but on their own terms. Ayn Rand's book *The Fountainhead* exalts individualism and warns of the dangers of collectivism.

Gans also argues that strong leadership is highly valued, because it is the way through which order and moral values are maintained. In all countries around the world, news media provide substantial coverage of their leaders.

As noted earlier in this book, the news also reinforces the value of order and social cohesion. Whenever a major disorder occurs, such as a riot or protest, the first thing the authorities do is call for calm. Of course, the media are the messengers of this social control message. The message is almost always the same: violence is never the way to solve problems and one must work peaceably for change.

Well, almost always.

There are some interesting historical exceptions to this rule.

REUTERS, TERRORISM AND OBJECTIVITY

The Sons of Liberty.[36]

U.S. historians could have called them America's first terrorists. After all, they used violence to achieve political goals before and during the War of Independence. They tarred and feathered British civilians and destroyed their property. They forced some British tax collectors to resign from their positions. They also were behind the famous Boston Tea Party.

Historian Todd Alan Kreamer points out that the British clearly viewed the Sons of Liberty as a terrorist organization. But American history books today do not characterize that group as a terrorist organization for one simple reason: America won the war.

To the victors go the spoils, including the power to define reality. So, today, the Sons of Liberty are known as patriots or freedom fighters, not terrorists.

The line between terrorist and patriot (or freedom fighter) is thin but not invisible to mass media scholars who study propaganda, culture and language. They know that U.S. government politicians and spokespersons often use highly emotive words to demonize their enemies and glorify their friends. "Terrorist" and "freedom fighter" are two of the most popular. Media research shows that journalists routinely and unquestioningly cite these terms in news stories, even outside of directly quoted material.

But once in a while a news organization steps out of the mainstream. That happened on September 25, 2001, when Reuters news service announced that it would no longer use the word "terrorist" or "freedom fighter" in news stories unless those terms were attributed to a source. In essence, the news agency called into question the power of political elites such as George Bush to define reality. Media rarely do that, especially after an event as horrific as the September 11 attack.

Nancy Bobrowitz, who was senior vice president for Reuters' corporate communications, said Reuters had, for several decades, a policy against using what it calls "emotive" terms without attribution. However, the policy

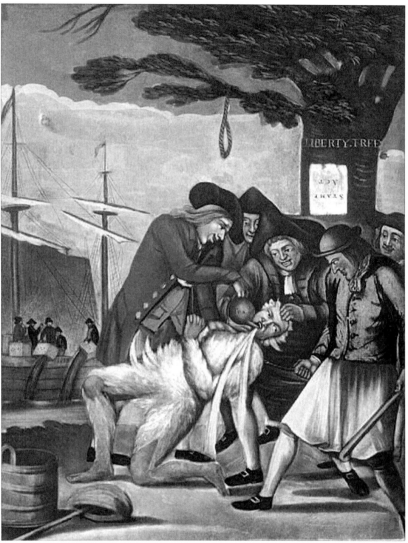

Five "Patriots" tar and feather of British Commissioner of Customs John Malcolm on Jan. 5, 1744, under the Liberty Tree in Boston. The painting shows the Boston Tea Party in the background, an event that occurred a month earlier. Some historians say the Sons of Liberty was the first terrorist groups in America.

apparently was not formalized until Reuters head Stephen Jukes sent out a memo to his staff in September saying "one man's terrorist is another man's freedom fighter."

Reuters' website added: "As part of a long-standing policy to avoid the use of emotive words, we do not use 'terrorist' and 'freedom fighter' unless they are in a direct quote or are otherwise attributed to a third party. We do not characterize the subjects of news stories but instead report actions, identity and background so that readers can make their own decisions based on facts."

Bobrowitz said Reuters must adhere to such a policy in part because Reuters has a "global audience." She said objectivity is important to gain the confidence and respect of readers around the world. A month later, the BBC World News Service agreed and instituted a similar policy.

However, none of the major U.S. news organizations has followed Reuters' lead. In fact, so far Reuters' decision has generated more criticism than support from U.S. journalists and their organizations.

"Journalism should be about telling the truth, and when you don't call this (September 11) a terrorist attack, you're not telling the truth," Rich Noyes, director of media analysis at the conservative Media Research Center, told the *Christian Science Monitor*.

To support their case, some critics of Reuters cite former *New York Times* columnist William Safire's definition of terrorism. Safire wrote that the term "terrorist" has its roots in the Latin "terrere," which means "to frighten." Safire added: "The most precise word to describe a person who murders even one innocent civilian to send a political message is terrorist."

This is a reasonable definition.

But if one accepts it, critics point out, then U.S. history must be re-written.

The Sons of Liberty would be just the beginning. In the late 19th and early 20th centuries, the list of other "terrorist actions" would include the forced annexation of Hawaii, police violence against labor union workers, state tolerance of lynchings of African Americans, the CIA-backed coup in Chile in 1973, the My Lai massacre in Vietnam, and military invasions in Carribean countries.

Of course, critics also would point out that the quintessential terrorist act was the dropping of atomic bombs on Nagasaki and Hiroshima, because they directly or indirectly contributed to the deaths of thousands of innocent civilians. Proponents of dropping the bomb justify these deaths as unfortunate casualties of war. They blame the Japanese.

But, as media scholars point out, historically, the ultimate arbiter of what is defined as an act of terror is who wins the war or the conflict. The inability of U.S. media to see this principle stems largely from the structural constraints they face. They serve American elites and institutions, and they ultimately must respond to their concerns. If they don't, then those institutions could stop giving the news media information and news.

THE MAINSTREAM BIAS AND SOCIAL CHANGE

One of the hallmarks of modern society — if not its identifying feature — is social change. But if the mass media contain a mainstream bias, how can change take place?

The short answer is that the media rarely serve as agents of radical change. They are better characterized as agents of reform.

One would be hard-pressed to argue that mainstream media are radical. The only possible exception to that rule is the American Revolution, when the "patriot" press played a key role in mobilizing and informing the colonists.

But historical and social scientific research on mass media clearly supports the idea that mass media can play a reformist role, and one that benefits not just elites but the poor and other disadvantaged groups. In fact, the reformist role helps explain, in turn, the stability and durability of capitalism as an economic institution.[37]

Mainstream mass media and corporate media in particular have played an important role in legitimating and sometimes facilitating (though rarely initiating) the goals of many social movements, which in turn have led to a number of social changes. The most notable example of this occurred at the turn of the century, with the rise of the so-called "muckrakers," who were responding to the Progressive Movement.

Media in Western nations also have played a role in legitimating decisions from the courts and government that expanded rights and opportunities for women, minorities, the working class, environmentalists, homosexuals and the poor. Such changes certainly have not eliminated inequalities, discrimination or injustices, but they have significantly altered the power structure in most Western countries during the 20th century.[38]

Although journalists tend to support the dominant system of values, research shows that they generally are more liberal than elites, as well as the general public, on a wide variety of social and political issues.[39] These findings suggest that media have the capacity at times to produce content that is critical of dominant groups and beneficial to disadvantaged groups.

Polls and historical research show that conservatives are more critical than liberals of investigative reporting and that journalists often are sensitive to the concerns of minorities and consumers groups, are critical of business, and believe that private business is profiting at the expense of Third World countries.[40] One analysis of U.S. network television news coverage of Latin America also failed to produce evidence of a conservative, status-quo bias.[41]

Media reports also helped legitimize rural protest groups in Minnesota, whose goal was to block construction of a power line that would serve a large, Midwestern metropolitan area.[42] Studies often find that media coverage influences governmental policy at the national level[43] as well as the local.[44] And a recent study found that, contrary to the expectations of the researcher, media coverage of separate protest marches in Washington sponsored by gay and lesbian organizations and pro-choice groups were much more favorable than unfavorable to each of those challenging groups.[45]

Although media need a consistent, inexpensive supply of news and depend heavily on political and economic elites for the news,[46] it is also important to point out that elites depend heavily on the media to achieve their goals. It is widely agreed, for example, that a state or national politician cannot be elected today without effective media coverage. Candidates rely less and less on the political party machine and more and more on direct coverage in media to get elected. This dependence, in turn, has lessened to some extent the power of the traditional political parties.

Another study showed that veteran reporters at mainstream newspapers can write stories that challenge components of the dominant ideology.[47] Studying Canadian press coverage of disarmament, peace and security issues, another reported that commentaries, columns and op-ed pieces often challenged the dominant view of bureaucrats.[48]

The news media often cover protests and demonstrations, such as the one outside of the 2008 Republican National Convention in Saint Paul, Minnesota. That coverage provides information and commentary that citizens and politicians often use when they vote or create policies.

And a study of the press in India suggests that the news media have the potential to challenge the status quo.[49] The researcher found that such challenges may not be direct or comprehensive, but some kinds of news stories may represent a challenge indirectly by contributing, for example, to public awareness of problems with the status quo, which in turn can promote discontent and support for social change.

Research also shows that alternative media often challenge dominant ideologies and contribute to mobilizing and promoting social movements or causes. Challenging the arguments of the "routines theorists,"[50] one participant observation study found that reporters at an alternative radio station could create oppositional news using conventional routines and reportorial techniques.[51]

A historical review reported that alternative media have helped to promote the American revolution, abolitionism, and equality for women, minorities, and gay rights groups.[52] And even though one study discussed earlier found that the mainstream mass media marginalize anarchist groups, the study also found that the alternative (nonmainstream) press idolized them.[53]

Research on the ideological effects of the media indicates that the media may have dysfunctional consequences for some groups, but this is not always the case and, furthermore, media consumers are not easily manipulated. Researchers found that English children's use of mass media leads to distorted perceptions of immigrants.[54] But two other studies conducted in the United States have reached opposite conclusions.

One, which was conducted during the 1960s, reported that the greater the number of mass media messages white Southerners attended to, the less likely they were to have strict segregationist attitudes.[55] Although this relationship was not particularly strong, it did hold up when controlling for education. Mass media, the researchers argued, often subvert traditional, patrimonial ways and usher in modern attitudes that promote social change.

Researchers behind the *Great American Values Test* concluded that a specially designed 30-minute television program broadcast in 1979 also was able to increase anti-racist beliefs and the importance of equality itself as a basic social value.[56] The researchers also found that people who have a high dependency on television changed their values more and contributed more money to groups that promote anti-racism and equality than people with low dependence on television.

A large body of research also indicates that media often impact public policy. Researchers at Northwestern University, for instance, found that investigative stories on police brutality "produced swift and fundamental revisions of regulations regarding police misconduct."[57] Another study found that media coverage of murder cases influences the way prosecutors handle cases.[58]

Another study suggests that television may actually promote beliefs that oppose economic inequalities.[59] The data, obtained from personal interviews with a probability sample of U.S. adults in 1986, show that people who benefit most from the system — men, whites, conservatives, and those who have high incomes, education and occupational prestige — are most likely to favor economic inequalities. The data suggest that television viewing reduces support for beliefs that promote economic inequality, even when controlling for all of the other factors.

Sociologist William Gamson's peer group study also suggests that people often use media to challenge and criticize established authorities. He challenges both the radical view that working people are incorporated by the dominant ideology and the mainstream social science view that working people are uninterested in politics and unable to engage in well-reasoned discussions. Using data collected in peer group sessions with 188 "working people," he concludes that "(a) people are not so passive, (b) people are not so dumb, and (c) people negotiate with media messages in complicated ways that vary from issue to issue."[60]

Mainstream corporate media may also help promote the causes of social movements.

MEDIA AND SOCIAL MOVEMENTS

Although investigative journalism is often cited as a source of social change, it is not the most significant source in modern society. Social movements, many sociologists would argue, are much more important. Without social movements, today's world would be much different.[61]

Consider, for instance, what it was like to be a woman before the late 20th century. Nowhere in the world did women have the right to vote. They had limited access to a college education — many schools would not accept women. But even if a woman had a college education, she didn't have access to the best jobs in the public or private (corporate) world. Teaching school was her best bet.

Or consider what it was like to be an African American living in pre-Vietnam War America. African Americans could not eat in many restaurants. They had to sit at the back of the bus. They could not drink out of water fountains reserved for whites. Their children could not attend the best schools. They were denied access to good jobs. And, in some areas of the Deep South, they lived in fear for their lives.

Today, there is little question that opportunities and social conditions for women, African Americans and many other historically oppressed groups have improved in the United States and most Western countries. Women are guaranteed the right to vote. Minorities and women have better access to jobs and education. Factory laborers are no longer required to

Social movements are one of the most important sources of social change in society. In this 1967 photograph, Martin Luther King, Jr., is speaking against the Vietnam War at University of Minnesota's St. Paul Campus of the University of Minnesota. *(Photo by Minnesota Historical Society, used with permission)*

work 16 hours a day. Pollutants and emissions from factories and motor vehicles are much more highly regulated. People now have access to contraceptives. The elderly have social security and health care. The stigma associated with being homosexual has lessened considerably, and many corporations and governments have extended employment benefits to same-sex partners.

To be sure, these changes and the passage of time have not eradicated discrimination, inequality, income disparities, disregard for the environment, unwanted births, lack of access to opportunity, poor health care and poverty. Sociocultural patterns are deeply embedded, and elites and the institutions they control nearly always resist change, because it usually means a loss of political, social and economic power. But elite resistance to challenges from less advantaged groups is not always effective in preventing social change that benefits those groups.

As the preceding examples show, social movements often have played a pivotal role in altering, however subtly, the balance of power between

How the Mass Media Really Work

traditional elite groups and the masses. That's one reason why U.S. civil rights leader Jesse Jackson says he remains upbeat and optimistic — despite past and current problems, the civil rights movement, in his view, has won significant battles since the 1960s.[62]

To be sure, social science research clearly demonstrates that all social systems have ideological and coercive means of social control, and that the content of mainstream mass media generally supports those ideologies and those in power. We know that all modern social movements need the mass media to achieve their goals in a representative democracy. Media play an important role in legitimating (or delegitimating) the goals of social movements and accelerating (or decelerating) public attention to the social problems movements identify.

We also know, thanks to media researcher David L. Protess and his colleagues at Northwestern University, that investigative reporting is most likely to promote change when journalists and policy makers actively collaborate to set policymaking agendas prior to story publication.[63] However, we don't know a whole lot more about the conditions when mass media may help promote or hinder social change, partly because this topic generally has been ignored by critics of corporate and global media.

Nevertheless, despite the shortage of research, several statements can be made. One is that, historically, mass media have tended to ignore social movements until they gain power. Although the civil rights and women's movements were founded in the 19th century, they did not garner significant favorable media coverage until the 1950s and 1960s. This coincides with a substantial growth in the size and power of those movements. The same thing happened to the environmental movement. Not until 1962, with the publication of Rachael Carson's *Silent Spring*, which drew attention to the problems of pollution, did mainstream media begin giving substantial coverage to environmental issues.

However, since then, mainstream media — especially media in large, pluralistic cities — have published or aired many stories that have lent support to the goals of these movements, and news coverage has been much more favorable.[64] Television entertainment programming in the United States also has become more favorable to women and those with alternative lifestyles.

Overall, then, it is clear that mainstream mass media are no agents of radical change. But throughout the 20th century, corporate media have published many stories that have helped promote or legitimize social reforms. As Herbert Gans sums it up:

> News is not so much conservative or liberal as it is reformist; indeed, the enduring values are very much like the values of the Progressive movement of the early twentieth century. The resemblance is often uncanny, as in the common advocacy of honest, meritocratic, and anti-bureaucratic government, and in the shared antipathy to political machines and demagogues, particularly the populist bent.[65]

And comparing the media to legal systems, sociologist Jeffrey Alexander observes:

> In distinguishing the news media from the law, the significant point is the media's flexibility. By daily exposing and reformulating itself vis-à-vis changing values, group formations, and objective economic and political conditions, the media allows "public opinion" to be organized responsively on a mass basis. By performing this function of information-conduit and normative-organizer, the news media provides the normative dimension of society with the greatest flexibility in dealing with social strains.[66]

Indeed, relative to most other social institutions in society — including the church, government, the legal system and schools — the news media are more responsive to alternative, nonmainstream groups and ideas. This helps social systems adapt and change.

THE FUTURE OF (RELATIVE) OBJECTIVITY

Studies show that mainstream journalists depend heavily upon powerful political and corporate elites for the news. In fact, about two-thirds percent of all news stories are estimated to originate with such sources.

As noted in this chapter, this dependence creates a bias in the news — one that favors those in positions of power in the system and excludes those who lack power. Historically, the latter has included minorities, women, the poor, labor unions, environmentalists, homosexuals, anti-globalization groups, and anti-war groups.

Although the ethic of objectivity produces a bias that favors mainstream values and institutions and, thus, is anything but "objective" in an absolute sense, the ethic is likely to remain the most important value guiding news gathering well into the 21st century. That's because, in relative terms, the ethic of objectivity does produce a journalism that incorporates more points of view or opinions than other approaches.

Recall, that, during the 19th century, most newspapers in Europe and the Americas were highly partisan, usually siding with and sometimes being financially supported by political parties. Many contemporary critics of journalism wish for that kind of press again — one that allegedly contained a robust debate.

But, as might be expected from a partisan press, the stories and columns in those publications were often vitriolic, inaccurate and self-serving. Not only that, they also excluded the other point of view. You only got one side of the story. Moreover, most people didn't get more than one side to a story because they just read their own political party's paper. They didn't read the other party's paper, and this, of course, had the effect of limiting the debate.

The ethic of objectivity changed that.

Increasingly, newspapers became less partisan and restricted opinion and commentary to special pages. News stories now contained not just one point of view, but two or more views. Of course, to a certain extent, this took some of the bite out of the partisanship. But, at the same time, it improved the accuracy of the news accounts and, more importantly, brought the story to a broader range of people. Now people who were members of different parties could read the same publication and get the views of not only the leaders of their parties but also the opposition.

Paradoxically, then, the ethic of objectivity actually broadened the debate on public issues and this is its great strength.

Unique Media Roles

Although all forms of mass media serve as institutions of control and change, each performs a unique function. Newspapers play the biggest role when it comes to public affairs; movies are powerful storytellers; and broadcast media are good at entertaining. The Internet and new technologies are blurring the lines between these media, but they nonetheless are likely to live on in the near future.

The various roles of print media are discussed in the next chapter, followed by a chapter on broadcast media. The last chapter discussed the role of the Internet and new technologies.

Chapter 3
ROLE OF PRINT MEDIA

The mosquito control plane flew over Olga Owens Huckins' two-acre bird sanctuary in Duxbury, Maryland, and dropped its payload of DDT.[67]

The insecticide was particularly effective at killing mosquitoes.

But it didn't stop there.

"The 'harmless' shower bath killed seven of our lovely song-birds outright," Huckins later wrote. "We (Huckins and her husband) picked up the three dead bodies the next morning, right by the door. ... The next day three were scattered around the bird bath. ... On the following day one robin dropped suddenly from a branch in the woods."

Huckins said she was too "heart-sick" to hunt for other dead birds. "All these birds died horribly ... . Their bills gaping open and their splayed claws were drawn up to their breasts in agony."

The year was 1957.

Huckins was so outraged that she wrote a letter to *The Boston Herald* and sent a copy to Rachel Louise Carson, a friend who was a biologist. She asked Carson to find someone in Washington D.C. who could help.

At the time, the public knew little about the dangers of DDT and other pesticides. Although many biologists and environmental scientists were aware of the dangers, the mainstream mass media

Rachel Carson

DDT nearly wiped out the bald eagle in the United States, but now the bird is widely seen in many states. *(Photo by Yathin S Krishnappa, used with permission)*

had ignored many pleas to look into the problem. In 1945, for example, Carson herself proposed writing an article on the dangers of DDT for *Reader's Digest.* The conservative-leaning magazine turned her down.

But Carson, who had worked for the U.S. Fish and Wildlife Service, could not ignore her friend's plea. She contacted *The New Yorker* magazine, which suggested that she write the article herself.

Carson ended up writing a book.

She called it *Silent Spring,* a title originally intended for the book's chapter on birds.

Yet, the book, published in 1962, was anything but silent.[68]

Carson's basic theme was that indiscriminate use of pesticides and other chemicals could destroy life on earth. Chemicals were getting into the food chain and threatening all forms of biological life. She criticized the government for spraying without first informing citizens so they could take precautions. She also criticized the government for not conducting more research into the impact of chemicals on wildlife and ecosystems. And she criticized the practice of applying more chemicals when insects develop resistance to chemicals.[69]

When word got out that Carson was writing *Silent Spring*, the U.S. chemical industry launched an aggressive public relations campaign, criticizing Carson and the book. The chemical companies also threatened to withdraw advertising from media that favorably reviewed the book. A government official also criticized Carson, calling her a "spinster."

But the negative publicity backfired, creating even more interest in her book, which generated a whopping 40,000 in advance sales.

President John F. Kennedy asked the Science Advisory Committee to examine the effects of pesticides, and the Committee issued a formal report that backed up most of Carson's claims. By the end of 1962, more than 40 bills had been introduced in various states to regulate the use of pesticides. In 1970, the U.S. government created the Environmental Protection Agency. In 1973, DDT was banned in the United States. And perhaps most importantly, *Silent Spring* helped mobilize environmental groups and movements around the world.

Unfortunately, Carson did not live long enough to see most of these social changes. She died of cancer in 1964.

BOOKS: IDEA WAREHOUSES

Books perform many different roles or functions for individuals and organizations.

For example, books on popular fiction and literature are often a source of inspiration and entertainment. The phrase, "curling up with a good book," expresses this process quite adroitly.

Books can also relax people and reduce loneliness. In social settings, books often become the topic of conversations that unite people and make them feel they share common interests and values. Classic works of literature serve as a source of cultural identity. People revere such works and this reverence helps make them feel integrated into a community or society.

Beyond serving a "bonding" function, scholarly and scientific books also help solve practical problems. The knowledge that accumulates in books is used by scientists to identify and solve social, medical, political and environmental problems. Advanced technology would not be possible today if many fundamental ideas about physics, chemistry and electricity were not compiled in books.

Although books serve many different functions for people and groups, it is important to point out that they, like all other forms of mainstream mass media, play a key role in helping maintain social order. They provide information and ideas that individuals and organizations use to achieve their goals, generally within the boundaries of the dominant values and norms of a society.

Harriet Beecher Stowe

But unlike other forms of mass media, books have at least one key advantage over other forms: in-depth analysis of ideas. In other words, they are "idea warehouses." As such, the book has a greater potential than other forms of media to effect social change. Take, for instance, Harriet Beecher Stowe's *Uncle Tom's Cabin*

HARRIET BEECHER STOWE: A SOCIAL CHANGE AGENT

"So you're the little woman who started this great war!"

That is what Abraham Lincoln reportedly told Harriet Beecher Stowe when he met her during the U.S. Civil War in the 1860s.[70]

Ironically, Stowe didn't look like a rabble rouser. She was less than five feet tall and the mother of seven children.

But her book, *Uncle Tom's Cabin* helped mobilize public opinion around the world against the injustice of slavery. The book sold more than a half million copies in the United States within five years and was translated into more than 20 foreign languages. Historians and scholars widely agree it is one of the most influential books in American history.

Stowe was born in 1811 in Litchfield, Connecticut, the daughter of a liberal clergyman.

Stowe was very bright. She learned Latin before age 10 and was teaching it at age 12. She helped her sister open a school and wrote a geography

How the Mass Media Really Work

CASSY MINISTERING TO UNCLE TOM AFTER HIS WHIPPING. Page 198.

An artists drawing of a scene from *Uncle Tom's Cabin*. Cassy is administering to Uncle Tom's wounds after a whipping. Historians say the book had a major impact on turning public opinion against slavery before the Civil War.

textbook before moving to Ohio at age 25. Stowe was very religious and promoted feminist causes as well. Many of the female characters in her writings are presented as equals to men.

Her husband, a teacher, was also an ardent opponent of slavery. To supplement his income, Stowe began writing short stories dealing with domestic life. The royalties enabled her to hire household help to assist with raising their seven children.

In Cincinnati, which was separated only by the Ohio River from a slave-holding community, Stowe met many fugitive slaves and listened to their stories. She also visited Southern states.

Uncle Tom's Cabin was published in serial form in the National Era magazine in 1851. The book was published the following year.

Religion plays a prominent role in the book. Stowe urges people to maintain a personal relationship with God and to love and care for others even if they are cruel and mean.

Uncle Tom's Cabin is the first book to feature a black person as the hero. But Tom did not fight for his freedom; rather, he sought freedom to serve

God. Although religion plays a prominent role in the book, Stowe builds a strong case for the emancipation of slaves.

Stowe also wrote *The Key to Uncle Tom's Cabin* (1853), which reinforced her arguments with a large number of documents and testimonies against slavery. Stowe also wrote many other articles, books and poems. She died in 1896 in Hartford, Connecticut, at the age of 85.

BOOKS AS AGENTS OF SOCIAL CHANGE

The books by Carson and Stowe had a tremendous influence on people and indirectly stimulated substantial social changes. These changes, it should be emphasized, were not radical or revolutionary. Rarely do mass media have such power.

But even if books have limited impact in the short term, it is difficult to dismiss their long-term impact. Who among us hasn't been personally or professionally changed by some books? Although the social impact of books is difficult to measure, few people would dispute the notion that great books can change the world. As mass communication historian John Tebbel puts it:

> [B]ooks ... have done more to shape the course of human affairs than any other product of the human mind because they are the carriers of ideas and it is ideas that change the world. Newspapers, magazines and other products of the press have played a similar role, but it is the book, a less transitory product, which gives permanence, or in some cases the illusion of it, to ideas and permits them to grow, flower and to multiply into intellectual infinity. One need cite only the sacred books of the world's religious faiths as proof.[71]

Indeed, the Bible, the Koran, the Tanakhand and other religious books have had a dramatic impact on people's lives.

Interestingly, when they were first introduced, rulers in many places around the world viewed them as a threat to their power and sought to ban or restrict them. However, as the ideas in these books took hold, the books went from being viewed as radical to conservative. Indeed, today most mainstream religious books promote traditional ideas and values. Books play a key role in regulating and controlling human behavior. In some cases, they also help prevent or slow social change.

But whether one views these or other great books as mechanisms of social control or social change or both, one cannot deny the fact that books have from the beginning of time served as a major repository of ideas.

THE SOCIAL IMPACT OF EARLY BOOKS

In the early 1800s, most of the books published in the United States — 70 percent or more — were written by British authors. But, by 1850, most — 80 percent — were written by Americans. Many of these authors became very famous. They included James Fenimore Cooper, Ralph Waldo Emerson, Nathaniel Hawthorne, Henry David Thoreau, Walt Whitman and Edgar Allen Poe.

Of course, much of the content of the books they wrote reinforced dominant values and institutions in society. But many of the books also contained themes that challenged the status quo and conventional ways of thinking.

For example, the main characters of Cooper's *The Last of the Mohicans* (1826) include noble Indians, not just villainous ones. At the end, the "evil" Mangua pays for his crimes when he is shot and killed by one of the heros. One of the main theme's of Emerson's *Self-Reliance* (1841) is that humans should trust their own intuitions and resist the limitations of mainstream institutions and conventional ideas.

In *The Scarlet Letter* (1850), Hawthorne condemns the Puritan ethic that cannot forgive missteps from the path of virtue. Forgiveness, in other words, is a virtue. And in *Walden* (1854), Thoreau, a student of Emerson, attacks America for its emphasis on materialism and a restrictive work ethic. The emphasis on materialism turns men into "machines" who "lead lives of quiet desperation."

After 1850, American women began making a mark as novelists. They included Stowe and Louisa May Alcott. Alcott wrote *Little Women* (1868), one of the first books to suggest that women can earn their own living and have an identity separate from their husbands, fathers or brothers.

Outside of the United States, the most powerful nonfiction book of the 19th century was Karl Marx's *Das Kapital* (*Capital*, 1867), which was a

Mark Twain's books reinforce dominant values in America, including friendship, freedom, justice and compassion.

stinging indictment of capitalism as an economic system. Marx basically argued that capitalism involves a process where a small number of capitalists (bourgeoisie) exploit the labor of millions of workers (the proletariat). He argued that revolution was inevitable and that the new economic order (communism) would signal an era of freedom for ordinary people.

The revolutions never took place in capitalist economies, but the book inspired revolutions in noncapitalist systems (Russia and China) and continues to inspire many scholars and people who see faults in modern capitalism.

At the end of the 19th century, the most influential novelist in America was Samuel Clemens, better known by his pen name Mark Twain. In fact, Ernest Hemingway and many other writers argued that *The Adventures of Huckleberry Finn* (1885) was the most influential book of the 20th century.

Several common themes run through this book and Twain's other masterpieces, which include *The Adventures of Tom Sawyer* (1876), *The Prince and the Pauper* (1882), and *A Connecticut Yankee in King Arthur's Court* (1889). Some of those themes — which include the importance of friendship, freedom and independence, justice and compassion — reinforce society's dominant values and norms. In *The Prince and the Pauper,* Twain also criticizes people who judge others by the clothes they wear, rather than by what's in their hearts and minds.

Karl Marx is vilified in the United States, but his writings have influenced many social activists and scholars.

How the Mass Media Really Work

Upton Sinclair's The Jungle prompted Congress and state legislatures to enact laws that improved meat packing and inspection.

But Twain also attacked some powerful traditional institutions and values. In *The Adventures of Tom Sawyer,* he takes aim at organized religion, which he believes is based on control and power and does little to stimulate true spirituality. In *The Adventures of Huckleberry Finn,* Twain attacks traditional values about Chivalry, arguing that the American Civil War itself was partly caused by romantic notions of honor and a false sense of glory.

IMPACT OF BOOKS DURING THE 20TH CENTURY

Assessing or measuring the impact of books on public policy or society is never an easy task. This is especially true of fiction works, which are sometimes dismissed simply because they are fiction. But during the early 1900s, several nonfiction books provided more direct evidence of the power of books to influence social policy (i.e., produce social change).

Perhaps the best example was Upton Sinclair's *The Jungle,* which chronicled unhealthy conditions in meat-packing plants in the United States. A socialist, Sinclair hoped his book would persuade people that such abuses would not occur under socialism.[72] But instead of "hitting them" in the head, his book hit them in the stomach. Congress and state legislatures responded by passing laws that improved methods of meat-packing and inspection.

W. E. B. Du Bois, a Ph.D.-educated sociologist, became the best-known champion of civil rights before World War II. He edited a magazine and wrote numerous papers and books, including *The Souls of Black Folks* (1903), which criticized Booker T. Washington's more conservative, or accommodating, approach to securing equal rights. Later, Du Bois was able to influence the U.S. Congress to pass laws that established legal action against lynchers, among other things.

In 1963, Betty Friedan's *Feminine Mystique* stimulated a national debate about the role of women in society and helped mobilize the women's movement. Alex Haley's *Autobiography of Malcolm X* (1965), which chronicles the life of an African American who draws upon Islamic religion to problems facing Black Americans, helps mobilize the civil rights movement.

In the world of fiction, John Steinbeck's *Grapes of Wrath* (1939) took aim at the California agricultural industry and stimulated a number of reforms that helped protect migrant workers in California.

Ernest Hemingway also became one of the best known and loved writers of the century. His *Farewell to Arms* (1929) is a powerful anti-war story, and it argues that there is no glory in modern warfare, where men are reduced to helpless targets. This argument has angered military institutions, which depend heavily on duty and glory to recruit new soldiers and maintain morale.

Hemingway's *For Whom the Bell Tolls* (1940) was more mainstream, criticizing fascism and brutality and extolling the virtues of commitment and camaraderie. Similarly, *The Old Man and the Sea* promotes more traditional values of courage, manhood and respect for nature.

In 1988, Toni Morrison's book *Beloved*, which chronicled the story of an escaped slave woman who killed her baby to save it from slavery, won the Pulitzer Prize for fiction. In 1993, Morrison became the first African American woman to win the Novel Prize in Literature. Oprah Winfrey was so moved by the book that she bought the movie rights, adapted it for television, and starred in the lead role.

Toni Morrison (Photo by Angela Radulescu, used with permission)

TONI MORRISON: COMBATING RACISM THROUGH BOOKS

An African American woman escapes slavery and settles in Ohio in the mid-1800s.[73] When her slave master catches up, she kills her newly born unnamed baby to save her from a life of suffering.

The dead baby, called "Beloved," haunts the house but, eventually, the spell is broken.

That is the rough storyline of Toni Morrison's book, *Beloved*, which in 1988 won a Pulitzer Prize for fiction. In 1993, Morrison won a Nobel Prize for Literature.

In her works, Morrison explores the experience of black women in a racist culture.

"Tell us what it is to be a woman so that we may know what it is to be a man," she wrote in her Nobel Prize acceptance speech. "What moves at the margin. What it is to have no home in this place. To be set adrift from the one you knew. What it is to live at the edge of towns that cannot bear your company."

Many people argue that Morrison's work has had a powerful effect on helping people understand what it is be black in America, especially black and female.

Morrison was born Chloe Anthony Wofford in Lorain, Ohio, in 1931. Her parents moved to the North to escape southern racism. As a child, she read voraciously. Her father was a welder and told her folktales of the black community.

In 1949, she entered Howard University and changed her name from "Chloe" to "Toni," saying that people found "Chloe" too difficult to pronounce. She continued her studies at Cornell University wrote her thesis on suicide in the works of William Faulkner and Virginia Woolf. She received her master of arts degree in 1955.

Morrison taught English at a university and then moved to Syracuse, New York, to work as a textbook editor. At Random House, she edited books by black authors and continued to teach at the State University of New York. In 1984, she was appointed to an Albert Schweitzer chair at the University of New York at Albany, where she helped young writers.

Morrison wrote her first novel, *The Bluest Eye*, in 1970. In 1992 she said she regretted changing her name when she published the novel. The story is set in the community of a small, Midwestern town. The central character is a black girl who prays each night for the blue-eyed beauty of Shirley Temple. The girl believes everything would be all right if only she had beautiful blue eyes.

Morrison gained international attention with the publication of *Song of Solomon* in 1977, which chronicled a black family from a male point of view. She has written three more novels since 1993. They include *Jazz* (1993), *Paradise* (1998) and *Love* (2003).

J. K. ROWLING: MAGIC AS SOCIAL CONTROL

When scholars think of books, they often think of the works by classic authors, such as Morrison. The public, on the other hand, often thinks of more popular works, such as those by Stephen King or Tom Clancy.

J. K. Rowling *(Photo by Daniel Ogren, used with permission)*

In either case, though, the result is the same: All books promote values and ideas, usually ideas that fall within the mainstream. This includes the famous Harry Potter series by Joanne Rowling, better known by her pen name, J. K. Rowling.[74]

The story of Rowling could have been the subject of a Horatio Alger book. During the late 1800s and early 1900s, Alger was famous for his rags-to-riches books. Historians point out that his books reinforced the idea that capitalism was a good economic system because everyone had a chance to get rich, which is largely a myth still perpetuated today.

In the mid-1990s, before she was famous, Rowling was so poor that she had to skip meals to provide enough food for her daughter. By the turn of the new millennium, she was one of the richest women in the world, earning hundreds of millions of dollars a year.

Potter, the main character in her books, is a boy hero with the powers of a wizard. The books draw upon themes as old as the lessons in the *Iliad* and *Odyssey* by Homer. Potter continually confronts evil and defeats it.

Some religious groups have criticized the books for promoting witchcraft. But the public has generally ignored such criticism, and the books have been credited with stimulating reading among young people.

The books have been translated into more than 70 languages and combined have sold more than 500 million copies in 200 countries.

Rowling has won many honors and has been featured on many national television programs. But a decade ago she was single mom in a Catch-22. She couldn't work because she couldn't afford daycare, and she couldn't afford daycare because she wasn't working. So she and her daughter survived on $105 a week in public assistance.

She was born in England in 1965. From an early age, she enjoyed telling stories to her sisters. She wrote her first story, about a rabbit, when she was 5 or 6 years old.

In school, she was terrible at sports but loved English and foreign languages. She wrote a lot in her teen years but never showed much of it to her friends. She attended Exeter University, where she studied French, presumably to enter a career as an administrative assistant. But that was a disaster, she said, because she was a very disorganized person.

"The worst secretary ever."

When she was 26, she went abroad to teach English. She married and had a daughter, but the marriage ended and she found herself having difficulty making ends meet.

The idea for the Harry Potter books came to her in 1990, while she was riding a train.

"Harry just strolled into my head fully formed," she said.

She worked on the book for several years, often while her daughter napped. Several publishers rejected the manuscript.

The values and lessons promoted in the Potter books are very mainstream. They include liberty, independence, free will and choice, sacrificial love, and the evils of materialism.[75]

NEWSPAPERS: SOCIETY'S GUARD DOGS

Security guard Frank Wills never thought of himself as a hero. But don't try telling that to the Democrats.

On June 17, 1972, Wills was making his nightly rounds when he discovered a piece of masking tape over the lock of a door on the first floor of the building he was patrolling. He removed the tape and discovered several other doors that were taped to stay open. When he returned to the first door, he found the tape he removed had been replaced.

Wills called police at 1:47 a.m.

When police arrived, they followed the trail of tape to the Democratic National Committee headquarters, whose offices were located in Wills' building, the Watergate office-apartment-hotel complex in Washington D.C. Police arrested five men who had broken into the offices. Later it turned out four of the burglars were Cuban exiles and one was a former CIA surveillance expert. They were carrying cameras, pens filled with tear gas, eavesdropping equipment and $6,500 in crisp $100 bills.

For two years newspaper reporters followed the story, which eventually tied the burglary to President Richard Nixon. The burglars, acting under orders of Nixon's re-election campaign, had been searching for information to embarrass Democratic presidential candidate George McGovern. They also intended to bug the phones and offices.

But the dirty tricks didn't end there.

The reporters also discovered that Nixon's administration had been spying illegally on U.S. citizens, harassing political opponents, forging campaign literature, and attempting to obstruct justice through a cover-up.

Nixon won the 1972 election, but he resigned two years later, on August 8, 1974, under pressure of impeachment and conviction.

A number of his assistants were convicted and spent time in prison. Nixon, however, never went to prison because he was pardoned by Vice President Gerald Ford, who became president after Nixon resigned. The pardon angered many Americans, and Ford lost the 1976 presidential election to Democrat Jimmy Carter. For a brief time, security guard Frank Wills, who earned $80 a week, was a hero, but he quit his job when his company refused to give him a raise. He died in poverty.

No story in the history of journalism has generated more praise for U.S. mass media. Bob Woodward and Carl Bernstein of the *Washington Post* took the lion's share of credit, helping their newspaper win a Pulitzer Prize. They also wrote a best-selling book, called *All the President's Men,* which was made into a successful movie starring Robert Redford and Dustin Hoffman.[76]

The Watergate story seemed to confirm watchdog theory. This is the notion that the news media are supposed to be watchdogs for the people, especially the powerless and those who have no organized voice in the system. News media are supposed to be adversaries, not advocates, of the government and the powerful. They are supposed to challenge authority and promote democratic ideals.

But how accurate is this ideal?

Do newspapers really challenge the dominant power groups, as suggested by the watchdog notion?

Moreover, what is the primary function of newspapers in a community?

Richard Nixon, leaving the White House after resigning as president in the wake of the Watergate scandal.

ROLE AND FUNCTION OF NEWSPAPERS

Most professional journalists do not see themselves as advocates of government or big business. They see themselves as defenders of truth and justice. They believe they represent the interests of ordinary citizens, not government bureaucrats or corporate elites.

This idea originated with the concept of the press as a Fourth Estate. In 1638, the term Fourth Estate was used to refer to the British Army. The other three were the three estates of Parliament: one representing the nobility, another the clergy and the third the House of Commons. How the term came to be associated with the news media isn't entirely clear.

Nineteenth-century writer Thomas Carlyle gives credit to Edmund Burke, an eighteenth century British statesman and political philosopher.[77] Burke once commented that in addition to the three estates there was the Reporters' Gallery in Parliament, "a fourth estate more important than they all. It is not a figure of speech or witty saying; it is a literal fact, very momentous to us in these times."

Some historians, however, doubt this report.[78]

The first reliable citation is an essay by Thomas Bington Macaulay in 1828, who wrote that "the gallery in which the reporters sit has become a fourth estate of the realm."

Whatever the origins, the concept plays an important role in the ideology of contemporary journalism, and is closely allied with the watchdog concept — or the idea that the press should actively search for abuses of authority and power.

More formally, the assumption behind the Fourth Estate concept, according to mass communication researchers George A. Donohue, Clarice N. Olien and Phillip J. Tichenor, is that the press acts "as a checking mechanism, constantly reminding the government groups about where ultimate sovereignty resides and ensuring that the obligations of the social contract are observed."[79] In this country, these ideas are often traced to Thomas Jefferson, the third U.S. president.

Jefferson believed that even though individuals may make mistakes, the majority of the populace could make sound decisions if given access to accurate and truthful information. He advocated education and argued that the press was an essential source of information and guidance and should be free from governmental control. In addition to educating the individual, the press should serve as a check on the government, to prevent it from infringing on the rights of the individual.

No experiment can be more interesting than that we are now trying, and which we trust will end in establishing the fact, that man may be governed by reason and truth. Our first object should therefore be, to leave open to him all the avenues to truth. The most effectual hitherto found, is the freedom of the press.[80]

Although the Fourth Estate and watchdog concepts are widely recognized in journalism, many scholars who study newspapers and news media reach just the opposite conclusion. Some even believe journalists act more like lap dogs for the rich and powerful than watchdogs for the poor and weak. The lap dog theory sees newspapers and other media as powerful agents of social control.

The truth, we shall argue here, actually lies somewhere in-between the watchdog and lap dog theories — in what three mass communication researchers at the University of Minnesota have called the guard dog theory. Newspapers clearly generate content that supports dominant values and institutions. They help support the status quo (i.e., the powerful institutions and groups in a community). But they also publish content that, at times, challenges those in positions of power and occasionally benefits the less powerful, the less privileged.

GUARD DOG THEORY

More formally, University of Minnesota mass communication researchers Phillip J. Tichenor, George A. Donohue and Clarice N. Olien liken the media to a guard dog. The basic idea is that media serve as a guard dog not for the entire community but for the political and special interest elite groups that hold power.

The "Minnesota Team" argued that the watchdog theory — which sees media as representing the average citizen — is fundamentally a myth, "in the sense of a sentinel of the general community keeping watch over central powers of government." The Minnesota Team also rejected the neo-Marxist or critical theory perspective, which tended to see media as lap dogs of political or economic elites. This couldn't be the case because, the Team pointed out, the media often attack or criticize powerful elites (Watergate is a good example), and elites in turn often are critical of the mass media (see for comparisons between the models).

Instead, the researchers argue that mainstream media are "a sentry not for the community as a whole, but for those particular groups who have the

How the Mass Media Really Work

COMPARISONS BETWEEN THE WATCHDOG, LAP DOG, AND GUARD DOG MODELS

Characteristic	Canine Analogy		
	Lap Dog Model	Guard Dog Model	Watchdog Model
News media relationship to elites	Media are advocate for elites; rarely critical of them	Media are mostly advocate, but can be adversary of elites	Media are adversary of elites; strongly critical of them
Social control and social change functions of news media in society	Media are powerful agents of social control; they inhibit change that might benefit disadvantaged groups or the public	Media support status quo and rarely initiate change, but they can facilitate change that benefits disadvantaged groups and the public	Media are powerful agents of change for the disadvantaged and public, and they are agents of control for (watchdogs of) elites
Policy Outcome	Media inhibit democracy	Media do good and bad things for democracy; depends on who benefits from coverage	Media enhance democracy

power and influence to create and command their own security systems."[81] Guard dog media "are conditioned to be suspicious of all potential intruders, and they occasionally sound the alarm for reasons that individuals in the master households, that is, the authority structure, can neither understand nor prevent. These occasions occur primarily when authority within the structure is divided."

The press is most likely to "bark" at elites when they are attacked by another powerful elite group (such as when Democrats criticize Republicans), or when elites in power violate the laws and norms (as in Watergate). The media's role is not to protect individual elites or organizations, per se, but, rather, to protect "the system." Any individual actor is expendable, but attacking or challenging the system itself (e.g., values, norms) is much more problematic. Mainstream media provide broad-based support for dominant institutions and values, such as responsible capitalism, representative democracy and family values.

From a broader perspective, the Minnesota Team sees the mass media as one institution among many (police, courts, schools, churches, businesses) that plays an important role in helping maintain society and the status quo. Media provide information that social actors use to achieve their personal and professional goals. Thus, the guard dog model is fundamentally a social control model.[82]

One implication of the guard dog model is that social change comes slowly, because elites usually resist changes that might affect their power and wealth. Also, change usually comes only when elites have an interest in changing the system. If elites have no interest in change, then there often is little media coverage.

WATERGATE AND GUARD DOG THEORY

Watergate is a good example.

On the surface, it may seem strange to argue that Watergate is a good example of how newspapers reinforce the status quo. After all, didn't the news media bring down the most powerful individual in the world?

Yes, but the resignation did not lead to radical change. Watergate is a prime example of how media help maintain a system. And to understand why this is the case, we first need to make a distinction between individual problems and social structural problems.

Almost from the beginning, the problem of Watergate was defined primarily as an individual problem, not as a problem of the social structure. In other words, the media spotlight was focused on the illegal actions of various individuals connected with the Nixon administration, who were defined as "bad actors." The media did not focus on the social structure as the source of problem — that is, that there was something wrong with the laws or structure of the American system of democracy.

This distinction is important.

When problems are defined in individual terms, problems are resolved by punishing or controlling the individuals. This generally does not lead to much social change. But when the problem is defined as systemic, or part of the social structure, then the social system must be changed to correct the problem, and this can have a much greater impact on people's lives now and in the future.

The claim that media coverage of the Watergate scandal is an example of social control ironically was confirmed by Vice President Gerald Ford the day after Nixon resigned and Ford became president. "Our long national nightmare is over," Ford said, adding that Watergate demonstrates "our system (of governance) works." He praised the press, and then urged the country to turn to other issues.

In short, the problem of Watergate did not stem from the system itself, Ford declares. It stemmed from a handful of individuals who violated the rules. The media played a crucial role in defining which rules were broken, and to that extent reinforced the status quo.

In Watergate, the moral lesson was that politicians should not engage in dirty tricks, or violate the trust of the people, or cheat, lie or steal.[83] These acts violate rules and laws. By drawing attention to the "abuses of power" that occurred during

The mastermind behind the Watergate burglary was G. Gordon Liddy, who had worked for the CIA and President Nixon. He and the five burglars were vilified for their role in bugging Democratic National Headquarters. *(Photo courtesy of Miami Dade County Archives, used with permission)*

Watergate, the media played an important role in reminding others about the rules and reinforcing the power of these institutions to control people.

Media coverage, in other words, reinforced the status quo.

From a broad perspective, all investigative reporting can be seen as helping to support the social system. That's because all investigative stories have a moral lesson embedded within them. They either draw attention to the violation of some law or norm or they suggest that the system needs a law or norm to correct a wrong.

But social systems are not static.

They change, and investigative reporting can help promote change that contributes to social order.

Watergate and Social Change

Admittedly, the Watergate scandal did not change the social system a whole lot. The institution of the Presidency continues to be very powerful — in fact, probably more powerful today than at any time in history. And many politicians still engage in dirty tricks (e.g., the latest fashion in the United States is negative political advertising).

But it would be unfair to say the Watergate story had no effect on the system. In the months and years after Watergate, Congress (and many states) passed a series of "good government" bills or rules designed to restore faith in the political process. Among other things, these actions

- limited individual contributions to candidates for federal office to $1,000 for each primary, election and runoff, and to $5,000 for political action committees;
- required candidates running for federal office to identify people and organizations that contribute $100 or more to a campaign;
- eliminated office "slush" funds, limited spending on direct mail to constituents, and eventually banned honoraria;
- required elected officials to file annual reports detailing some aspects of their income and investments; and
- resulted in the enactment of an independent prosecutor law.

To be sure, none of these changes has radically altered the distribution of power in American society. Some say the office of the president is even stronger today than it was then.

As such, some scholars argue that investigative journalism is politically conservative. They point out that stories rarely address questions of what has gone wrong in the system, who should be accountable, and how things should be changed. In many cases, journalists consider such matters as going beyond the bounds of "objectivity" in reporting (see Chapter 2).

News Reporting and Social Change

Many other examples in which investigative reporting has had little or no impact on the system could be cited. However, there also are many

Frederick Remington's painting of the charge of Teddy Roosevelt (on horse) and the Rough Riders at San Juan Hill. Roosevelt called the reform-minded journalists of his day "muckrakers."

examples that have contributed to significant social change — change that has benefited the disadvantaged and disenfranchised.

For example, during the early part of the 20th century, capitalism was clearly "out of control." Factory workers in Europe and the United States worked up to 16 hours a day, were paid poor wages and worked in unsafe and unsanitary conditions. Few laws regulated industry. But the abuses drew the attention of a small group of journalists, dubbed "muckrakers" by Teddy Roosevelt, who gave them that derogatory title because they had exposed corruption in the U.S. Senate.

Turning Teddy on his head, so to speak, the journalists appropriated the muckraker title as a badge of honor. Their newspaper and magazine stories led the federal and many state governments to enact a number of laws or regulations that broke up monopolies in the oil industry, placed greater sanitary regulations on the meat-packing industry, improved working conditions for factory workers, recognized the right of laborers to unionize, limited working hours for children, improved housing conditions and increased penalties for government abuse of power.

From a systemwide perspective, these reforms no doubt helped to "cool down" radical groups and reduced the potential for violent or revolutionary change.

During the 1960s and 1970s, mainstream media increasingly began covering social movements seeking greater rights and opportunities for women and protection of the environment. Beginning in the 1970s, journalists at many large, corporate newspapers across the United States investigated reports of police brutality, and their stories helped contribute to the formation of many civilian review boards.

Philadelphia Inquirer reporters Donald L. Barlett and James B. Steele also made a name for themselves with a number of investigative reports on the criminal justice system and Washington's relationship with special interest groups.

Today, the interests of investigative reporters are championed by an organization called Investigative Reporters and Editors (IRE), which is based at the University of Missouri (see Internet Resources listing at end of this chapter for more information).

Although investigative reporting often promotes social change, it is important to point out that everyday journalism often has the same impact. For example, mass media historian Dolores Flamiano found that during the early part of the 20th century mainstream newspapers and magazines "helped to bring the concerns of the birth control movement to a larger, more heterogeneous audience."

During the 1950s, some newspapers, like *The New York Times*, *The Nashville Tennessean* and *The Atlanta Constitution*, were publishing news reports about acts of discrimination and racism against African Americans. But most newspapers paid little attention to the problems facing minorities in America.

In summer of 2004, one newspaper — *The Lexington* (Kentucky) *Herald-Leader* — even admitted that it failed to cover the civil rights movement during the 1950s. Why? Because, scholars have found, newspapers take their cue (and news) from powerful white political elites, who at that time were refusing to grant status to civil rights leaders or their movement.

But newspapers and television news began to cover the civil rights movement more after the U.S. Supreme Court and Congress legitimated the civil rights movement with a series of court ruling and laws. By the early 1960s, *The News York Times* gave prominent coverage to the civil rights movement and to Martin Luther King's "I Have a Dream" speech.

A protestor offers a flower to military police on guard at the Pentagon during an anti-Vietnam War demonstration in 1967. For many years mainstream news coverage marginalized anti-war protestors, primarily because the politicians whom journalists quoted overwhelmingly supported the war. The coverage turned more favorable toward protestors in the early 1970s when three-fourths of the public and many moderate politicians turned against the war.

In 1968, journalists in Vietnam rebuffed U.S. military propaganda about the Tet Offensive, and their reports helped turn public opinion against the war — so much so that after those reports were published or broadcast a majority of citizens opposed the war.[84] "The media's negative assessment proved more convincing than Washington's statements of victory because it confirmed the sense of frustration that most Americans shared over the conflict," according to Vietnam historian Sandra C. Taylor.

ALTERNATIVE NEWSPAPERS AS AGENTS OF CHANGE

During the 1960s, critics of the Vietnam War pointed out that coverage of the war in mainstream daily newspapers was biased — that it had a pro-U.S. involvement slant.

Although there were some exceptions, these charges were generally accurate. The heavy dependence that journalists had on the White House and on the U.S. military generally produced news that legitimated and supported U.S. involvement in Vietnam and Southeast Asia.

In response, some critics started up their own newspapers, which were often dubbed "underground" newspapers, because they criticized U.S. foreign policy as well as promoted use of drugs like marijuana and the so-called "hippie" lifestyle. Many of the alternative newspapers, which published either weekly or monthly, also promoted civil rights, women's rights and gay rights.

The underground newspapers drew intellectual strength from poets and writers like Allen Ginsberg, Jack Kerouac and Eldridge Cleaver and from musicians like Woodie Guthrie, Pete Seeger, Bob Dylan and Joan Baez. The most prominent underground newspaper was the Village Voice, which was founded in Greenwich Village.

After the Vietnam War, most of the underground newspapers went out of business, but some survived by turning more of their attention to music and the arts. They also toned down their criticism of the "establishment," which made them more palatable to advertisers, most of whom had no interest in supporting "radical" causes. This is a good example, by the way, of how the profit-motive helps control and limit the distribution of critical ideas in a society.

Today, most large cities in the United States have at least one weekly newspaper that caters to the arts and entertainment business in a community. But it is rare to find one that can match the "critical edge" of the newspapers that were published during the Vietnam War.

OTHER NEWSPAPER FUNCTIONS

The guard dog function is not the only role or function newspapers and the mass media can perform.

The mass media are often said to be an informer, or a forum for the exchange of ideas and information, a transmitter of culture, an entertainer, a recorder of past events, an educator, an interpreter of complex events, a source of community solidarity, a promoter of democracy, a source of advertising for consumers, a promoter of social reform, and a shaper of the public agenda.[85]

But notice that all of these functions or roles have implications for social control — for integrating people and groups into the dominant culture.

Some people see the newspapers and other media as performing a negative or dysfunctional role, such as a manipulator of public opinion or a debaser of culture. Violent content also is often thought to produce aggressive behavior in children[86] and a perception of the world as a mean and scary place in adults.[87]

Newspapers and other media can have dysfunctional consequences for individuals, to be sure. But when taken as a whole, research shows that media content clearly supports powerful groups and their interests and, at times, can criticize them.

From a historical perspective, it is fair to say that newspapers — more than any other medium — have broadened the role that ordinary citizens can play in political affairs. Three hundred years ago people around the world had very little say in their own governance. Power was extremely centralized. Kings, emperors, nobles, despots, military leaders and tribal chiefs ruled.

But the printing press helped decentralize control over knowledge and information, and newspapers in many countries played a key role in giving ordinary citizens a greater role in everyday political affairs. Metaphorically, the newspapers helped create a "public sphere," one in which political ideas and social problems could be discussed and debated. Newspapers helped create a world of "politics for everyone," albeit that role is somewhat limited for ordinary citizens.

MAGAZINES: SPECIALIZED CONTROL

When Ida M. Tarbell's father heard she was going to write a series of articles about The Standard Oil Company for *McClure's* magazine, he pleaded with her not to do it.[88]

In 1897, Standard Oil controlled 90 percent of the oil production in the United States. The company, headed by John D. Rockefeller, had run many competitors out of business, including her father's business partner, who had shot himself to death. Now Frank Tarbell was struggling to pay off his partner's debts.

"Don't do it, Ida," he pleaded. "They will ruin the magazine."

Other friends and associates gave similar warnings.

But Ida was not easily frightened.

She was independent, college-educated, and talented. She believed injustice should be confronted and defeated.

John D. Rockefeller

So, with the support of S. S. McClure, her magazine publisher-boss, Tarbell began investigating Standard Oil. For five years, she dug into files of previous lawsuits and obtained a copy of a congressional investigation that had been suppressed. She interviewed scores of current and former business partners and clients.[89]

The end result was one of the greatest and most powerful investigative stories of all time — a 19-part series that set into motion a series of events that led to the break-up of the world's greatest oil trust. Tarbell's first story appeared in *McClure's* magazine in November 1902. She profiled Rockefeller, who was revealed to be a conniving, deceitful, greedy and dishonest man.[90]

More importantly, Tarbell's articles revealed that Rockefeller had made secret deals with the railroad companies

Ida Tarbell

to have his company's oil shipped at discount. This was illegal, because the railroads were monopolies and were required by law to charge the same rates to everyone.

But Rockefeller's underhanded scheme enabled him to bankrupt or buyout scores of smaller refineries. Rockefeller even had deals with newspapers. More than 100 newspapers in Ohio, for instance, had signed contracts with Standard Oil, guaranteeing that they would print editorials and news in favor of the company in exchange for advertising.

Standard Oil tried to discredit Tarbell after the

McClure's Magazine published exposés of abuses in capitalism.

stories began appearing. Rockefeller and company spokesmen called her "Miss Tarbarrel." They fed stories to newspapers that belittled and criticized her. When her articles were published into a book two years later, an oil industry publication subsidized by Standard Oil headlined its review: "Hysterical Woman Versus Historical Facts." A Harvard University economist criticized Tarbell's book and called her "a mere gatherer of folklore." Standard Oil distributed 5,000 copies of his attack.

But all of these attempts to destroy Tarbell failed. She had truth on her side, and the public could sense that. They loved her, and, for a time, she was one of the most famous women in America.

Nearly two dozen anti-trust lawsuits were filed against Standard Oil from 1904 to 1906. The U.S. Bureau of Corporations launched an investigation and in 1906 handed a report to President Theodore Roosevelt that confirmed Tarbell's findings.

The tide had turned against Rockefeller and Standard Oil, and the bad news kept pouring in. Newspaper publisher William Randolph Hearst came into possession of documents which showed that Standard Oil had been bribing judges, Congressmen and U.S. Senators. Finally, in 1911, the U.S. Supreme Court issued a decree ordering the breakup of Standard Oil, because the court determined that the company's goal had been "to drive others from the field and exclude them from their right to trade."[91]

McClure's magazine prospered during this time. Its circulation eventually exceeded 500,000, making it one of the two biggest magazines in America.

Tarbell and other journalists at the magazine had a disagreement with McClure and left in 1906. They purchased and edited *American Magazine*. Tarbell also lectured and wrote several popular biographies, including eight books on Abraham Lincoln. She served on numerous governmental committees throughout her life.

She remained single to preserve her independence and freedom. She died in 1944 at the age of 87. *McClure's* magazine went out of business in the 1930s.

ROLE AND FUNCTION OF MAGAZINES

Few stories in the history of magazine journalism have had as much impact on the political process as Tarbell's "History of the Standard Oil Company." Her stories prompted government authorities to break-up of Standard Oil, and they also indirectly prompted changes in anti-trust laws that gave the U.S. government greater authority to regulate monopolistic practices in the private sector.

Like newspaper investigative stories, Tarbell's exposé on Standard Oil may be seen as performing a guard-dog function for society. It helped construct (or reconstruct) a social problem (abuse of power by big business) that policymakers were encouraged to solve for "the good of the entire community or society."

Yet magazines have a social control function that is distinct from newspapers and other media. Most notably, magazines typically offer more specialized content and more in-depth coverage.[92]

For example, in terms of political content, magazines clearly offer a wider variety of choices than daily newspapers, radio or television. There are magazines that cater to political activists or junkies on the extreme left end of the spectrum (communist) as well as on the extreme right (fascist), and the middle, too. Although many people abhor extremist perspectives, civil rights advocates point out that freedom of expression can be likened to a "safety valve" that reduces the potential for violence and revolution.

Of course, books can compete with magazines in terms of specialization and depth. However, magazines publish more regularly and, thus, create "ongoing communities of special interest" — something that is more difficult to do with books. Every week or month those communities are given a fresh supply of information or entertainment content on that topic of interest. And there seems to be a magazine out there to serve every unique interest.

For example, magazines like *Time* specialize in news and politics, while *Good Housekeeping* and *Redbook* provide a wide range of advice on domestic living and home life. There are serious literary magazines, like *The New Yorker*, and those that spoof culture, such as *Mad* magazine. There are magazines that cater to car lovers, literary afficionados, quilt makers, sailors and body builders. Some magazines also keep people up to date on the latest celebrity gossip and give them advice on parenting and coping with life changes.

Of course, all of these magazines — even the nonpolitical ones — have implications for social control. Entertainment and hobby magazines help people relax and escape from the stresses of life.

But magazines can, from time to time, also shake things up. As this chapter will point out, the muckraking era in the early 1900s provides one of the most prominent examples.

Capitalism Out of Control

At the turn of the century, capitalism was on a roll.[93]

Business was booming.

Railroads were expanding.

Industrial output was growing rapidly. Factories were turning out all kinds of new products and time-saving devices.

Many people dreamed of leading the life of a Horatio Alger book character — someone who becomes fabulously rich through hard work. Of

Two women on the picket line during the "Uprising of the 20,000," a garment workers strike in New York City in 1910.

course, some did. John D. Rockefeller, Andrew Carnegie, Jay Gould, J. P. Morgan, Cornelius Vanderbilt and Daniel Drew built financial empires in the oil, railroad, steel, shipping and banking industries.[94]

But appearances were deceiving.

In fact, life for many urban residents was less than ideal. Poverty was widespread, even among employed workers. Many factories and businesses paid low wages and required workers to work 14 or more hours a day, six to seven days a week. The wages were so low in some cases that everyone in a family, including children, had to work in order to survive.

Housing conditions also were awful.

Access to health care was often nonexistent.

New immigrants especially suffered. They were forced to accept the worst and lowest paying jobs.

Labor unions were despised. Most newspapers editorialized in favor of business owners and capitalists; they seldom sympathized with striking workers, who they usually described as anarchists or dangerous radicals.[95]

The burgeoning factory system was producing wealth, as Adam Smith had predicted in his 1776 classic book, *The Wealth of Nations*.[96] But, as Karl

Marx correctly pointed out in the mid-1800s,[97] the wealth went not to the workers or ordinary people — it went to the capitalists, or what he called the "owners of the means of production." The "robber barons" got richer and richer while many workers, or proletariat, lived in poverty.

Not all was well in America.

In fact, at the turn of the century, millions Americans called themselves "socialist" or "communist" or identified with left-wing political parties. To them, capitalism was out of control. It could not solve many economic, political and social problems, despite what the free-market economists said. And it could not be trusted to police itself.

THE MUCKRAKING MAGAZINES

One consequence of this discontent was the progressive social movement, which lasted from about 1890 to 1915.[98] Although the term has its roots in religious concepts, the progressive movement wanted greater democratic participation for individuals. It also believed in science. And it wanted to check the power of large businesses and restore the power of the individual entrepreneur or craftsman.

This, then, was the state of affairs in America when Ida Tarbell began investigating Rockefeller and the Standard Oil Company. But her story was only part of the picture. Dozens of other journalists were investigating unfair businesses practices, as well as corruption in city and state government, poor sanitation in meat packing plants, fraud in patent medicines, and poor housing, working and health conditions. They included:

- David Graham Phillips (1867-1911), a former newspaper reporter, book author and freelance writer who exposed graft and corruption in the U.S. Senate in his 10-part series, "The Treason of the Senate," which was published in *Cosmopolitan* magazine. The series documented how rich businessmen bribed senators.
- Jacob Riis (1849-1914), a New York newspaper reporter who exposed child labor abuses, industrial water pollution, and slum housing conditions. Riis mastered photography and his pictures convinced others the problems were real. He wrote and took

Muckraker Upton Sinclair (in white suit and armband) is arrested in 1914 at the Rockefeller Building in New York City for protesting conditions of Colorado coal miners.

pictures for several books, including *How the Other Half Lives, The Children of the Poor,* and *The Battle with the Slum.*

- Lincoln Steffens (1866-1936), a former newspaper reporter and managing editor of *McClure's* magazine who investigated corruption in government in numerous cities (Chicago, Cincinnati, Cleveland, Minneapolis, New York, and Pittsburgh) and in state government (Illinois, Missouri, New Jersey, Ohio, Rhode Island, and Wisconsin). His 1904 book on corruption in city government, *The Shame of the Cities,* was a best-seller.

- Upton Sinclair (1878-1968), a novelist who hoped his exposé of unsanitary Chicago meat-packing factories would motivate people to join the socialist party. However, instead of "hitting them in the head," his book, *The Jungle,* hit them in the stomach. The government responded by invoking legislation that increased safety and health standards at meat-packing facilities. Sinclair wrote many other books and eventually won a Pulitzer Prize in 1942 for *Dragon's Teeth,* a book about the rise of Hitler.

How the Mass Media Really Work

These and other exposés encouraged legislation that protected children and the environment, gave women the right to vote, reformed the judicial system, increased anti-trust prosecutions, and improved the safety of food and drugs. In fact, their stories were so powerful that, as briefly mentioned in Chapter 4, President Theodore Roosevelt ridiculed the investigative reporters, calling them "muckrakers." In those days, a muckraker was a person who spread or picked up manure. But the journalists took the insult as a badge of honor, and to this day the term has had a positive connotation in the field of journalism.

Today, few magazines specialize in investigative reporting. One notable exception is *Mother Jones*, which was launched in 1976 by the non-profit Foundation for National Progress. But, ironically, the decline of muckraking since the turn of the century may stem in part from its own success. The reforms instituted in response to the muckrakers' exposés helped cool down some radicals and social movements. Since then, other reforms — such as expanding rights for labor unions, women and minorities — also have been interpreted as playing a role in cooling down some social movements.[99]

MAGAZINES, CIVIL RIGHTS AND POLITICS

Before the Civil War, a number of magazines also promoted the abolition of slavery and the rights of African Americans. They included *National Era*, the *National Anti-Slavery Standard*, the *Saturday Visiter* (sic), and the Anglo-African Magazine. Harriet Beecher Stowe's *Uncle Tom's Cabin* first appeared in serial form in the *National Era*.

Another good example of an abolitionist publication was the *National Reformer*, which was the organ of the American Moral Reform Society, an interracial organization. It was edited by William Whipper, the son of a black servant and her white employer. The *Reformer* advocated a number of reforms, including abolition, equal rights for blacks and women, temperance and nonviolence. Arguing the cause of slavery for the South was *DeBow's Magazine*.[100]

Although the magazine industry continued to become more specialized as the 19th century came to a close, political and social commentary, which had always been a staple of magazines, didn't die out. In fact, a number of magazines devoted to critical review prospered during this time and are still

Abolitionist newspaper editor Elijah P. Lovejoy was killed when a proslavery mob attacked him and a colleague in this house in Alton, Illinois on November 7, 1837.

in existence. They include *Atlantic Monthly* (1857), *Harper's New Monthly Magazine* (1850, now called *Harper's Magazine*), and *The Nation* (1865).

The muckrakers' investigations and the progressive era effectively came to a close with the start of World War I. The nation's attention shifted to the war in Europe and to stopping Germany's imperialist policies. During times of war, research has shown that social movements usually are forced to put their goals on hold for the good of the entire country.[101] The number of new magazine start-ups also dropped.

But after the war several new magazines offering specialized content or a unique approach emerged on the scene. One of those was *Reader's Digest*, which appeared in 1922 and carved its niche by purchasing the rights to books and articles from other publishers and condensing them for easy reading. The magazine was very conservative, moralistic and anti-communist, which meant it tended to serve a conservative readership base.

But it was extremely successful. At one point, it achieved a circulation of 20 million.

The first modern news magazines were founded in the 1920s. Henry Luce created *Time* in 1923. His successful formula involved summarizing the

How the Mass Media Really Work

big news stories of the week and classifying them into more than 20 different departments or sections. *Time* also had conservative leanings.

Newsweek, which had more liberal and Democratic ties, was founded in the early 1930s. In contrast to newspapers, which were closely tied to the ethic of objectivity, news magazines "colored" their stories with opinion and analysis.

The New Yorker, which positioned itself as a magazine of humor and literary fare for the sophisticated urbanite, was founded in 1925. Some of the best writers in this country have written articles for it, including James Thurber and E. B. White, who together coauthored in 1933 a tongue-in-cheek piece titled, "Is Sex Necessary?" Today, *The New Yorker,* which also publishes nonfiction articles on current affairs, is considered by many critics to be the best literary magazine in the world.

Photojournalism came of age in the 1930s. Although magazines had been publishing woodcut pictures since the 19th century, the idea that photos themselves could tell a story really began with several European magazines and Henry Luce's *Life* magazine, which was founded in 1936. *Life,* a weekly picture magazine, was so successful in the 1950s that it alone generated one-fifth of all U.S. magazine advertising revenues. *Look,* another photo magazine, appeared the following year.

Economic growth and the growth of the stock market during the early 1900s stimulated interest in business news. *Forbes* magazine was founded in 1917 by Scottish immigrant B. C. Forbes, who was then a columnist for Hearst newspapers. In 1929, McGraw-Hill Publishing Company founded *Business Week,* which became the leading business and financial news magazine.

None of the magazines targeted to African Americans and founded before the Civil War survived it. Several other magazines founded in the early 1900s — *Voice of the Negro* and *Colored American* — had financial difficulty.

But in 1910, W. E. B. Du Bois, an executive for the National Association for the Advancement of Colored People, founded *The Crisis,* which achieved a circulation of more than 100,000 in eight years. Du Bois, who is revered today as one of the greatest civil rights champions in the history of the United States, edited the magazine until 1934. *The Crisis* challenged the concepts of white supremacy and black inferiority at a time when these ideas were widely accepted. NAACP still publishes the magazine.

W. E. B. Du Bois: A Radical Force for Change

In May 1919, William Edward Burghardt Du Bois was angry.[102]

W. E. B. Du Bois

Although many African Americans had served in the U.S. Armed Forces during World War I and some had lost their lives, those returning were treated like second-class citizens at home. They were denied jobs because they were black. Some were lynched by white mobs for taking jobs in the North. And those that remained in the military were denied promotions.

"By the God of Heaven, we are cowards and jackasses if now that the war is over we do not marshal every ounce of our brain and brawn to fight the forces of hell in our own land," Du Bois wrote in a famous editorial titled, "Returning Soldier," and published in the magazine *Crisis,* which he edited. "We return. We return from fighting. We return fighting! Make way for Democracy! We saved it in France, and by the great Jehovah, we will save it in the United States of America, or know the reason why."

Congress listened.

It passed legislation to inaugurate black officer training schools, establish legal action against lynchers and set up a federal work program for returning veterans.

Du Bois was a famous sociologist and black protest leader. But it was his journalism and books that moved people to action.

Du Bois was born in 1868 in Massachusetts. He endured many racial insults as a child. At age 15, he became the local correspondent for the *New York Globe,* a position he used to urge Blacks to politicize themselves.

How the Mass Media Really Work

Two years later, he attended college in Nashville, and it was there that he witnessed discrimination and racism in its most extreme forms. After graduation, he entered Harvard graduate school, attended school in Germany and became the first black man to earn a Ph.D. at Harvard. His dissertation, *The Suppression of the African Slave Trade in America,* remains the authoritative work on that subject.

He took a teaching job and conducted empirical research on African American life in America, writing numerous papers and books, including *The Souls of Black Folks,* which criticized Booker T. Washington's more conservative, or accommodating, approach to securing equal rights. Du Bois became more radical as time passed, but he never joined the communist party.

He founded and edited for 25 years *Crisis* magazine, which was published by the National Association for the Advancement of Colored People (NAACP), a group he helped create in 1909. Du Bois was a superb writer. His mission was to make people aware of the problems that faced African Americans. He wanted racial equality and he fought tirelessly all his life to achieve that goal. But he became disillusioned at the end of his life, and he renounced his U.S. citizenship and moved to Ghana, where he died in 1963.

Historians today widely agree that Du Bois is the most important black protest leader in the first half of the 20th century, and he continues to influence many contemporary civil rights leaders.

MAGAZINES AND SPECIALIZATION

When television arrived on the scene in the 1950s, the most popular magazines were *Reader's Digest, Life, Look, Collier's*, and *Saturday Evening Post.* Like television, all of them appealed to large, general audiences.

But only one of them — *Reader's Digest* — survived beyond the 1970s. *Collier's* closed in 1956, the *Post* in 1969, *Look* in 1971, and *Life* in 1972.[103] The irony is that all of the magazines had large circulations when they folded.

Saturday Evening Post, for example, had a circulation of about 6 million and a pass-along rate of 14 million readers (meaning each magazine was read by more than two people). The main problem was a loss of advertising.

Advertisers dropped general magazines and went to television, partly because it drew extremely large audiences, was more engaging and more cost effective per consumer.

But not every manufacturer wanted to reach large audiences. As people's needs for goods and services became more unique and specialized, manufacturers began producing more specialized products and services to meet those needs. Manufacturers needed cheap and efficient ways of reaching their specialized target markets, and magazines were ideally suited to meet that need. Thus, television had relatively little impact on specialized magazines, because those magazines could deliver specialized audiences to advertisers for a much lower cost.

One of the best success stories was *Ebony*.

The magazine, founded in 1945 by John H. Johnson, targeted middle-class African Americans. The magazine imitated the format of *Life*, publishing a lot of pictures and news stories. Its circulation grew dramatically and now exceeds 2 million. *Ebony* is published by Johnson Publishing Company, which also publishes the newsmagazine *Jet*, and is the world's largest Black-owned publishing company.

Another successful specialized magazine established after World War II was the *National Review*, launched in 1955 by conservative William F. Buckley, Jr. The *Review* was targeted to conservatives and had a circulation of more than 100,000 by 1977.

But perhaps the most phenomenal success story of the 1950s was Hugh Hefner's *Playboy*, a magazine launched in 1953 and targeted to men. *Playboy* featured partially nude photos of women and articles written by leading writers. The first issue featured Marilyn Monroe on the cover and sold more than 51,000 copies. *Playboy*'s circulation reached 7 million in 1972, but afterward began to decline because of competition from *Penthouse* and *Hustler*, which offered more explicit erotic photography.

Magazines and the "New Generation"

Magazines on the left of the political spectrum struggled during the conservative, anti-communist 1950s. But they made a comeback during the 1960s and 1970s, when sentiment against conservative politics and the Vietnam War grew. *The Nation* (1865) and *The New Republic* (1914), for example, attracted new customers, especially from younger, college-educated people.

Magazines geared to serving the interests of young people also emerged during the 1960s and 1970s. *Rolling Stone,* which focused on music and politics, was founded in 1967. By 1977, the magazine had a circulation of 500,000 and was a $10-million-a-year operation.

In 1965, *Cosmopolitan* magazine, faced with declining circulation, hired Helen Gurley Brown to

Helen Gurley Brown in 1964

remake the magazine. Brown, the author of the best-selling book *Sex and the Single Girl*, turned the literary *Cosmopolitan* into a magazine for young, career-minded women. Circulation climbed and today *Cosmopolitan* has about 3 million subscribers.

Occasionally, magazines on the left could also shake up the status quo. One of those was *MS.* magazine, which was launched in 1971 and promoted the belief that when women are liberated, men will be too. The magazine was edited by Gloria Steinem, who became famous after she went undercover as a "bunny" in a Playboy club and later wrote about her "degrading" experience. *MS.* magazine reached a circulation of 500,000 by 1983, but eventually went out of business and since has been revived as an adless monthly.

Another magazine that bucked the status quo was *The Progressive*, which became internationally famous when it tried in 1979 to publish an article titled, "The H-bomb Secret: How We Got It — Why We're Telling It." Although the article was based mainly on public sources and experts said no one could build a bomb with just the information in the article, the U.S.

government filed a lawsuit to block publication. A U.S. district court sided with the government, but the case became moot after another publication published the article and the government dropped its lawsuit.

Although some magazines have challenged the status quo, most reinforce mainstream values. *Newsweek* coverage of the attacks the World Trade Center and Pentagon in 2001 provides a good example of the social control function of magazines.

NEWSWEEK AND 9/11: MOBILIZING OPINION AGAINST AN ENEMY

On the morning of Sept. 11, 2001, *Newsweek* editor Mark Whitaker was assembling a team of reporters and assigning stories when Donald Graham, chairman and CEO of the Washington Post Company, which owned *Newsweek*, called.[104]

"Buddy, this is going to be one of the biggest stories you'll ever cover," Graham said. "Do what you have to do."

Whitaker later said the comment giving him carte blanche to cover the terrorist attack "was hugely inspiring." The magazine published a special newsstand issue titled "Attack on America" two days after the attacks. This was followed up with three regular issues: "God Bless America," which examined of the after-effects of the attacks under the photo of firefighters raising the flag at the World Trade Center ruins; "Trail of Terror," which examined Osama bin Laden's organization; and "Why They Hate Us," a look at the Arab perspective.

Newsweek's coverage earned it the prestigious National Magazine Award for "General Excellence." The coverage also demonstrated how news magazines help mobilize public opinion and boost morale during times of crisis.

In the "Attack on America" issue, a *Newsweek* writer wrote that "Tuesday, Sept. 11, 2001, will indeed be a 'date which will live in infamy,' as Franklin Roosevelt said almost 60 years ago, after the bombing of Pearl Harbor. But the analogy ends there. Last Tuesday's events are even more gruesome and tragic than what happened on Dec. 7, 1941."

For the "God Bless America" issue, *Newsweek* editor at large Kenneth Auchincloss wrote a piece ("We Shall Overcome") on patriotism and the nation's renewed sense of unity.

NEWS-WEEK

10 CENTS · FEBRUARY 17, 1933 · $4 A YEAR

TUESDAY: FLEW 5,341 MILES

THURSDAY: VON PAPEN BALANCES

MONDAY: HITLER'S MIGHT

MONDAY: WOLEY WAKES

All mainstream news media are dependent upon centers of power for the news. The cover of the first issue of Newsweek, published on Feb. 17, 1933, illustrates this principle. It included photographs of four major world leaders: Adolf Hitler (Germany), Franklin Roosevelt (United States), Joseph Stalin (Soviet Union) and Franz von Papen (Germany).

In the "Trail of Terror" issue, *Newsweek* quoted President George W. Bush: "Either you are with us or you are with the terrorists." *Newsweek* also wrote that, "In the coming months, years and perhaps decades, America's global war against terrorism will demand radical thinking on how to fight an enemy whose goal is to instill fear and confusion, whose armies are militia networks strewn across the globe and whose war finances are untraceable bundles of cash. The American people must accept at the outset that capturing or killing one individual will not rid them or the world of the scourge."

And this, from a reader in the Oct. 15, 2001, issue: "Thank you for publishing in your last three issues the pictures of the terrorist attacks and their aftermath that kept me from sleeping. I needed to see the reality of the horror. I am moved that you did not decide that your readers could not handle the reality of this unspeakable terror."

As of 2013, *Newsweek* was owned by IBT, a private company. Only a digital edition is now available in the United States.

SPECIALIZATION AND "ZINES"

As the 20th century came to a close, the trend toward specialization in the magazine industry accelerated. From 1990 to 2000 alone, there was a net gain of more than 3,800 new magazines. Nearly all of these magazines were targeted to specialized (as opposed to general) audiences.

One of those was *Brill's Content*, a magazine launched in summer 1998 by Steven Brill, creator of Court TV. The purpose of the magazine, he wrote, was to serve as a critic of the mass media. "It's time to hold journalists accountable, it's time we embarrass them into doing their jobs the way they're supposed to — with integrity, honesty, fairness and accuracy." But the magazine closed in 2001, the victim of poor advertising revenues.

The 1990s was also the decade of zines (pronounced "zeens") — low cost magazines that focus on alternative cultures and offbeat subjects. One example was *Kicks*, a magazine about obscure 1960s rock groups and grade-B horror movies. Another was *The Optimistic Pezzimist*, which is for people who collect Pez dispensers. Desktop publishing and copy machines have made small-press runs financially viable.

How the Mass Media Really Work

As the magazine industry entered the 21st century, most major publishers began offering online versions of their hard-copy product. Newsletters and scientific journals followed suit. And now some newer magazines are publishing exclusively on the Internet (see sidebar story about *Newsweek* magazine), raising questions about the future of the industry.

Chapter 4
ROLE OF MOVIES AND RADIO

George Orson Welles was only 24 when he signed a contract with RKO Radio Pictures in the summer of 1939 to produce his first movie.

To say he was talented was a gross understatement.

He had already become famous in the New York theater community for his creative and offbeat productions of classic plays. He also became nationally known after his October 1938 Mystery Theater radio production of *War of the Worlds*, which was so realistic that nearly a million people across the country panicked, believing the earth was being invaded by Martians.

Yet, Hollywood didn't exactly greet Welles with open arms.

Orson Welles

Welles was called an "upstart" because he had no film-making experience. But to his credit, he ignored the insults. Instead, he hired respected screenwriter Herman J. Mankiewicz to help him develop the idea for his motion picture.

Mankiewicz and Welles went through seven re-writes. But the hard work paid off. *Citizen Kane* is today rated as one of the greatest motion pictures of all time.

The film tells the story of Charles Foster Kane, an aging newspaper tycoon whose arrogance alienates him from everyone who loved him. The movie was loosely based on the life of William Randolph Hearst, who had built a newspaper empire in the late 19th and early 20th centuries. On his deathbed in his Gothic mansion in Florida, Kane utters his last word, "Rosebud."

What is "Rosebud?"

Through the use of flashbacks, a magazine reporter covering the life of Kane searches doggedly to discover the meaning of the word and the man behind it.

We authors won't reveal the movie's ending for the benefit of those who haven't seen it. But "Rosebud" has become the most famous prop in Hollywood. It was sold to producer/director Steven Spielberg in 1977 for $60,500.[105]

For two years, Welles hid the fact that the movie was based on the life of Hearst. He was worried in part about what Hearst would do. And this was no exaggeration fear.

When word leaked out just before completion of the film in 1941, Hearst newspapers, wire services and radio stations banned all mention of *Citizen Kane* as well as all other films produced by RKO and refused to accept advertising for the movie. A group of Hollywood executives, fearing the wrath of Hearst on their operations as well, even offered RKO a cash settlement to destroy the film.

But it was too late.

Welles had sneak-previewed the film to so many prominent people that it was impossible to expunge it. The film opened in theaters in 1941 and received good reviews and did well in large cities. But the Hearst boycott and Hollywood control of theater bookings hurt the debut. RKO eventually reported a loss of $150,000.

The film was re-released in the mid-1950s, and in the early 1960s an international panel of leading film critics selected *Citizen Kane* as the No. 1 film of all time. The film is acclaimed not only for its script and acting (Welles played Kane), but for its wondrous use of light and photography. The angles, shadows and perspectives in this black-and-white movie are still widely copied by cinematographers today.

Welles had a fabulously successful career as a movie producer, director, actor and writer, although he was never again able to match the acclaim he achieved with *Citizen Kane*. Welles also came to symbolize the successful

Orson Welles starred as the self-destructive Charles Foster Kane. One of the themes of the movie is that money and fame cannot buy you happiness.

Hollywood outsider — the man who placed art above profits and commercial success. Welles died in 1985.[106]

RKO Radio Pictures struggled financially for most of its 25-year existence. The company ceased production in 1953 and was sold to Desilu Productions in 1957.

MOVIES: MORALITY PLAYS

No motion picture in the history of film-making has generated more acclaim and attention than *Citizen Kane*. The technical aspects of the film — such as the camera angles, lighting, and set details — are, indeed, masterful.

But the heart of this film is not in the technical details. It's in the story. And this is a story about a man who climbs the ladder of success only to find he is alone at the top. Wealth and power cannot buy happiness. True happiness can be found only in loving others and in enjoying the simple things in life.

If that sounds moralistic, that's because it is.

Citizen Kane is a morality play. In other words, it deals with questions of right and wrong. And the moral lesson in this movie is an old one. Greed and arrogance are bad.

For thousands of years, artists and playwrights have employed similar themes in their works of literature and art, including popular works such as the sinking of the *Titanic* (see Chapter 1). *Citizen Kane* is unique only in that it conveys the moral lesson through the life of Charles Foster Kane, a newspaper tycoon.

Almost all motion pictures contain messages about right and wrong, good and bad. This includes serious films like *American Beauty* and popular movies like *The Lord of the Rings*.

American Beauty is the story of a man going through a mid-life crisis, but in the end he finds redemption. Redemption — or the idea that people who stray from the "path of righteousness" can redeem themselves — is a major and powerful theme in many motion pictures.

The *Lord of the Rings* movies pit "evil" forces against the "good" forces, and "good" always wins in the end. It's also a story about importance of friendship and loyalty.

Motion pictures are morality plays. They tell stories that deal with issues of right and wrong. In general, these stories promote or reinforce dominant norms and values in a culture, such as love, friendship, trust and honesty. They define the boundaries of acceptable behavior and they reinforce social order.

Of course, motion pictures aren't the only mass medium that tells stories and deals with questions of right and wrong. As noted in Chapter 3, investigative news stories contain moral lessons as well. They point out that something is wrong and needs to be fixed or corrected.

But in terms of teaching those lessons no mass medium format is more compelling than motion pictures. This power is so widely recognized that even encyclopedia entries pay homage to it:

"Motion pictures are the most important narrative art form of the 20th century, having taken on the functions served earlier by dime novels, serial novels, staged melodramas, wax museum displays, epic paintings, and professional storytelling. These earlier forms ... were supplemented by comic books, radio, and television, but it is the motion picture that came to dominate them all."[107]

Motion pictures have this power partly because they engage not one but two human senses — seeing and hearing. Print media engage only the former and radio only the latter. Television engages both senses and that certainly accounts in part for its power and popularity.

But motion pictures are even more engaging than television because they are shown on a "big screen," which draws the viewer into the experience even more. The late movie critic Roger Ebert even argues that *Citizen Kane* can only be fully appreciated on the big screen, because there are many props and items that cannot be easily seen on the small (broadcast television) screen.[108]

MOVIES AND SOCIAL CONTROL

People often complain about the motion picture industry. Many argue that movies make children aggressive, stereotype certain groups, and promote commercialism and materialism.

It would be difficult to argue that movies do not have these dysfunctional effects on some people on some occasions. However, it would be difficult to argue that all of the effects of movies are dysfunctional for society. If that were so, then one might expect complete social decay and disorder in a short period of time.

Instead, when viewed from a detached perspective, one can see that the greatest effect of movies is reinforcement of dominant norms and values in a society. Like other forms of art and literature, movies usually tell a story that contains a moral lesson.

For example, in the Christmas classic *It's a Wonderful Life,* George (played by Jimmy Stewart) faces a financial crisis and wishes he had never been born. An angel grants his wish and then shows George what the world would have been like without him. The experience transforms George and he then comes to appreciate his life. As the angel puts it: "See George, you've really had a wonderful life. See what a mistake it would be to throw it away?"

This film is just one example of the power that motion pictures play in reinforcing dominant values in society. During World War II, Hollywood

Donna Reed, James Stewart and Karolyn Grimes starred *in It's a Wonderful Life*, whose moral lesson is that family and friends are more valuable than money and wealth.

made movies to help the war effort and to maintain morale "back home." During the Vietnam War, Hollywood produced *The Green Beret,* which starred John Wayne and idealized the U.S. military. In recent years, the new enemy in movies are "the terrorists."

Movies, like other forms of mass media, reinforce values about the importance of family and friends, of obeying the law, and of being honest and grateful. In fact, it is very difficult to find a movie that does not support these values.

Movies also can have other prosocial effects. Research shows that movies, like television, have taught many children how to groom and dress, play sports, and interact with others. Although not all of the content of motion pictures results in prosocial effects, movies in general reinforce dominant values of a society and, as such, their biggest impact is maintenance of society.

How the Mass Media Really Work

Of course, most people do not think about social control when they go to the movies. To them, the movies are simply entertaining — a form of relaxation. But it is important to point out that "being entertained" is itself an effect. To the extent that movies help people relax, then they are contributing, however subtly, to social order.

Take, for instance, the movies made by Hollywood legend Steven Spielberg. Most people don't realize it, but most of his movies contain a strong social control message: family values are good.

STEVEN SPIELBERG: PROMOTING FAMILY VALUES

Even before turning 18, Steven Spielberg was a success.[109]

At age 12, he had completed his first scripted amateur film. At age 13, he won a prize for a 40-minute war movie called *Escape to Nowhere*. And at age 16, his 140-minute science-fiction production, *Firelight*, generated a $100 profit in a local theater.

Steven Spielberg *(Photo by Romain DuBois, used with permission)*

Yet, Spielberg's application to film school in the 1960s was rejected because his grades weren't good enough. As a youth, Spielberg was more interested in watching television and in producing amateur films than in studying. But failure to gain entry to film school didn't deter Spielberg.

He enrolled as an English major at California State University in Long Beach, and after scrounging up $15,000 from friends, Spielberg produced *Amblin'*, a 24-minute film about a pair of hitchhikers. *Amblin'* won several film awards and was shown at the Atlanta Film Festival in 1969. Executives at Universal-MCA were so impressed that they gave him a seven-year contract in the television division. Spielberg, only 20 years old, made history as the youngest person to obtain a long-term contract from a major production studio.

In the movie *War of the Worlds*, a Boeing 747 crashes. The scene is now a set in the Universal Studios backlot in Hollywood. One of the key values in the movie is the importance of family. *(Photo by Miles Peterson, used with permission)*.

Today, Spielberg is consistently rated one of the top producer/directors in the world. He earned Best Director and Best Picture Oscars for *Schindler's List*, which details the true-life story of a German factory owner who saved thousands of Jewish citizens during World War II, and a Best Director Oscar for *Saving Private Ryan*, which chronicles the efforts of one World War II soldier whose mission is to find and bring home the only surviving son of a family whose three other sons were killed in action. *The Color Purple*, which told the story about two sisters separated at an early age, earned 11 Oscar nominations.

Many Spielberg movies contain a lot of action and adventure. But the key value promoted in these movies as well as many of his other movies is family values.

In 2005, Spielberg released *War of the Worlds*, an adaption of H. G. Wells classic book that focuses on a divorced father who regains the love and respect of his children after fighting to keep them safe from cannibalistic aliens.

A *Hollywood Reporter* survey of studio executives in 2000 rated Spielberg the most "bankable director" of more than 800 rated.

Spielberg was born December 18, 1946 — the son of an electrical engineer father and a concert-pianist mother. He seems to have inherited the pragmatic craftsmanship of his father and the artistic and creative talent of his mother.

After signing the contract with Universal, Spielberg directed some television shows and, in 1972, the made-for-TV movie *Duel*, which starred

How the Mass Media Really Work

Dennis Weaver as a salesman menaced by a diesel truck. Spielberg directed his first feature film, *The Sugarland Express*, in 1974. The film won a Cannes Film Festival Award for Best Screenplay. He followed that in 1975 with *Jaws*, the blockbuster movie about a great white shark. In 1977, he wrote the screenplay for and directed *Close Encounters of the Third Kind*, the science fiction adventure that netted him a Best Director Oscar nomination.

Not everything Spielberg has directed has been successful. His first attempt in 1979 at comedy, *1941*, was a disaster. But in 1981 he and friend George Lucas followed this up with *Raiders of the Lost Ark*, which netted him another Best Director Oscar nomination. A year later he released *E.T.: The Extra-Terrestrial*, which became the biggest domestic moneymaker.

Responding to critics who said he could not make a serious adult film, he directed in 1985 the screen adaptation of Alice Walker's *The Color Purple*, which garnered 11 Oscar nominations, although none for Spielberg. That movie exposed the evils of gender discrimination and the goodness of family love and friendship.

The Academy gave him the Irving G. Thalberg Award in 1987. Around the same time he divorced actress Amy Irving and married *Indiana Jones and the Temple of Doom* leading lady Kate Capshaw.

Spielberg directed two blockbusters in 1993: *Jurassic Park* and *Schindler's List*. *Jurassic Park* grossed $100 million in just the first nine days and eventually shattered *E.T.*'s record. *Schindler's List* earned his first Best Director Oscar. His second came with *Saving Private Ryan*, which was released in 1998. *Amistad*, a movie about an 1839 shipboard revolt by African slaves, earned him a Golden Globe nomination.

In 1994, Spielberg joined with David Geffen and Jeffrey Katzenberg to form DreamWorks, which released *Amistad, Saving Private Ryan* and *American Beauty*, the latter of which won the Best Picture Oscar for 1999. In 2002, Spielberg directed *Minority Report*, which starred Tom Cruise and has been called one of his finest films. He also produced the critically acclaimed *Lincoln* (2012) and *War Horse* (2011).

MOVIES AND SOCIAL CHANGE

Although family values permeate Spielberg's movies, this doesn't mean that they can't also stir the conscience and move people to action.

Schindler's List and *Amistad*, for example, admonished bigotry.

During the 1920s and 1930s, movies helped acclimate people to an increasingly urban and industrialized society. Although half of the population of the United States lived in rural areas, the settings for most movies took place in big cities and usually portrayed cosmopolitan life in a glamorous way. This enticed many people to move to urban areas in search of a better life. By 1960s, only five percent of the population earned a living through farming and the nation was overwhelmingly urbanized.

Another good example of the social change function took place during the 1960s and 1970s, when many independent filmmakers (not associated with one of the seven big film studios) produced movies that were critical of U.S. involvement in the Vietnam War and supported the women's and civil rights movements. More recent movies like Sherman Alexie's *Smoke Signals* (1998) also help to dispel myths about Native Americans. And Michael Moore's documentaries on General Motors, on the gun industry, and on the Bush Administration and 9/11 have raised people's consciousness about the abuse of power in America.

Although all mass media produce content that generally supports the dominant values and norms in a society, in relative terms, motion pictures often "push the envelope" even more. Part of this tendency stems from the fact that filmmakers and scriptwriters on the whole tend to be more liberal than the population at large. Art and literature have always attracted people who are critical of the status quo. Film offers a way to air alternative ideas.

At the same time, movies also have generated criticism for promoting too much change. During the 1920s, religious organizations and parents were concerned about the effects of the portrayal of sex, crime and violence in the movies were having on young people..

To head off the criticism, studio heads formed a self-regulatory organization called the Motion Picture Association of America (formerly called the Motion Picture Producers and Distributors of America). Although MPAA didn't have the power to censor, the MPAA promoted a "Production Code" that placated critics for a time.

However, the controversy boiled over again with the release in the early 1930s of the Payne Fund Studies, the first social scientific studies of the effects of movies.[110] These studies showed that movies which contained scenes of horror and violence scared many children, giving them nightmares.

How the Mass Media Really Work

The studies also found that movies presented moral standards that were more progressive and more sexually liberated than traditional values. The film industry responded again by strengthening its Production Code, which quieted critics for a time.

But conservatives and religious groups have never stopped complaining completely about the alleged "immoral" content in movies and television programming. Liberals also complain that too much emphasis is placed on materialism and commercialism.

During the 1950s, the movie studios began producing motion pictures with conservative, anti-communist overtones. They tried to deflect attacks from right-wing politicians, especially Sen. Joseph McCarthy of Wisconsin, who accused the film industry of being sympathetic to communists. The House Un-American Activities Committee (HUAC) called more than 100 Hollywood witnesses from 1950-52, some of whom testified against their colleagues. However, eight screen writers and two directors, later known as the Hollywood Ten, refused to testify and were sentenced to serve up to a year in prison.

The studios, to their discredit, then blacklisted many producers, writers, directors and stars who were suspected of communist associations. This destroyed the careers of many innocent people. The "red scare" didn't subside until 1954, when broadcaster Edward R. Murrow challenged McCarthy and showed that many of his accusations were false (more details later in this chapter).

Actor James Dean also became a legend in the 1950s, even though he only had three major movie roles (*East of Eden*, 1955; *Rebel Without a Cause*, 1955; *Giant*, 1956) before dying in automobile accident in 1955. Dean came to symbolize a restlessness that eventually took hold in the 1960s' social movements that opposed the Vietnam War and favored equal rights for women and minorities. Films such as *Dr. Strangelove* (1963), which condemned nuclear weapons, reinforced the goals of these movements.

Despite these trends, civil rights and women's groups often criticize the film industry for failing to advance diversity goals. To the dismay of many feminists, many movies still portray women as subordinate to men, as victims and as sex objects. Men often are portrayed as the saviors.

Actor James Dean in a trailer for the film East of Eden. Dean came to symbolize a restlessness that took hold in the 1960s' social movements.

Civil rights groups also complain that the movies often portray African Americans as drug dealers and criminals, Native Americans as savages, and Muslims as terrorists.

Stereotypes are form a social control. They marginalize groups that are excluded from the top echelons of the power structure.

RADIO & RECORDINGS: FOR LOVE AND POLITICS

Edward R. Murrow stood on the roof of a building near the British Broadcasting Corporation in London as the German bomber passed overhead. The year was 1940, and Adolf Hitler's air force was bombing the city night after night in what came to be known as the "Battle for Britain."

"Off on my left, I can see the faint-red angry snap of anti-aircraft bursts," Murrow said, speaking into a microphone that transmitted his live radio report to millions of people back in the United States, which was not

President Harry Truman and Edward R. Murrow during a segment of *This I Believe*, in which guests talk about the values that are important to them. Such programming reinforces dominant values in American society.

yet involved in World War II. "Four searchlights are swinging over in this general direction. The plane's still very high. ... Just overhead now the burst of the antiaircraft fire. Still the nearby guns are not working. The searchlights now are feeling almost directly overhead. Now you'll hear two bursts a little nearer in a moment. ... There they are. That hard, stony sound."[111]

For five years Murrow reported the war. He began his broadcasts with the simple declaration: "This is London." He spent several more evenings reporting from rooftops as the bombs burst around him and ignited numerous fires that did massive damage to London and other English cities from June 1940 to April 1941. Thousands of civilians and several hundred British fighter pilots were killed. On December 25, 1940, he reported, "This is not a merry Christmas in London. I heard that phrase only twice in the last three days."

On one occasion, the BBC Broadcasting House suffered a direct hit. The bomb smashed through an upper story window and came to rest on the floor. The bomb squad attempted to defuse the bomb, but it went off, killing seven people and injuring several others. Murrow knew most of them. He was on the radio as the wounded and killed were taken out of the studio. He described the scene and the smell of iodine that permeated the studio.

Murrow also flew more than 40 combat missions aboard Allied bombers and paratrooper planes. After the war, he visited a recently liberated concentration camp and reported: "I pray you believe what I have said about Buchenwald (concentration camp). I reported what I saw and heard, but only part of it. For most of it, I have no words."

Murrow went on to become the most famous and trusted U.S. journalist of the war. His quiet, monotone voice enhanced his credibility. The poet Archibald MacLeish would later tell Murrow, "You burned the city of London in our houses and we felt the flames that burned it."[112]

After the war, Murrow was promoted to vice president and director of public affairs of CBS. In 1951, he took his radio program "Hear It Now" to television and called it "See It Now." His television show made history in 1954 when it condemned Sen. Joseph R. McCarthy for falsely accusing people of being communists (see discussion later in this chapter). Murrow, who smoked three packs of cigarettes a day, died of lung cancer in 1965 at the age of 57.[113]

RADIO NEWS AND SOCIAL CONTROL

Many historians argue that Murrow's live radio reports from London played the crucial role in swaying American public opinion against Nazi Germany.

But Murrow's broadcasts almost didn't happen.

When Murrow first proposed the idea, the British Air Ministry turned him down, because it was worried Murrow might say something to compromise British national security. Control of information is a primary concern during times of war.

But Murrow wouldn't take "no" for an answer. He went to the top of the political power structure — to Winston Churchill, the British Prime Minister. Churchill also recognized the value of controlling information. But,

How the Mass Media Really Work

instead, he saw Murrow's reports as an opportunity to generate sympathy in America for the British.

Of course, this was not the first time mass media was used to influence public opinion during a war. In the late 1890s, New York newspapers played a major role in drumming up support for U.S. involvement in the Spanish American War.[114]

But never before had a major war been reported "live," as it happened. Leaders around the world quickly seized upon this new-found power. Radio was used to drum up sympathy for the home country and hate for the enemy. In other words, radio became a tool of propaganda for both sides. It was a mechanism of social control.[115] And still is, even during peacetime.

Perhaps the most notable example today is talk radio, which usually involves a host who interviews guests and takes listeners' calls.

Talk radio hosts always have a point of view, sometimes controversial. Rush Limbaugh and Dr. Laura Schlessinger, for example, promote conservative values. They differ only in that Limbaugh deals primarily with political issues, whereas Dr. Laura's program dispenses conservative personal advice on love, marriage, family and relationships.

Of course, not all of the political content on radio is controversial. Radio is often the first place people turn to in times of crisis, such as threatening weather conditions. Radio news, like newspaper and television news, often is viewed as "objective" and informative.[116] Indeed, National Public Radio, which provides programming to the nation's noncommercial and educational radio stations, and commercial radio networks like ABC and CBS are highly respected for their news coverage.

But as discussed in Chapter 2, even so-called "objective" news is not really objective in any absolute sense.

Rush Limbaugh *(Photo by Nicolas Shayko, used with permission)*

News reports tend to frame the world from the perspective of those in power, because journalists rely heavily on them for the news. Murrow's reports are a good example. He depended upon British authorities for information, and this explains in part why his reports reflected a pro-British point of view.

Music and Social Control

But politics and news aren't the only content on radio. In fact, radio's most unique niche today is music. More than 80 percent of on-air radio content is music.[117] Listening to music is the No. 1 pastime activity while driving or riding in a car. Millions of people wake up to radio music and news. And millions more listen to it throughout the day as they work.

Needless to say, most people enjoy listening to music because it entertains and relaxes them. But this does not mean that music has no implications for social control, or is less important in this regard than news programs or talk shows. As noted earlier in this book, entertainment is also a form of control. People who are entertained and relaxed have fewer reasons to stir up trouble (e.g., join anti-establishment or revolutionary movements). Moreover, the lyrical content of music generally reflects and reinforces the values and beliefs of a society.

Musicians write about the beauty of love, friendship, honor, respect, peace and duty, and the ugliness of war, discrimination, hate, and dishonor. Of these, the greatest is romantic love.

Love sells.

That's because a sizable portion of tape and compact disc buyers are young people, who often are searching for love or for a marriage partner. At any one point in time, about three-fourths of the songs on the best selling lists are about love and relationships. Every genre of music — jazz, blues, rock-n-roll, bluegrass, rap, hip-hop, classical, pop, punk, country, folk, swing — sings about the beauty and trials and tribulations of love.

Live music was the most popular form of programming in the 1920s. RCA hired the Philadelphia Orchestra under Eugene Ormandy, and NBC created its own orchestra under the leadership of Arturo Toscanini. Jazz, big

The social control functions of music go back to antiquity, as this painting on a 2,500-year-old Greek vase shows.

bands, and country music also became very popular. Dance crazes, such as the Charleston, stimulated demand for records. Then, as today, the lyrical and thematic content of music focused heavily on love, relationships, having a good time and how to get over bad times.

Dramatic and Comedic Programming on Radio

However, in the late 1920s, the radio networks began producing more dramas, comedies, soap operas, game shows, talk shows, and news programming. Many of these programs attracted larger audiences, which in turn generated higher advertising revenues. One of the most popular programs was "Amos 'n' Andy," which was based on the life of two black men (although the real-life actor-comedians were white). The comedy has been severely criticized for portraying racial stereotypes. But during the Great Depression the problems of the black man were generalized to other citizens as well.

Other comedic programming quickly followed. Former vaudeville comedians Fred Allen ("Town Hall Tonight" and "The Fred Allen Show"),

Jack Benny ("The Jack Benny Program"), and George Burns and Gracie Allen ("The George Burns and Gracie Allen Show") became national stars, and later transferred their radio programs to television. The light-hearted nature of their programs offered many people respite from the tough economic times — a decade in which up to a third of the population was unemployed.

Dramatic and mystery programming, such as "Charlie Chan," "Sherlock Holmes" and "The Shadow" were also very popular. "The CBS Mystery Radio Hour" made history in 1938 with its dramatic adaptation of H. G. Wells's science-fiction story, *The War of the Worlds.*

WAR OF THE WORLDS: THE POWER OF RADIO

On Oct. 30, 1938, Martians invaded the earth.[118]

Or at least that's what one million people in the United States thought.

They were listening to CBS's "Mercury Theater on the Air," which was broadcasting a radio drama adaptation of H.G. Wells' classic book War of the Worlds on Halloween. Many listeners didn't hear the introduction and the intermittent disclaimers. Some had tuned in late, because they didn't like a guest who was being interviewed on another radio program. And what they heard was the realistic-sounding voice of the "Secretary of Interior," who said:

> Citizens of the nation: I shall not try to conceal the gravity of the situation that confronts the country, nor the concern of your Government in protecting the lives and property of its people. ... Fortunately, this formidable enemy is still confined to a comparatively small area, and we may place our faith in the military forces to keep them there. In the meantime, placing our trust in God, we must continue the performance of our duties ... so that we may confront this destructive adversary with a nation united ... .

The Martians had destroyed the police and military forces that had confronted them and were now spraying New York with poison gas. A minute later an announcer came on and said "you are listening to the CBS

Brazilian artist Henrique Alvim Corrêa made this drawing for the novel *The War of the Worlds*. It shows a Martian fighting-machine battling the warship Thunder Child.

presentation of Orson Welles and the Mercury Theatre on the Air," but by then many people had stopped listening.

In New York, hundreds of people fled their homes. In Concrete, Washington, the power went out when the Martians were supposed to be cutting communications lines, which led to mass hysteria. In Birmingham, Alabama, people went to church and prayed. In Boston, the newspaper (Globe) was deluged with calls from frightened people. In Rhode Island, many people called the electric company and urged them to turn off all lights so the city could protect itself against the Martians.

One million people panicked, according to estimates. One woman broke her arm after falling down some stairs. But there were few injuries and no one was killed.

Lawsuits were filed against CBS, the Mercury Theatre and Orson Welles, who had produced the program and served as a narrator. But none went to trial because there was no precedence for such claims.

The FCC adopted a resolution banning the use of "on the spot" news stories in dramatic programming. CBS apologized. Mercury Theatre survived and became very popular.

But the incident was not forgotten.

For many people, it reinforced the idea that mass media in general and radio in particular was a powerful medium. Shortly after the incident, researcher Hadley Cantril and others studied the broadcast to discover the conditions that led people to panic and believe the drama was real.

They estimated six million adults heard the broadcast, and, of them, about 20 percent, or slightly more than one million, panicked. They also found that those who panicked tended to be less educated, more religious, and more emotionally insecure. Ironically, these findings suggested media effects may be more limited than previously thought.

To be sure, not all music supports dominant values and institutions. Punk and rap musicians, for example, are criticized occasionally for producing lyrics that challenge or attack traditional values or institutions, such as the police. One example is the rapster Eminem, whose songs have denigrated women and homosexuals. Many musicians also compose lyrics that glorify or encourage sex out of wedlock, which angers some people who hold traditional religious values.

However, it is important to point out that these same songs almost always support a more fundamental value: love. And this is a value upon which almost everyone can agree.

RADIO, MUSIC AND SOCIAL CHANGE

Music genres reflect the integrating power of music.

Many working-class people like country music; highly educated and upper class people often like classical music; young people are drawn to rock, punk, hip-hop, alternative, rap and grunge; and minorities and professionals are disproportionately drawn to blues and jazz. These genres create a community and often help make people feel more connected to society. In fact, music plays such an important role in most people's lives, that it is difficult to conceive of a world without it.

Folk musician Woody Guthrie wrote lyrics that criticized capitalism and influenced many songwriters during the 1960s and 1970s.

But not all news or music programming serves as an agent of control. Political news or music has often served to motivate people to change the world.

One of the best examples was folk musician Woody Guthrie, who wrote the famous song, "This Land Is Your Land." Music scholar Dan Erickson points out that the original version contained the lines: "In the squares of the city; In the shadow of a steeple; By the relief office; I'd seen my people. As they stood there hungry, I stood there asking, Is this land made for you and me?"[119] However, many popular renditions and performances of the song censor that verse and another which pokes at private property ownership.

Guthrie influenced many folk and rock musicians who, during the 1960s, protested U.S. involvement in the Vietnam War. Their songs reinforced the goals of the anti-war movement and protest groups. It would be incorrect to say that protest music alone helped bring an end to the Vietnam War. But it clearly helped bond people together in a common cause and indirectly brought about social change.

THE ROCK 'N' ROLL OF CHANGE

In 1953, Bill Haley and his band, "The Comets," were struggling musicians. They had one moderate hit, "Rock the Joint," which sold 75,000 records. But their next release, "Crazy, Man, Crazy," shot into the U.S. Top 20 and gave the group national recognition. More importantly, it launched a new music genre, rock 'n' roll.

Rock 'n' roll was a term used to describe the movements of sexual intercourse. But today it is associated with one of the most commercially successful trends in modern music.

The roots of rock 'n' roll go back to classical blues, gospel and country western music. But most people didn't care about that. They liked "rock" because it was fun to dance to. Within a year or two, teenagers abandoned the more traditional music of Patti Page ("Tennessee Waltz"), Doris Day and Bing Crosby, and began listening to a new band of musicians.

In 1954, Bill Haley and the Comets released "Shake, Rattle and Roll" and "Rock Around the Clock." The latter sold more than 25 million copies, a phenomenal number, and ensured that "rock 'n' roll was here to stay."

Other performers quickly followed and had even more success. Two were African Americans. Chuck Berry wrote the hits "Maybellene," "Sweet Little Sixteen," "Rock and Roll Music," "Roll Over, Beethoven," and "Johnny B. Goode." Little Richard wrote the hits "Good Golly Miss Molly," "Long Tall Sally," "Tutti-Frutti" and "Lucille."

But Elvis Presley became the king of rock 'n' roll.

Before he became famous, Presley used to listen to the "Grand Ole Opry" and watch black musicians perform the blues live. In 1954, Presley recorded the first of 15 songs, five of which had considerable local success. In 1956, Elvis recorded "Heartbreak Hotel," the first of 45 rpm records that sold more than a million copies.

Elvis Presley singing "Jailhouse Rock."

He appeared on television but the networks would show him only from the waist up because gyrating hip action on stage was considered too provocative. "Elvis the Pelvis" drove audiences wild when he performed live. During his life, Elvis sold more than 500 million records. He died of an accidental drug overdose in 1977.

Rock 'n' roll became a dominant music genre on radio during the 1960s, a time of increasing social unrest.

Social movements that promoted civil rights, women's rights, and environmental protection and criticized U.S. involvement in the Vietnam War became increasingly vocal. These and other liberal groups demanded more justice and equality. Young people also were experimenting with marijuana, LSD and other drugs. They rejected traditional values that frowned on sex before marriage. Needless to say, music reflected and reinforced these changing values and trends.

The Beatles — John Lennon, Paul McCartney, George Harrison and Ringo Starr—led the way with songs about justice, equality, love, peace, sex and drugs. In the early 1960s, the group wrote love song songs, such as "Love Me Do," "Please Please Me," "She Loves You" and "I Want To Hold Your Hand."

Later, the Beatles turned to writing more serious and controversial works. In 1967, the group released the album, "Sgt. Pepper's Lonely Hearts Club Band," which became the definitive psychedelic soundtrack. Today, many critics consider "Sgt. Pepper" to be the best rock album of all time. Beatlemania lasted until 1970, when the band broke up after McCartney left to pursue a solo career.

The 1960s and 1970s saw the emergence of new, more specialized forms of music, including the hard-driving dancing beat of disco (The Bee Gees), the soulful sounds of Motown (Diana Ross and The Supremes), the aggressive urban dance beat of funk (Sly and the Family Stone); the iconoclastic sounds of punk (Sex Pistols), the social conscious lyrics of folk-rock (Bob Dylan); and the Afro-Jamaican sounds of reggae (Bob Marley).

In the 1980s, rap/hip-hop (LL Cool J) became popular and has remained one of the dominant music genres throughout the 1990s and 2000s (Puff Daddy and DMX). The term hip-hop, by the way, refers to a cultural movement that contains four major elements: deejaying, rapping, graffiti painting, and b-boying (a dance style).

How the Mass Media Really Work

Chapter 5
ROLE OF TV AND INTERNET

The episode on the *Jerry Springer Show* was called "Secret Mistresses Confronted."[120]

The syndicated television show, which was tape recorded in May 2000, featured Ralf Panitz, his ex-wife Nancy Campbell-Panitz and his current wife Eleanor. All three had been living together since Ralf and Nancy divorced. But Nancy didn't know that Ralf secretly had married Eleanor. To get Nancy on the show, Ralf told her that he was going to publicly renounce Eleanor on air.

But that never happened.

Instead, Ralf and Eleanor announced they had been married two months earlier. Eleanor then hurled insults at Nancy. "Are you going to leave us alone? I want you to leave us alone ... You're old. You're fat." Nancy left the stage and the audience booed her.

Three months later, Ralf went home after watching the program on television in a local bar. He and Nancy had an argument. He beat her to death, according to police.

Ralf was convicted of second-degree murder and sentenced to life in prison. In July 2002, Nancy's family filed a lawsuit against Springer and his company, claiming they contributed to Nancy's death.

The incident brought back memories of a 1995 Jenny Jones Show program, in which a man murdered another man after learning on the show that he was the subject of his victim's homosexual fantasies. A jury ordered *The Jenny Jones Show* to pay $25 million in damages to the family of the murdered man.

Critics call Springer's show "trailer trash television" because, according to *The Los Angeles Times*, it "deifies dysfunction, exploits unsophisticated guests and gives a promotional forum to the sexually confused and promiscuous, porn stars, adulterers, criminals, Ku Klux Klan member and various other ne'er-do-wells."[121]

The show titles seem to support these criticisms: "I Am Pregnant by a Transsexual," "I Want Your Man," "Paternity Test: I Slept With Two Brothers," and "Prostitutes vs. Pimps!" And producers don't mind when fights break out on the show, because they know that increases the show's ratings.

ARE TV TALK SHOWS DESTROYING MORALITY?

Talk shows have been around since the origins of television.

Tonight first aired in 1954 and was hosted by Steve Allen and Ernie Kovaks (later by Johnny Carson). Phil Donahue launched the first audience-participation show in 1967, which lasted on various networks until 2003.

But talk shows didn't draw a lot of attention until the 1980s, when Oprah Winfrey took her Chicago show national in 1984. *Oprah* quickly overtook Donahue's show in the ratings, and she went on to become the most successful woman in television history. Other talk shows followed, but most *(Geraldo, Sally Jesse Raphael, Maury Povich)* had to employ gimmicks or sensational tactics to attract audiences.

But all of these programs have been upstaged by Jerry Springer, whose show, which was launched in 1991 and is still in syndication, became infamous for featuring guests who assault each other with fists and chairs.[122]

Springer's show and others frequently are criticized for promoting anti-social values.

But a close viewing shows they almost always reinforce traditional norms and values. The audiences play an active role in this process, booing and cheering what they see as acceptable and unacceptable behavior. Talk show hosts are keenly sensitive to this and sometimes deliberately say things to stimulate outrage or succor from audiences.

Even Springer recognizes this.

A family watches television in 1958. Then, as now, television is a powerful agent of social control, consuming an average of four hours out of each adult's day.

"Our audience always boos the bad guy and cheers the good guy," he told *The Los Angeles Times*. "Our show becomes a little morality play. ... if you are concerned about what lessons come out of our show, we make it clear that violence is no good. We make it clear that infidelity, promiscuity, drugs and prostitution are bad."[123]

Of course, this doesn't appease critics. They prefer more talk shows like Oprah, which consciously avoid lurid topics.

But all talk shows and "real-life" courtroom dramas such as *People's Court* and *Judge Judy* perform the function of reinforcing dominant values about right and wrong. If they didn't, nobody would advertise on them.

TELEVISION: THE GREAT ENTERTAINER

Americans spend more time with television than with any other mass medium, which leads many scholars to the conclusion that it is the most powerful medium of social control and social change.

During prime time evening hours, more than 75 million Americans are "glued to the tube." The typical child over age 4 watches more than 20 hours a week, or about three hours a day. The typical adult watches more than 30 hours a week, or about four hours a day.[124]

Television is the No. 1 leisure time activity among both children and adults. In fact, many children spend more time watching television than they do in the classroom.

Why do people watch so much television?

The No. 1 reason is to relax or be entertained.

Research shows that television viewing can reduce stress and help some people escape loneliness and boredom. Thus, it would be unfair to argue that watching television has only adverse effects.

Watching television is not necessarily a bad thing. People need to relax to be physically and mentally healthy. Commercial television and public television also provide public affairs and educational programming that many critics find appealing.

But, it is important to point out, "being entertained" also is a way of controlling people. People who are relaxed and entertained are, quite simply, less likely to be dissatisfied with the status quo, and less like to be socially and politically active.

In fact, two sociologists in the 1950s gave this phenomena a name. Paul F. Lazarsfeld and Robert K. Merton called it the "narcotizing dysfunction" of the mass media.[125]

"It is termed dysfunctional rather than functional on the assumption that it is not in the interest of modern complex society to have large masses of the population politically apathetic and inert," the sociologists wrote.[126] Mass media make people apathetic and inert because it decreases the amount of time "available for organized action." According to Lazarsfeld and Merton:

The individual reads accounts of issues and problems and may even discuss alternative lines of action. But this rather intellectualized, rather remote connection with organized social action is not activated. ... mass communications may be included among the most respectable and efficient of social narcotics. They may be so fully effective as to keep the addict from recognizing his own malady.[127]

The narcotizing function becomes more pronounced as viewing time increases. People who watch a lot of television are often called "couch potatoes," meaning they are lazy and passive. They are going to be less likely to question injustice and wrongdoing, and, thus, are going to be easier to control.

That's because entertainment television tends to avoid controversial issues, such as poverty, lack of universal health care, racial discrimination and corporate abuse of power. Television also rarely criticizes powerful institutions and values systems.

Instead, shows like *West Wing* and *Homeland* , which revolve around life in the White House, help legitimize powerful institutions, even though history shows that powerful institutions often do not act in the interests of ordinary people.

SOCIAL CONTROL IN EARLY YEARS OF TV

Most early TV entertainment programming provided strong support for the social control model. This included light-hearted family/comedic shows such as *The Adventures of Ozzie and Harriet*, *Amos 'n' Andy*, *The Life of Riley*, *Howdy Doody*, *Kukla*, and *Fran and Ollie*.

None of these shows criticized dominant values or beliefs.

One small exception was *I Love Lucy*, the most spectacular success of the early 1950s, which starred Lucille Ball. *I Love Lucy* contained portrayed Lucille as a well-intentioned but bumbling housewife.

However, the show, which ran from 1951 to 1956, also portrayed her as a strong-willed woman who could not easily be manipulated by her husband. Lucy served as a role model for future shows that portrayed women as being less dependent upon men.

American actors (clockwise from front) Ozzie Nelson, Harriet Nelson, David Nelson and Ricky Nelson starred in the ABC television series "The Adventures of Ozzie and Harriet" in the early 1952. The show reinforced traditional values about the roles of men, women and children.

Westerns (*Gunsmoke, Bonanza* and *Death Valley Days*) and crime dramas (*Perry Mason* and *Dragnet*) were extremely popular in the mid- to late 1950s. *Gunsmoke* was the most popular, lasting 20 years.

How the Mass Media Really Work

All of these westerns towed the mainstream-value line. Breaking the law was almost always bad; police or sheriffs were almost always good.

Most TV news programming in the 1950s also was geared to support the two major mainstream political parties, the Democrats and Republicans.

Broadcast legend Edward R. Murrow first appeared on television in 1951, hosting *See It Now*, a program based upon his popular radio show *Hear It Now*. The TV program was one of the first regular network shows to be broadcast nationally.

In 1953, Murrow also hosted a popular interview show called *Person to Person*, in which he interviewed movie stars and famous people in their homes. And in 1954, Murrow became famous for helping to marginalize a right-wing extremist.

MURROW MARGINALIZES A RIGHT-WING ACTIVIST

In February 1950, a quiet and undistinguished senator from Wisconsin charged that 205 Communists had infiltrated the U.S. State Department.[128]

Although Joseph R. McCarthy could not identify a single "card-carrying Communist" in the U.S. government, he was able to generate a great deal of publicity and public support for his anti-Communist campaign. Many

innocent people were forced to resign from their jobs, including Hollywood screen writers and directors.

At the time, many political elites knew McCarthy was a liar and self-appointed witch-hunter. However, few, including President Dwight D. Eisenhower, were willing to criticize him. They feared reprisals and a public backlash.

Broadcaster Edward R. Murrow wasn't one them.

Edward R. Murrow

On March 9, 1954, he publicly criticized McCarthy on his television news program *See It Now*. That show was based on four months of research. Fred Friendly, Murrow's colleague and co-producer of *See It Now*, put together a mountain of evidence against the Republican senator.

Sen. Joseph R. McCarthy (standing) makes a statement at the Senate Subcommittee on Investigations' McCarthy-Army hearings, June 9, 1954. Edward R. Murrow's show on McCarthy helped bring about his downfall five months later, when the U.S. Senate censured McCarthy.

"We will not walk in fear, one of another," Murrow told his 12 million viewers. "We will not be driven by fear into an age of unreason if we dig deep in our history and doctrine and remember that we are not descended from fearful men, not from men who feared to write, to speak, to associate and to defend causes which were for the moment unpopular." Murrow concluded:

> "The actions of the junior Senator from Wisconsin have caused alarm and dismay amongst our allies abroad and given considerable comfort to our enemies, and whose fault is that? Not really his. He didn't create this situation of fear; he merely exploited it, and rather successfully. Cassius was right: 'The fault, dear Brutus, is not in our stars but in ourselves. ... Good night, and good luck."

McCarthy's influence diminished substantially after that program and after a nationally televised hearing on McCarthy's charges of subversion. In

How the Mass Media Really Work

late 1954, the Senate condemned him for conduct "contrary to Senate traditions." McCarthy died in 1957, a discredited man.

The *See It Now* program, which first aired in 1951, was popular with everyone except CBS executives, who were concerned about alienating corporate sponsors. CBS Board Chairman William S. Paley pulled the plug on the program in 1958.

Many supporters of the program were outraged.

New York Herald Tribune television critic John Crosby wrote that "See It Now ... is by every criterion television's most brilliant, most decorated, most imaginative, most courageous and most important program. The fact that CBS cannot afford it but can afford *Beat the Clock* is shocking."

Contemporary media sociologists, however, see the incident as another example of how mainstream media corporations accommodate the needs of powerful organizations that fund them, which in turn lessens the power of the news to shake up the status quo.

TV's Mainstream Journalists

In 1956, NBC assigned two broadcast journalists to cover the Democratic and Republican presidential political conventions.

Chet Huntley and David Brinkley would go on to become two of the most respected mainstream journalists in the country, co-anchoring the news NBC evening news for 14 years. NBC became the first network to offer a 30-minute evening news broadcast.

In 1960, television for the first time broadcast the presidential debates. Media and political experts widely agree that John F. Kennedy outshone Richard Nixon during the debates, largely because of his cool demeanor and good looks. Since then, political campaign managers have made "television image" a major part of their marketing campaigns.

Although Huntley and Brinkley were popular newscasters in the 1960s, the biggest star was Walter Cronkite, who was promoted from reporter to the evening anchor position at CBS in 1962. Cronkite eventually would become the "most trusted journalist" — and most mainstream journalist — in America, according to polls.

Chet Huntley *(Photo in the public domain)*   David Brinkley *(Photo in the public domain)*   Walter Cronkite *(Photo by Rob Bogaerts)*

During the 1970s, one of the most popular news programs on television was CBS's *60 Minutes*, which debuted in 1968. The show took on many controversial topics, but its focus was investigatory and reformist, not radical.

The most popular woman newscaster of the 1970s was Barbara Walters. She co-starred in NBC's *Today* show and later co-anchored the ABC evening news with Harry Reasoner.

Walters went on to host many other television programs, interviewing hundreds of famous personalities and world leaders, a journalistic practice that, as pointed out earlier, helps reinforce the status quo.

In 1991, Iraqi dictator Saddam Hussein ordered a military invasion of Kuwait. Several weeks later, a U.S.-led coalition launched a counterattack. President George H. W. Bush's administration asked American television networks to leave Iraq. Every network except one complied, providing evidence to critics that mainstream television news bows to authority and reinforces mainstream values such as patriotism.

The exception was Ted Turner's Cable News Network, which broadcast live reports 24-hours a day from Bagdad, where coalition planes were dropping bombs and Iraqi anti-aircraft guns were firing back. It was high drama, and CNN's ratings soared. Almost overnight, CNN had established itself as the television news leader, eclipsing the three big networks (ABC, CBS and NBC), which had big-name stars like Dan Rather, Peter Jennings, and Tom Brokaw.

How the Mass Media Really Work

Twelve years later, in 2003, the United States sent troops back to Iraq and ousted Hussein from power. CNN and the other networks were there, providing news heavily-laden with the American perspective.

But one exception was Al-Jazeera, the first independent satellite television network in the Middle East and the station Osama bin Laden picked to broadcast his messages. Al-Jazeera was widely criticized in the West, but it became the most trusted source of news about the war among people who lived in the Middle East.

TELEVISION GROWS UP

In the late 1950s and early 1960s, one of the most popular television entertainment programs was *Leave It Beaver*, a family situation comedy seen through the eyes of a small boy named "Beaver Cleaver."

Beaver lived an idyllic household, where his mother wore dresses when she cleaned the house, his father never raised his voice in anger, and his older brother almost always treated him with respect. When the show ended in 1963, it seemed that America itself had also lost much of its innocence.

President John F. Kennedy was assassinated in 1963, and for the next 15 years Americans would be divided by a number of controversies, including the Vietnam War, racial and gender discrimination, and environmental degradation.

Television was not untouched by these events. For the first time, Americans were first-row spectators to riots in major U.S. cities and to a war in a foreign land.

Images of injured and dead U.S. servicemen were particularly disturbing. So was the My Lai Massacre, in which American soldiers gunned down innocent women and children. Many historians and scholars believe such images helped sway public opinion against the war.

But it would be incorrect to say that television deliberately set out to challenge U.S. government policy or to sway public opinion against the war. Television then, as now, was a business, run by executives who sought to make a profit. TV executives were not eager to broadcast news or entertainment programming that criticized powerful people or alienated lots of viewers or advertisers.

U.S. Army photograph of the aftermath of the My Lai massacre in 1968. News of the massacre helped sway public opinion against the Vietnam War.

In fact, the networks were quick to censor programs that criticized the so-called "establishment," which included the president, the government, and the military and industrial complexes.

CENSORSHIP OF TELEVISION PROGRAMMING

One of the best examples was the *Smothers Brothers Comedy Hour*, a CBS show that starred Dick and Tom Smothers and aired from 1967-69.

In folk songs and comedy sketches, the brothers and their guests poked fun at the military, the police, middle-class America, President Lyndon Baines Johnson and the government. Almost everyone thought it was funny except CBS censors, employees whose job it was to cut offensive content.

For example, they eliminated:

- a scene from a Mother's Day special which ended with the words, "Please talk peace" (reference to Vietnam War);
- an interview with Dr. Benjamin Spock, who was an advocate for draft evaders;

How the Mass Media Really Work

Tom and Dick Smothers poked fun at the military, police, middle-class, and President Lyndon Johnson during the three-year run on CBS television in the 1960s. The show was canceled partly because executives were worried about alienating advertisers and losing their broadcast licenses *(2004 photo by Erik Schultz)*.

- images from the 1968 police-instigated riot outside the Democratic Party convention in Chicago.

Although it had high ratings, the *Smothers Brothers* show was canceled in 1969. The network justified its decision by making reference to a network policy that "prohibits appeals for active support of any cause" (even if it was "peace"). The truth, though, was that CBS executives were worried about alienating advertisers and losing their broadcast licenses.

In an ironic twist, the censors at CBS helped canonize the Smothers Brothers as symbols of the struggle for free speech on television. To this day, Dick Smothers lectures on the topic to groups across the country.

On Dec. 4, 2002, Bravo aired *Smothered*, a documentary special about the Smothers Brothers' censorship struggles.

The Smothers Brothers isn't the only example of censorship on television. In most cases, the censors are less concerned about politics than on offending conservative, Christian values. For example:

- In 1944, NBC censors shut off the sound feed while Eddie Cantor and Nora Martin were singing "We're Having a Baby, My Baby and Me." The censored lines were:

  > Martin: *Thanks to you, my life is bright. You've brought me joy beyond measure.*
  > Cantor: *Don't thank me. Quite all right. Honestly, it was a pleasure.*
  > Martin: *Just think, it's my first one.*
  > Cantor: *The next one's on me.*

- In the 1950s comedy *I Love Lucy*, Lucy and Ricky slept in separate twin beds and kept one foot on the floor when kissing. Censors also would not allow use of the word "pregnant" on the air. Instead, she was "expecting."
- In the late 1950s, the *Ed Sullivan Show* showed Elvis Presley singing from the waist up, because censors thought his wiggling torso was too sexually suggestive.
- In the early 1960s, a dance scene between a white male actor and a black female actor was cut from the television show, "East Side, West Side."
- For their appearance on the *Ed Sullivan Show* in 1967, the rock group Rolling Stones had to change the lyrics of "Let's Spend the Night Together" to "Let's Spend Some Time Together."
- In 1981, comedian Charles Rocket was fired from the *Saturday Night Live* program after he accidentally said "fuck" on the program.
- In 1989, the made-for-TV movie "Crimes of Passion II" was never broadcast because of advertising boycotts organized by "Americans for Responsible Television," which opposes sex and violence on television.
- In 1992, during a live performance on *Saturday Night Live,* singer Sinead O'Connor ripped up a photograph of Pope John Paul II after singing Bob Marley's "War" and remarked, "Fight the real enemy." The photo tearing scene was cut when the program was rebroadcast.

How the Mass Media Really Work

Censorship is one way of creating control. Another effective approach is to avoid covering controversial issues altogether. Entertainment television excels in this regard.

For example, in the 1950s network programming refused to provide on-air opportunities for minorities. Advertisers would not sponsor programs hosted by minorities.

One exception was Hugh Hefner's *Playboy's Penthouse,* a syndicated television program that began broadcasting in 1960 that often featured black musicians like Sammy Davis Jr., Nat King Cole and Ray Charles.

Hugh Hefner in 2010 *(Photo by Glenn Francis, used with permission)*

In the 1960s, opportunities on television for women were a little better than they were for minorities. This included Lucille Ball's second series (*The Lucy Show,* without ex-husband Desi Arnez), *The Ann Sothern Show* (a comedy), and Carol Burnett's variety show.

In 1968, singer Diahann Carroll became the first black female to star in a comedy series. *Julia* was a young, independent, widowed nurse (her "husband" had been killed in Vietnam) who was raising a little boy.

Black Entertainment Television (BET), the first cable network targeted to African American audiences, was launched in 1980. The network continues to produce television and radio programming targeted to black audiences.

The first Spanish-speaking television station, KMEX (Univision) was founded September 29, 1962. KMEX won the first Edward R. Murrow Award and is the first TV station to create a Spanish-language morning talk show ("Los Angeles al Dia").

During the turbulent 1960s and 1970s, most entertainment television ignored the Vietnam War as well as social movements promoting civil, women's, gay and environmental rights.

Instead, they aired family-oriented comedic and science-fiction programming. This included *The Andy Griffith Show, The Beverly Hillbillies, The*

Addams Family, My Favorite Martian, Bewitched, I Dream of Jeannie, Star Trek, Outer Limits, and the *Twilight Zone.*

The first prime-time cartoon show, *Rocky and His Friends*, appeared in 1959. Children saw the show as pure entertainment, but Rocky and Bullwinkle's main adversaries were Soviet-Union-like spies Boris Badenov and Natasha Fatale. The show subtly reminded children that America's greatest enemy was communism.

Other cartoons, such the *Flintstones, Alvin and the Chipmunks,* and *The Jetsons,* were less propagandistic but, nonetheless, reinforced values about the importance of family and friends.

Overall, though, the content of entertainment television tends to conform to the mainstreaming rule more than other forms of mass media content, partly because television has always tried to reach large rather than segmented audiences. And, as a rule, *the more people a mass medium tries to reach, the less offensive it must be.*

IS TELEVISION DYSFUNCTIONAL?

Although television avoided controversial issues during the 20th century, some of its programming still generated complaints from parents and religious activists.

The most frequent complaint was that its content was too violent. Studies showed that westerns, crime dramas and cartoons contained a lot of violent acts, including assaults and murders.

But the issue did not get a great deal of national attention until 1969, when the Commission on the Causes and Prevention of Violence issued a report suggesting that violent programming on television "can and does have adverse effects upon audiences."[129]

After riots broke out in many U.S. cities, President Lyndon B. Johnson appointed two separate commissions to look into the causes of violence.

In 1969, one of those commissions, the National Commission on the Causes and Prevention of Violence, issued a report that placed part of the blame on television.

In response, television executives countered that the violence was make-believe and that there was no evidence to show that violent programming had adverse effects on children or adults.

A soldier stands guard on a corner in Washington D.C. in 1968 near the ruins of buildings destroyed during riots after the assassination of Martin Luther King, Jr. The Commission on the Causes and Prevention of Violence put some of the blame on television, which rarely gave attention to problems facing minorities and the poor.

But in 1982 the debate peaked when the National Institute of Mental Health published *Television and Behavior: Ten Years of Scientific Progress and Implications for the Eighties,*[130] which, after reviewing more than 3,000 scientific studies, concluded that the evidence overwhelmingly supported charges that televised violence increases aggressive behaviors in many children.

The findings, however, have had relatively little impact on television programming, partly because the First Amendment helped insulate television from regulatory control. In fact, mass communication researchers report that there is more violence on television today than 30 years ago.[131]

To be sure, television can produce anti-social effects on some people, at some times, and in some places. But such effects do not outweigh the prosocial control and change functions of the medium.

Entertainment television shows began to deal with more controversial topics during the 1970s.

At the head of the pack was the satirical comedy *All in the Family,* whose lead character (Archie Bunker) was a blue-collar bigot. The show dealt with many sensitive issues, including abortion, racism and homosexuality. Although the program was clearly intended to be a parody, research showed that, ironically, many politically conservative viewers identified with Bunker's archaic value system. The moral of the story here is that people's perceptions and value shape the way they interpret information, sometimes in ways different than was intended.

Saturday Night Live also satirized many topics and people, including sex and religious leaders.

Roots, a miniseries based on Alex Haley's popular book about several generations of black Americans, fostered greater appreciation for the plight of blacks. So did *Good Times,* a gritty comedy about a black family living in a ghetto.

Also popular, but much less political, were the comedies *Happy Days,* which followed the lives of a group of fifties-era teenagers, and *The Brady Bunch,* a sappy comedy about a family with six children.

Historically, situation comedies have been the most popular fare on television. This was also the case during the 1980s. The (Bill) *Cosby Show* led the pack. It was a wholesome comedy that featured an upscale African American family.

But television as a whole would never return to the "innocent" 1950s.

Cheers, for example, featured the escapades of an unmarried, sexist, womanizing bar owner called "Sam Malone" and his voyeuristic patrons. *Roseanne* portrayed a working class family in which the mother and father often argued and shouted at the kids and dealt with real-world problems like drugs and sex.

But the most outrageous comedy of the time was *Married...with Children,* which featured a father who was a professional failure, a vain mother, the lustful son, and a promiscuous daughter. Although critics attacked *Married...with Children* as being anti-family, a closer viewing shows that virtually every episode contained a moral lesson that reinforced traditional family values or other system values.

The 1980s also saw the rise of Oprah Winfrey, who would serve as a powerful prosocial agent of control for American women.

Oprah Winfrey: Helping Women Solve Problems

At age 13, Oprah Winfrey got into trouble and was sent to a juvenile detention center.[132] Some people say it was the best thing that ever happened to her.

The center was too crowded to accept her, so she was sent to live with her father, a strict disciplinarian. He forced Oprah to learn five new words before dinner each day and to read a book and write a report on it once a week.

Three years later Oprah won an oratorical contest that gave her a scholarship.

Oprah Winfrey in 2011 *(Photo by Greg Hernandez, used with permission)*

Fifteen years later she received Golden Globe and Oscar supporting actress nominations for her performance as Sofia in Steven Spielberg's adaptation of Alice Walker's masterpiece, *The Color Purple*.

Twenty years later she would host the most popular syndicated television show in the world — one that is focused mainly on entertaining women and helping them solve their problems.

Thirty years later her media empire would be valued at more than $1 billion, making her the most successful female entertainer in U.S. history.

Oprah credits her father with turning her life around.

"My father, Vernon Winfrey, is one of the most honorable men I know." She was born in 1954, the daughter of Vernita Lee and Vernon, who were not married. At age 4, she began her public speaking career. She toured churches in Nashville, reciting sermons of James Weodon Johnson while other children sang.

Vernita and Vernon separated and Oprah lived on a pig farm in Mississippi with her maternal grandmother until age 6, when she went to Milwaukee to live with her mother. Oprah had little supervision and got into trouble. A cousin also sexually molested her.

When she went to live with her father in Nashville, she was pregnant. She lost the child.

But her father, who was a barber and city council member, laid down some rules. Oprah responded. She became a good student. At age 17, she was crowned "Miss Fire Prevention" in Nashville. While visiting a radio station one day, she was invited to read copy. The station hired her to read news on the air.

At 19, Oprah, who was now a sophomore at Tennessee State University, was crowned Miss Black Tennessee. In the same year she was hired as Nashville's first female and first black TV-news anchor.

After graduation, she took an anchor position in Baltimore, but she wasn't well suited for the job. Sometimes she would cry when reading sad news. The station moved her into their morning talk show program. She found her niche.

In 1984, she became host of A.M. Chicago, a morning talk show. The name eventually was changed to The *Oprah Winfrey Show*, and, in 1986, the program was syndicated. Soon thereafter her program surpassed Phil Donahue as the nation's top rated talk show. Oprah was only 32.

Oprah went on to star in many prime-time TV specials, home videos and movies. She also set up her own television, film, video and print production companies (all of which have "Harpo" — Oprah spelled backwards — in the name). In 1996, Oprah set up a book club that catapulted virtually every selection to the top of the best-selling list.

She has won scores of awards and contributes 10 percent of her fortune to charitable causes.

In 2000, Oprah launched a magazine, titled *O: The Oprah Magazine*. In the same year, she co-founded Oxygen, a U.S. cable television network targeted to women. In September 2002, she debuted in *Oprah After The Show* on Oxygen.

But the foundation of her empire has been the *The Oprah Winfrey Show*, which until 2010 was seen by more than 30 million viewers in 160 countries. More than 1 million people also visited her website, Oprah.com, every day.

"She's certainly the most influential person on television," said Dick Kurlander, vice president of Petry Television, a company that offers consulting services to TV stations. "She's extremely credible."

TELEVISION PUSHES THE ENVELOPE

Entertainment television programming during the 1990s and 2000s couldn't be called radical by any measure, as it rarely challenged powerful corporate and political groups. In fact, shows like *CSI: Crime Scene Investigation*, *Sopranos* and *Law & Order* glorified police and the court system.

Reality shows like *Survivor*, *Who Wants to Marry a Millionaire*, *The Mole*, *The Osbournes*, *The Anna Nicole Show*, *Big Brother* and scores of others were very predictable. Like audiences for talk shows, the at-home audiences for reality shows evaluated the contestants or participants through the prism of society's dominant values and beliefs. Contestants who behaved well were usually liked; those who violated the rules or treated other contestants with disrespect were disliked. Audiences loved it when these people were eliminated from the competitions.

Television continued to promote mainstream values and ideas as the 21st century approached. However, some television programming did anger some conservatives and religious leaders.

The programming included *Ellen* and *Will and Grace*, which featured homosexuals in lead roles; *NYPD Blue*, which contained nudity and foul language; *Friends*, which revolved around sexual themes and innuendoes; *Men Behaving Badly* and *South Park*, which contained a lot of crude behavior and language; *Politically Incorrect with Bill Maher*, which was, indeed, often politically incorrect; and even *Seinfeld*, which had one show devoted to the topic of masturbation (i.e., who could hold off the longest before doing it).

The content on cable television represented an even greater challenge to traditional norms and values. Shows like *Sex in the City*, *Queer Eye for the Straight Guy*, and *Breaking Bad* included frank discussions about sex and illegal behavior.

The psychological and social effects of programs that present alternative, nontraditional lifestyles are complex.

But research has shown, for example, that white people who watched the television miniseries *Roots* were more sympathetic than nonviewers to the plight of black Americans. And shows that challenge mainstream values can contribute to the decline of traditional family values.[133]

Although conservatives often view the decline of traditional family values in a negative way, liberals point out that shows which push the mainstream value envelope can increases understanding and acceptance of people with alternative lifestyles and values. The passage of same-sex marriage laws in some states, for example, has not increased the number of homosexuals or led to a decline in the importance of family values.

The potential of television as a agent of social change may increase as more and more television channels become available through cable and the Internet. The FCC does not regulate these channels, so they have greater freedom to produce programming that challenges dominant values and institutions.

Objectivity and Broadcast News

As noted in the previous chapter, the ethic of objectivity is a powerful force in newspaper journalism. Print journalists strongly adhere to the principle that they should keep their own opinions out of their stories, should cover all sides to a story, and should give roughly equal coverage to all sides.

But broadcast journalists have never had the same level of commitment to "relative" objectivity. Their news reports often make editorial comments. Some even end their stories with what print journalists call the snapper — a statement that sums up the moral lesson for the viewer. This is particularly true after a tragedy, such as a disaster or major crime story.

Many print professionals and scholars believe broadcasting's departure from the ethic of objectivity hurts the credibility of broadcast news. However, the broadcast news industry doesn't seem to care much. It is focused on ratings, and broadcasters who connect with the values of their audiences seem to be more popular.

How the Mass Media Really Work

This is especially true of Fox Network's *The O'Reilly Factor*, which appeals to audiences with mainstream conservative values. Highly partisan shows like this have blurred the lines between news and opinion. But they reinforce conservative values and beliefs and, hence, serve as agents of control for their viewers.

INTERNET: MASS COMMUNICATION FOR EVERYONE

Tim Berners-Lee wasn't thinking about mass media when he invented the World Wide Web in 1990. He was just trying to help scientists exchange data over the Internet.

But Berners-Lee's invention did more than solve the problem of transferring documents and data between computers. He turned the Internet into a mass medium and created what we authors call the Second Information Revolution.

"It's hard to overstate the impact of the global system he created," declared *Time* magazine, which selected Berners-Lee as one

Tim Berners Lee *(Photo courtesy of the John S. and James L. Knight Foundation)*

of the 100 greatest minds of the 20th century. "He took a powerful communications system (Internet) that only the elite could use and turned it into a mass medium."[134]

Before the Web, about 600,000 people, mostly scientists and government officials, used the Internet, which was not very user-friendly. But Berners-Lee's software was relatively easy to use and gave Internet users the power to create their own Internet sites and link to other sites. In fact, anyone with a computer and modem (a device for connecting a computer to a phone line) could easily enter cyberspace.[135]

And they did.

Within five years, there were 40 million users. Mass media organizations were some of the first. The bigger newspapers and television news organizations set up Web sites and marketed their news directly to online consumers. Journalists also used the Internet for e-mail and to research stories.

Today, about 1 billion people around the world are connected to the Internet,[136] primarily through the Web. Most daily newspapers, magazines, book publishers, recording companies, and radio and television stations and networks have their own Web sites, which combine pictures, graphics, text and sometimes audio-visual content. It's getting harder to tell the difference between media formats.

Although Berners-Lee wasn't thinking about mass media organizations when he invented the Web, in less than a decade the Web has transformed the way mass media organizations do business. In fact, many media analysts believe the Internet and the Web will eliminate traditional distinctions between newspapers, books, magazines, radio and television, creating what media analysts call a convergence of technology.

Even more important, though, is the fact that the Internet is empowering ordinary citizens as never before, creating the Second Information Revolution

THE FIRST INFORMATION REVOLUTION

Johannes Gutenberg gets credit for the First Information Revolution. He invented the modern printing press about 1450 in Germany.

At the time, ordinary people had few rights and little power. Emperors, kings, nobles, lords, religious leaders and tribal chiefs ruled in most areas of the world — some with an iron fist. Most of them monopolized the production and dissemination of knowledge and ideas, which helped them maintain power over people. Uninformed people are easier to control.

But Gutenberg's printing press made it much more difficult for elites to control the production and distribution of knowledge and ideas. In fact, the printing press enabled people who were critical of those in power to easily and inexpensively produce and distribute their ideas.

Replica of a Gutenberg press.

The best example in those days was the Reformation of the 1500s. The followers of Martin Luther used the printed press to spread ideas that were critical of Roman Catholic Church.

The loss of power was slow at first. Political and religious authorities tried to control the distribution of printed material, especially material critical of them.

But by the 1700s the sheer amount of material being produced outpaced the ability of censors to control it. Literacy spread. So did ideas about democratic government, which helped ignite revolutionary movements in many European countries and in America.

Collectively, historians have called this phenomenon *The Enlightenment*, an intellectual movement that challenged traditional religious and political authorities and championed science and greater participation for individuals in political affairs (especially representative democracy). Newspapers, magazines and other print media played a key role in the Enlightenment. They were mediators of news and information.

When people or researchers needed information about a contemporary political or social issue, they would go the library and pull out the index for *The New York Times* or some other major newspaper. People and organizations relied heavily, sometimes exclusively, on traditional mass media — newspapers, books, magazines, radio, and television — for information about politics, business, and social affairs.

In the 20th century, mainstream political groups and the government relied heavily on mass media to get their messages to the public and policymakers. So did social movements and nonmainstream organizations. One problem, though, is that groups outside of the mainstream had greater difficulty getting coverage of their ideas and causes. The civil rights and women's movements, for example, did not receive significant media coverage until the U.S. Supreme Court decisions of the 1950s legitimized their right to seek equality.

Mass media reached the peak of their power in the late 1900s. That's when people and social movement organizations began to depend more and more on the Internet for information and knowledge and to communicate with each other. In fact, in some cases the Internet allowed them to circumvent the media altogether.

THE SECOND INFORMATION REVOLUTION

A good example of this occurred in South Korea in the mid-1990s, when the government of South Korea enacted in secret new laws that allowed South Korean companies to lay off union workers, change working hours and hire replacements for union workers who go on strike.

The labor unions, which had been excluded from the meetings, were furious. They staged a strike. But they had a problem. The mainstream media in South Korea would not help them get their message out to the world.

So they did the only thing they could: They created a web page and sent thousands of e-mails to groups around the world.

It worked.

Thousands of people and groups around the world condemned the South Korean government.

Labor unions went on strike in South Korea to protest laws that deprived them of workers' rights. This photograph shows a different group of protestors in Seoul in 2005. But the same principles are at work — citizens are challenging powerful elites and institutions, and such disputes become the fodder of news stories that draw attention to social problems and may help participants solve them.

"E-mail was the only way KCTU (Korean Confederation of Trade Unions) could send more than 1,000 copies of letters and petitions overseas every day," one leader of the movement told mass communication scholar Tae-hyun Kim. "Without the website," another leader remarked, "the whole strike could have remained as a domestic issue, and might not have been able to attract international attention."[137]

Mass media, particularly news media organizations, are often portrayed in traditional history textbooks as defenders of democracy, life, liberty and happiness. There certainly are some good examples of that (e.g., the muckrakers).

But, as this book has shown in previous chapters, mass media do not always identify with the underdog. In fact, more often than not they produce content that supports powerful institutions and elites and dominant value systems.

In other words, they perform a guard dog role.

Thus, 20 years ago, when a group with little power wanted to inform others of its plight, there wasn't much that group could do without help from the mainstream media. In fact, historical research shows that mainstream news media marginalized the civil rights, women's and labor movements for many decades.

But the Internet has leveled the playing field, at least a little.

Through e-mail, websites, blogs YouTube and Twitter, groups and individuals can communicate directly with large numbers of people.

They can bypass traditional mass media.

They can mass communicate.

And many are doing that.

A billion people around the world use the Internet for e-mail, shopping and research. The Internet fulfills needs that traditional media could not. For example, going the bookstore can take up a whole afternoon. Ordering a book online takes minutes. Researching a specific concept or term can take hours in the library. Doing an online search takes minutes. And e-mail helps people stay in contact with others and even generate new relationships.

The Pew American and Internet Life Project found, for example, that 84 percent of U.S. Internet users have contacted an online group.[138] Half say the Internet helped them get to know people they would not otherwise have met. Another third said groups have helped them meet people of different ages. And a fourth said they have met people from different ethnic or economic backgrounds than their own.

The study also found that a fourth go online to connect with their local community, by arranging church meetings, neighborhood gatherings, local sports events, or charity activities. Men were more likely to take part in online groups about professional activities, politics and sport. In contrast, women were drawn to medical support groups, entertainment groups, and local community associations. Six of 10 who visit online groups email the group regularly.

The content on mass media Web sites, like the content in traditional media, also generally supports and maintains dominant values and social institutions. The sources for online news stories tend to be powerful political and economic elites. The lyrics for songs at an online music site tend to reinforce dominant values about love and relationships. Advertising encourages people to purchase goods and services that, in turn, help support a free-market system.

In short, the Internet, like traditional mass media, helps people achieve their personal and professional goals more efficiently and effectively. In sociological lingo, the Internet reduces social distance. It helps integrate people and organizations into the dominant culture. It is empowering ordinary people.

In fact, when people today want to research or find information about a topic or organization, they often turn first to the Internet.

The Internet gives them easy, quick access the archives of the *Times* or many other newspapers. However, the searchers can also do one thing that they couldn't do prior to the Internet: They often can go to the original sources quoted in the newspapers. That's because most organizations and many individuals now have their own websites that provide information and news about contemporary issues as well as many other topics.

Now that might not seem very special to many people.

But to some scholars, including us, it signals the beginning of the second information revolution — one in which the mass media, which once siphoned off some power from political elites, is now itself losing some of its mediating power.

This might seem like a strange statement to make when the number and variety of mass media are growing and when criticism of mass media seems to be at an all-time high. But the loss-of-power argument is based on relative, not absolute, change. In other words, although mass media clearly produce more content today than in the past, they are less likely now to be the exclusive or primary source of information and knowledge about the world, thanks to the Internet.

In addition to circumventing the mass media, people and organizations can also communicate more effectively and easily with the outside world. Weblogs, or blogs, which are essentially online diaries, have become very popular. They enable anyone to become a journalist of sort, for very little cost.

Blogs also have been used to monitor the performance of the mainstream mass media. In 2005, CBS Evening News and former anchor

Dan Rather were strongly criticized after bloggers raised questions about the veracity of a National Guard document stating that President George W. Bush had failed to perform his duties when he was a pilot during the Vietnam War.[139] In fact, the role of the blogs as a "fifth estate" is now becoming the main topic of some new books.[140]

Former CBS anchor Dan Rather

To be sure, the world is a far cry from being ruled by ordinary people. The development of the printing press and other forms of mass communication have not eliminated social inequities or injustices. Great disparities continue to exist within and between countries.

The "information revolution" also has not ushered in direct democracy — a political system in which all citizens have a direct say in the day-to-day happenings in government. Political and economic power remains highly centralized in all Western countries. Elites still wield a disproportionate amount of power, and will continue to do so in the immediate future.

Mainstream mass media also remain powerful institutions in society. Many people and elites continue to see them as credible institutions.

But, in relative terms, ordinary folks today have far less dependence on elites or mass media organizations when it comes to news and information. For the first time in history, ordinary citizens can communicate their ideas easily and cheaply to virtually anyone in the world, making is somewhat more difficult for the powerful to control information, knowledge and ideas.

How the Mass Media Really Work

Appendix
MASS MEDIA SYSTEMS THEORY

The theory presented in this book represents a loose compilation of ideas and hypotheses from many different theoretical models, which collectively are referred to as Mass Media Systems theory. MMST is based on Social Systems theory in sociology. The fundamental question involves examining why society exists and what contribution various institutions and organizations make to the maintenance or destruction of that society or a social system within that society.

A social system may be defined as two or more social actors (individuals or collectivities) in an interdependent relationship. Interdependency exists when the attempt by one actor to achieve a goal depends upon the actions of another (or others). A good example in modern society is the dependence that politicians have on the media to obtain news coverage in order to win an election and, vice-versa, the dependence that journalists have on the politicians to report the events tied to the election. Many other social actors, in turn, depend upon these two social actors to achieve their goals (e.g., voters' need for information in order to select a candidate).

The idea of society as a system can be traced to the ancient Greeks.[141] Yet, despite being one of the oldest theoretical frameworks in the social sciences, social systems theory is not a highly codified system of propositions or theorems. In fact, some scholars argue that social systems theory is "neither a true description of reality nor a substantive theory nor an analytical procedure. Rather, it is a conceptual device designed to facilitate the entire scientific process, from the formation of propositions to the design of research."[142]

The position taken here might be described as middle-of-the-road. Systems theory can, indeed, greatly facilitate the study of media processes and effects, but it also offers at a general level an explanation for the existence and persistence of social systems. More specifically, systems theory attempts to explain social systems in terms of institutional arrangements, values, beliefs and power. This position is contrary to some economic models, which attempt to explain social systems primarily in terms of the marketplace or contractual arrangements. While implied or formal social contracts may contribute to the maintenance of a social system, systems theorists argue that they alone cannot explain a wide range of behavior or action, including much of that exhibited by the mass media.

Since the turn of the century, a handful of mass communication researchers have used a social systems perspective to study the mass media, especially the *news* media.[143] However, the vast majority of research has been and continues to be oriented toward psychological or social-psychological explanations and the micro-level of analysis.[144] Such studies are important for understanding the consequences of mass-mediated messages, but they cannot fully account for the role of mass media in society, because media are macro-level phenomena that cannot be reduced to the sum of the cognitions or social roles of the social actors within them. The whole, in other words, is greater (or lesser) than the sum of its parts.

Although a number of factors could be cited to explain the relative lack of interest in system research on the mass media,[145] a key factor is that many contemporary media scholars continue to associate modern systems theorizing with the functionalism of Durkheim, Lazarsfeld or Parsons and, consequently, believe that it is outmoded and inherently conservative.[146] While the history of social systems theory is inextricably tied to these early theorists, a systems or functional perspective does not necessarily imply a theoretical conservatism, as numerous theorists have pointed out.[147] Concepts like social action, choice, conflict, power, institution building and the construction of social reality all play an important role in modern systems theorizing. Systems theory is opposed to logical positivism, determinism, reductionism and atomism; however, empirical analysis and quantitative research methods can inform theory and vice versa.

The purpose of this appendix is to debunk some of the myths surrounding systems theory and to show how it can be used to better understand the role of mass media in society. More specifically, it will be argued that systems theorizing has undergone a synthesis in which many elements of consensus, conflict and symbolic interaction theories have been incorporated into one model. This new approach still emphasizes that the mass media — like police, schools and other major institutions — are agents of social control, but concern also has increased with studying the origins and development of media institutions themselves. Media institutions themselves are no longer taken for granted or perceived as being part of some natural order. They are a product of concrete historical conditions, social and cultural phenomena, and the goal-oriented social actors whose interests are interlocked with those of other groups in society. The history of systems theory, like the history of social systems themselves, can be viewed

How the Mass Media Really Work

as part of a dialectical process in which criticism along the way has infused new ideas that have allowed the theory to adapt and change.

INTELLECTUAL HISTORY

Following Buckley,[148] the history of systems theory may be divided roughly into four major models or periods: mechanical, organic, process and general systems. The differences and boundaries between these models are not always easy to identify or define. But, heuristically, the models are useful for organizing and understanding the changes that have occurred.

MECHANICAL MODEL

The first formal social system models emerged in the 17th century and were adapted from the natural sciences, which opposed supernatural, mystical, teleological and anthropormorphic conceptions of the world. Social physics, the social counterpart to the natural science system models, regarded the human being as an elaborate machine whose actions and thoughts could be analyzed with the principles of mechanics. Society, for example, was like an astronomical system, composed of people who were bound together by mutual attraction or differentiated by repulsion. Different societies or states were seen as systems of balanced oppositions. Social organization, power and authority were believed to be the result of natural forces (i.e., social atoms and molecules), rather than being the product of human actions and will (i.e., socially constructed).[149] A number of concepts and terms emerged from this period, including the notion of moral or social space, social coordinates, equilibrium, and centrifugal and centripetal forces.

Many of the mechanical theories, according to Buckley,[150] contained elements of specious analogizing. One exception was Vilfredo Pareto, who employed only the most general principles. He was one of the first to think of society as a system in equilibrium, as a whole consisting of interdependent parts.[151] A change in one part, Pareto argued, affects other parts as well as the whole.[152] Social equilibrium is maintained by three types of factors: (1) the extra-human environment (climate, soil, etc.), (2) external conditions (society's previous states and contact with other cultures), and (3) internal elements (race, interest, knowledge, values, ideologies). Pareto believed that if a social system is subjected to pressures of external forces, inner forces will then push toward the restoration of equilibrium.

Although most contemporary systems theorists have rejected the notion of natural equilibrium, the idea of a system as a whole consisting of interdependent parts remains fundamental. In the broadest sense, a system consists of two or more units that relate to each other in a structural relationship and form an entity whose elements are functionally interdependent.[153] The opposite of a system is random variability. A social system, in particular, may be defined as a bounded set of interrelated activities that together constitute a single social entity.[154] The activities may involve those of an entire society or those of just two people or social actors (e.g., a wife and husband). Thus, societies also are conceptualized as being composed of subsystems within sub-subsystems, etc. (e.g., the society, a community within the society, a church within the community, a family within the church, a wife within a family).

The mechanical model produced little in the way of systematic empirical research. Most 19th century scholars seemed content to draw upon analogies from mechanical systems (i.e., solar systems) to describe actions within social systems. Such explanations were highly deterministic and mechanistic. Furthermore, no systematic studies of the mass media using the mechanical model apparently exist. This is not too surprising, since the mechanical model was already in decline by the mid-19th century, before newspapers and social sciences had obtained major institutional status.

ORGANIC MODEL

The use of the organismic metaphor is very old, but serious scientific usage of it is usually traced to Herbert Spencer.[155] Basically, this is the notion that society is like the human body: It has a number of different specialized or differentiated parts that contribute to maintenance of the overall life of the organism. Many followers of Spencer went to great lengths to find the social counterparts to the heart, brain, and other parts of the body. Spencer was much more cautious.[156] Nevertheless, Spencer failed to emphasize that society is more like a species than an organism.[157] When the analogy is the organism, the parts are perceived to cooperate and do not compete in a struggle for survival. In contrast to the organic analogy, the species metaphor emphasizes competition and conflict, which, of course, leads to a very different characterization of society.[158]

Historically, structural functionalists have been the major proponents of organic model.[159] Talcott Parsons, Robert K. Merton, Edward Shils and many others analyzed relations between social systems, personalities and cultures.[160] They focused on how solidarity, trust, meaning and power are institutionalized

How the Mass Media Really Work

in the construction or production of the social order. Although all of these dimensions were defined as needs that every social system must cope with in order to survive, cooperation and consensus were given a much more prominent role than power and conflict in the regulation of social activities.[161]

In their quest to explain social order, organic theorists spent a great deal of time trying to identify the functional imperatives of social systems — i.e., the needs or requisites that all social systems must solve in order to survive. Parsons, for example, developed the "four-function paradigm," which contended that all systems face four major problems — adaptation, goal attainment, integration and pattern maintenance (later renamed latent pattern maintenance-tension management). To solve these problems, he argued that social systems have developed four major subsystems or institutions: the economy to satisfy the adaptation need (i.e., the acquisition of resources from the environment); the polity to solve the goal attainment need; culture (or public associations), such as religious institutions, to meet the integration need; and the family and educational institutions to satisfy the need for pattern maintenance. Mass media were said to satisfy primarily the need for integration, albeit they as well as all other institutions were said to contribute more or less to each of the four requisite needs. A social system that resolves each of these four system needs successfully was, according to Parsons, in a state of equilibrium, or a state of balance. As Theodorson and Theodorson put it:

> [Social equilibrium is] the concept that social life has a tendency to be and to remain a functionally integrated phenomenon, so that any change in one part of the social system will bring about adjustive changes in the other parts. The initial change creates an imbalance, but a functional adjustment of the parts occurs to recreate an integrated, adjusted and relatively stable system.[162]

The equilibrium assumption led many of the functional theorists to take for granted the creation and emergence of values, norms and institutions. As a consequence, any behavior that deviated from the dominant system of values and rules was considered deviant and undesirable. The goal of social science research under such an approach was to eliminate or control such behaviors. Needless to say, the equilibrium assumption became a lightning rod for criticisms that systems theory was conservative and helped support an oppressive, inequalitarian status quo. Parsons, in particular, was frequently criticized for allegedly advancing a theory that appeared to be ideologically conservative, a label he dismissed but was never able to shake.[163]

Although the organic theorists placed a great deal of emphasis on how institutions maintain social order, they did not ignore social change, a point that is sometimes overlooked by critics. Organic theorists adopted a neo-evolutionary model of social change, in which structural differentiation and functional specialization were the primary agents. The organic theorists acknowledged that revolutionary change was possible; however, they could not account for such change because they viewed it as too complex to explain given the current state of knowledge. Parsons writes:

> ... a general theory of the processes of change of social systems is not possible in the present state of knowledge. The reason is very simply that such a theory would imply complete knowledge of the laws of process of the system and this knowledge we do not possess. The theory of change in the structure of social systems must, therefore, be a theory of particular subprocesses of change *within* such systems, not of the over-all process of change *of* the systems as systems (emphasis in original).[164]

One of the substantive areas particularly influenced by structural functionalism was comparative research on modernization in the 1950s and 1960s.[165] These studies sought to explain differences between traditional and modern societies, arguing that traditional societies were perceived as being restrictive and limited, whereas modern societies were seen as being much more adaptable to a wide range of internal and external problems, especially social and technological change. These theories assumed that the organizational dynamics of economic, political and industrial institutions provide the dynamic force of structure in any complex society. Mass media were seen as playing an important role in breaking down traditional authority and ways of life and ushering in modern values and norms.[166] Furthermore, as the world becomes more urbanized and industrialized, societies become more similar. This view was highly consistent with classical evolutionary theory, which stressed that most societies passed through relatively similar stages toward a common end-stage of modernity.[167]

Following the organic frame of reference, many mass communication researchers before and after World War II attempted to define the major functions that media perform for society. In the 1940s, Lasswell wrote about three major functions: (1) surveillance of the environment; (2) correlation of the parts of society in responding to the environment; and (3) transmission of the social heritage from one generation to the next.[168] Wright added a fourth: entertainment.[169] And Lazarsfeld and Merton added two more: status conferral and the enforcement of social norms (ethicizing).[170] Following Merton,[171] many theorists recognized that media and other institutions may have dysfunctional consequences for social systems or social actors. DeFleur argued, for example, that the function of low-taste content in mass media was "to maintain the financial equilibrium of *a deeply institutionalized social system which is tightly integrated with the whole of the American economic institution*" (emphasis on original).[172] Nevertheless, the underlying theme in such research was that media coverage, as a whole, contributed to social order.[173]

PROCESS MODEL

The process model began to take shape at the turn of the century and is represented in the writings of Albion W. Small, Charles H. Cooley, Robert E. Park, George H. Mead and E. W. Burgess. However, the process model was overshadowed by the organic model (e.g., structural functionalism) until the 1960s, when symbolic interactionism emerged as a widely respected perspective. Berger and Luckmann's classic book, *The Social Construction of Reality*, also helped tremendously to legitimize this perspective.

The process model views society "as a complex, multifaceted, fluid interplay of widely varying degrees and intensities of association and dissociation."[174] Structure is not something distinct from society but, rather, a temporary representation of it at any one point in time. Societies and groups continually shift their structures to adapt to changing conditions. The process model generally is opposed to the notion of equilibrium, since this idea implies that a social system could and should reach a stable or static state. Rather, society is seen as constantly changing and dynamic.

At the turn of the century, Small argued that human experience "composes an associational process," whereby social actors pursuing their own goals "enter into certain more or less persistent structural relationships with each other," also known as institutions, that carry out social functions. "These social structures and functions are, in the first instance, results of the previous associational process; but they no sooner pass out of the fluid state, into a relatively stable condition, than they become in turn causes of subsequent stages of the associational process."[175] Small predicted, somewhat presciently, that the future of sociology "is marked by the gradual shifting of effort from analogical representation of social structures to real analysis of social processes."[176]

Park viewed society as the product of interactions between individuals who are controlled by traditions and norms that arise in a process of interaction. Social control is "the central fact and the central problem of society. ... Society is everywhere a control organization. Its function is to organize, integrate, and direct the energies resident in the individuals which compose it."[177] Park distinguished four major social processes: competition, conflict, accommodation and assimilation. A relatively stable social order, according to Park, is one in which the mechanisms of social control have succeeded in containing antagonistic forces in such a way that they accommodate each other. However, overall accommodation can never be permanently achieved because new social actors are likely to emerge and claim their share of scarce resources.

Writing in the 1950s, Nadel also criticized the equilibrium model, arguing that the social structure must be viewed as an "event-structure."[178] He concludes:

> ... it seems impossible to speak of social structure in the singular. Analysis in terms of structure is incapable of presenting whole societies; nor, which means the same, can any society be said to exhibit an embracing, coherent structure as we understand the term. There are always cleavages, dissociations, enclaves, so that any description alleged to present a single structure will in fact present only a fragmentary or one-sided picture.[179]

Mass media research on the process model historically has focused heavily on how the mass media construct realities and how use of those realities contributes to social integration. For example, during the early part of the 20th century, Park examined the role of the immigrant press in helping newly arrived immigrants acclimate to community life in America.[180] During the 1950s, Janowitz also analyzed the integrative role of the urban weekly, concluding that community ties contribute to reading the paper and reading contributes to integration. He concluded that urban and suburban life, in contrast to the picture created by the mass society model, entails a rich combination of community and traditional ties mixed with modern occupational roles.[181]

GENERAL SYSTEMS THEORY (GST)

The general systems model can be traced to the writings of de la Mettrie, an 18th century physiologist who argued that organization was the fundamental feature of the physical, biological and social worlds.[182] However, GST did not became a potent force in the social sciences until the 1950s, when the Society for General Systems Research was formed.[183] The emergence of this organization represented the culmination of concern that specialization in the sciences was leading to the fragmentation of knowledge. GST was an attempt to integrate the various scientific disciplines by focusing on the principles of organization per se instead of what it is that is organized (i.e., physical or social phenomena).

How the Mass Media Really Work

Like organic and process models, the general systems model posits that social systems are capable of adapting to changes in their natural and social environments. However, GST places much more emphasis on the ability of social systems to transform their structure and form, rather than returning to some sort of equilibrium state, as organic models often postulate. GST also recognizes that systems may dissolve — adaption is not a necessary condition of system strain.

To adapt to changes in the environment, social systems and their actors must obtain feedback information from the environment about the consequences of various actions, social configurations and processes. According to Buckley, feedback-controlled systems are referred to as goal-directed because it is the deviations from the goal-state itself that direct the behavior of the system rather than some predetermined internal mechanism.[184] Feedforward describes the process when social actors in a system attempt to anticipate the probable consequences of proposed activities for the system and its environment before enacting those activities. Thus, systems are dynamic; that is, they can change in response to changes in the environment. Two basic terms are used to characterize change: morphostasis and morphogenesis. The former refers to those processes in a system that tend to preserve or maintain a system's given form, organization or state. Morphogenesis refers to those processes that tend to elaborate or change a system's form, structure or state.

Two key types of morphostasis are homeostasis and equilibrium. A social system is said to be homeostatic, or self-maintaining, if it acts to counter disruptive forces from the environment or its subsystems, as a means of maintaining some crucial system feature or features. Only certain features are protected, not the entire system. Usually these features are characteristics of the system that are important for its survival. Homeostatic actions operate to maintain the system in a "steady state." But if the actions are not successful, the key features being maintained will be changed or destroyed. Pressures also will generate for additional changes in other parts of the system, which may lead to radical alteration or dissolution of the system.

Most organic theorists postulated an inherent tendency toward equilibrium among all the parts of the system. However, general system theorists abandoned this idea and use equilibrium as a heuristic device, i.e., a starting point for analyzing changes in a system. Olsen defines equilibrium as a condition that "exists in a social system when all the parts maintain a constant relationship to each other, so that no part changes its position or relation with respect to all the other parts."[185] Dynamic processes such as homeostasis and morphogenesis may operate with the system, but basic relationships between constituent parts do not change through time. Disruptive stresses and strains may upset the equilibrium, but systems attempt to neutralize or destroy the disruptive forces. The difference between equilibrium and homeostasis is that the latter process refers to only one or a few selected features of the system that are protected, while in equilibrium every part is preserved in constant relation to the total system. In other words, a change in one part will produce changes in all other parts.

Most contemporary system theories emphasize that the equilibrium is dynamic; that is, at any particular time, one subsystem or institution may be more influential than another. At election time, for example, the mass media in a democracy are accorded unusual deference because of the importance that information is perceived to play in contributing to maintenance of the social system.[186] Contemporary theories also do not assume that a social system has a fixed equilibrium; that is, social structures do not always return to a steady state — they may disintegrate in response to environmental or internal stress and strains.

A social system is characterized as morphogenic, or developing, if the system as a whole moves toward increased order, complexity, adaptability, unity or overall effectiveness. A morphogenic system shows increased ability to deal effectively with its environment and its own subsystems. As such, it grows structurally, in terms of complexity and internal ordering, and functionally, in terms of its ability to control its activities and achieve its goals. Both homeostatic and morphogenic processes depend upon feedback, or flow of information from the environment, to operate. Neither process excludes rational thought or purposeful goal-striving, but such features are not a necessary condition for a social system to survive. System growth and change is often a process in which random occurrences that prove beneficial to the system (i.e., in terms of achieving goals) are incorporated and retained, while nonbeneficial occurrences are discarded. Social actors involved in these processes are not necessarily aware of the consequences of their activities for system maintenance or development, or the consequences that different forms of social organization may have on the system or its parts.

Several notable works in communication and sociology were produced during the 1960s and 1970s.[187] General systems theorists criticized organic theorists for placing too much emphasis on social order and not enough on social change. Such theories emphasized not only the structure-maintaining features of social systems but also the structure-elaborating and changing features of unstable systems (i.e., morphogenesis). In other words, in order for a social system to maintain a steady state (i.e., its position of power, control, influence, etc.), it may have to change its structure. General systems theory still has its protagonists in sociology[188] and organizational communication.[189] However, the effort to create a grand systems theory has ultimately failed, Turner

How the Mass Media Really Work

contends, because even though all systems of the universe may possess common properties, it is the unique properties and process of the systems that are more interesting to scientists.[190]

CRITICISMS OF SOCIAL SYSTEMS THEORY

During the 1950s and 1960s, many of the assumptions and postulates of systems models, especially structural functionalism, came under assault. The criticisms can be summarized under six major topics or themes.

First, the approach was criticized for employing illegitimate teleologies. An explanation is said to be teleological when it attempts to explain social processes, especially social change, by reference to end states or results. An illegitimate teleology exists when causal models assume that purposes or goals cause the processes or structures without documenting the causal sequences or mechanisms that gave rise to the processes or structures.[191] Durkheim's theory of the division of labor,[192] for example, is often criticized for employing an illegitimate teleology because he implied at various points that social solidarity — the end state — causes the division of labor to emerge out of competition.

Second, systems models were criticized for being tautological; that is, for having circular statements. Turner argues that this is most likely to occur with the use of terms like equilibrium and requisites.[193] Thus, a social fact is often said to contribute to maintenance of the system — to fulfill some need — and the cause of the social fact is the need it fulfills.

Third, structural functionalism was criticized for being ahistorical and Western-centric. Modern Marxists pointed out that the modernization process was not universal or present in every society. Rather, it was a unique historical situation connected with capitalism and Western expansion and the establishment of an international system of hegemonic and dependent societies. This criticism led to the development of dependency and world system theories.[194]

Fourth, many system theorists assumed that people are easily socialized. In a widely cited essay, Wrong argued that socialization provides people with a social identity, but at the same time they are creative and have the ability to evaluate social reality critically and take an autonomous stand toward concrete social roles. "When our sociological theory over-stresses the stability and integration of society we will end up imagining that man is the disembodied, conscience-driven, status-seeking phantom of current theory."[195]

Fifth, structural functionalism was criticized for being conservative — for supporting the status quo — because it placed too much emphasis on consensus in goals and values as the main integrating mechanism in social systems.[196] Social action or ideas that conflicted with dominant goals and values in a social system were perceived as deviant rather than the self-determining actions and interests of disenfranchised groups and individuals.   And sixth, the approach was criticized for failing to explain social conflict and change, particularly radical change. The possibility that integrative and regulative mechanisms will fail was recognized by structural functionalists, but social change was assumed to occur gradually.[197] Conflicts, when they occurred, were characterized as anomalies that various institutions — such as schools, police, courts and media — would address and correct to bring the system back into a state of equilibrium. As noted earlier, Parsons, in particular, has been criticized for neglecting the role of power.[198]

All of these criticisms have had some validity at one point or another. However, as Turner points out, none are insurmountable. The problem of teleology can be overcome with detailed causal analysis of how needs are actuated in the development of social structures.[199] The problem of tautology can be surmounted by focusing on how variations in social wholes are caused by variations in critical parts and vice versa, and abandoning the assumption of equilibrium. The problem of ahistoricity is not that structural functionalism is incompatible with historical analyses but, rather, so few analyses have tried to merge the two.[200] The problem of over-socialization can be addressed by focusing more on the creation of structures, not just the functions they perform. Although many functionalists have been rightly criticized for taking a conservative view, there is nothing inherent in functionalism that should lead to a conservative viewpoint, since system maintenance may be viewed as either enabling or repressive.[201] And while it is true that classical structural functionalism did not place a great deal of emphasis on explaining rapid social conflict and change, as noted earlier, criticism that it ignored the role of social change is unfounded. Parsons and others adopted a neo-evolutionary perspective which viewed change as a continual process of structural differentiation and functional specialization. Contemporary theories also have modified this slightly to place greater emphasis on the processes of de-differentiation and dissolution of structure as well.[202]

Despite these qualifications, the criticism of system models during the 1950s, 1960s and 1970s was accompanied by the growth of a number of alternative theoretical models. They included the conflict model of Ralf Dahrendorf,[203] the exchange model of George C. Homans,[204] and the symbolic structuralist model of Claude Levi-Strauss.[205] Refinements and improvements also were made to Marxist and symbolic interactionist models during this time. While there were many differences between these models, Eisenstadt points out

How the Mass Media Really Work

that they all shared one major feature: an unwillingness to accept the natural givenness of any single institutional arrangement in terms of the systematic needs of the social systems to which they belonged.[206]

The conflict and symbolic-interactionist models stressed that an institutional order is developed, maintained and changed through a continuous process of interaction, negotiation and struggle among those who participate in it. Greater autonomy also was granted to groups, organizations and individuals — their goals and values may differ considerably from those of the dominant groups and institutions. In short, the argument was that the explanation of any institutional arrangement has to take into account power relations, negotiations, struggles, conflicts and coalitions.

These alternative models have altered the course of systems theory. But it is important to point out that they have not displaced many of its central tenents, particularly the idea that social control is a fundamental need in any social system. Perhaps the greatest shortcoming of early models was not that they were wrong, but that they focused too narrowly on value consensus and the natural givenness of institutional arrangements in generating social order.

CONTEMPORARY SYSTEMS THEORY

Olsen argues that three major factors distinguish social system models from other types of models.[207] First, they place primary emphasis on the totality of the whole system; in other words, the whole is assumed to be greater than the sum of the parts. Emphasis on the whole does not preclude examination of the parts, but the parts can only be understood in relation to the larger whole that they constitute. Second, to define a social system, it must be bounded in some way to separate it from its environment. Such boundaries are always at least partially open to the natural and social environments in that they exchange materials, energy, individuals or information. Eisenstadt emphasizes that such boundaries are open and fragile, not closed and rigid. Social systems and the subsystems within them are in a continuous process of change (construction and deconstruction).[208] And third, the parts of a social system must be interdependent or interrelated to some degree, even though the patterns and degrees of the ordering can vary. As long as the parts of a system have some amount of functional autonomy, they can be analyzed as systems in their own rights or as subsystems of another system. These subsystems, in turn, may be composed of many sub-subsystems, etc.[209]

Unlike mechanical systems (e.g., gas-powered engines), Olsen points out that social systems are capable of adapting to changes in their natural and social environments. Social actors are assumed to be goal-oriented. Behavior is not determined or set by some outside factor or force.[210] However, the range of social action is not unlimited. Cultural, social, psychological, biological and physical elements of any system constrain or enable social action. For example, in most situations social actors have the choice of violating a social value or norm; however, the penalties or sanctions associated with such an action reduce the probability of nonconforming behavior. At the same time, rewards associated with following the norms increases the probability that people will obey. Thus, behavior in such circumstances is not determined, but the probability that action will be consistent with the dominant norm or value increases as the sanctions or rewards associated with the action increase.[211]

Currently, neofunctionalism is one of the most important intellectual movement in systems theory.[212] Alexander, one of the movement's leaders, argues that neofunctionalism: (1) models society as an intelligible system whose parts are symbiotically connected to one another and interact without *a priori* direction from a governing force; (2) concentrates on action as much as on structure, focusing on expressive activity and the ends of action as well as on practicality and means; (3) is concerned with integration as a "possibility and with deviance and processes of social control as facts" — equilibrium is a reference point for analysis; (4) posits that the distinctions between personality, culture and society are vital to social structure and the tensions between them as a continuous source of change and control; (5) implies a recognition of cultural, social and psychological differentiation as a major mode of social change and of the individuation and institutional strains that this historical process creates; and (6) implies the commitment to the independence of conceptualization and theorizing from other levels of sociological analysis.[213] Alexander adds that although each of these six theses can be identified with other lines of work in the social sciences, no other tradition can be identified with all of them.

As noted earlier, another important characteristic of modern social system theories is that they no longer take the development of institutions for granted. The process of institution building, Eisenstadt argues, is affected by three factors: (1) the level and distribution of resources among different groups (i.e., the type of division of labor); (2) the kinds of elites or institutional entrepreneurs that are available, or competing, for the mobilizing and structuring of such resources and for the major groups generated by the social division of labor; and (3) the nature of the conceptions of "visions" (or ideology) which inform the activities of these elites and which are derived from the major cultural orientations or codes prevalent in a society.[214]

According to Eisenstadt, the most important elites in any society are the political elites, because they deal most directly with the regulation of power. This

How the Mass Media Really Work

group consists primarily of elites in government. They are followed by elites whose activities involve the construction of meaning and trust (e.g., churches, schools, media). Elites or, more accurately, coalitions of elites exercise control over basic resources in society through control of the major economic, political and cultural institutions. This control is achieved through a combination of organizational and coercive measures, along with the structuring of cognitive maps (or rules) of the social order (e.g., through the mass media) and the major reference orientations of social groups. The major characteristics and boundaries of social systems are shaped by the different coalitions of elites and the modes of control they exercise. These modes of control include such things as the structure of authority, the conception of justice, the structure of power and the principals of social hierarchization.[215]

Although different coalitions of elites construct the boundaries of social systems and other collectivities, no such construction is stable, according to Eisenstadt. Conflict is inherent in any setting of social interaction because of, first, the scarcity of natural and social resources; second, the plurality of actors; and third, the multiplicity of institutional principles and cultural orientations.[216] Any social setting involves a plurality of elites, movements and groups with differential control over natural and social resources who struggle continuously for control and ownership over such resources. Social conflict and competition is intensified by social differentiation, which produces groups with differing orientations and interests.

Building on the work of the early theorists and structural functional approaches, contemporary theories of organizational growth and change have focused heavily on a neo-evolutionary perspective.[217] They vary in the extent to which structural and human agency factors shape or determine organizational structure and its outcomes. Two of the most prominent are the adaptation and selection models.

The adaptation model was a response to classical management theory, which viewed organizational performance as a product of rational decisions by managers to maximize productivity and efficiency.[218] Classical management theory fell into disfavor because it was unable to identify the principles that achieve optimal organization. Complicated tasks often exceeded the ability of any individual to find appropriate solutions. In contrast, the adaptation model proposed that organizations adapt to complexity in the environment by developing more differentiated structures. Dividing complicated tasks or decisions into subtasks or subdecisions enabled managers to make decisions within the limits of bounded rationality. In other words, organizational structures create environments that allow people to function within their abilities. This version of the adaptation model is a cognitive theory. Another version, called the resource-dependence model, contends that organizations struggle for power and resources with each other, and the outcome of this competitive process shapes organizational structure.

The adaptation model focuses on how organizations adapt to changing environmental conditions. The selection model, in contrast, attempts to explain why some organizations fail and dissolve. This model assumes that organizations are incapable of purposeful change. Several varieties of the selection model exist, but one of the most prominent is the human ecology model. Borrowing concepts and ideas from the biological sciences, this model was developed to understand better how organizations compete and coexist on limited resources in an ecological community.[219]

Basic concepts in the model include population, guild, niche and community. A population is a species. For the media ecologist, a population is a set of organizations that correspond to a medium or communication industry.[220] Thus, daily newspapers would be considered one population. A set of populations that compete for the same resources is called a guild. Hence, newspapers, radio stations, television stations and other mass media — to the extent that they compete for the same resources, such as advertising dollars or audiences — would comprise a guild. A community is a system in which the populations interact with each other and their environment. A niche is the function or role of the population within the community.

The concept of niche breadth refers to the number and amount of resources that a particular population consumes. Niche overlap is the degree to which two populations depend on the same resources. Competition refers to the indirect effect of the use of resources by one population on the availability to another. The theory assumes that resources available to the populations are finite.[221]

Overall, research suggests that many elements of organizational structure tend not to change in response to the environment.[222] This is especially true of large organizations, which have more resources to resist environmental pressures.[223] However, proponents of the selection model argue that there is prima facia evidence for its validity, since it is well known that the mortality rate among small organizations is much higher than for large ones. Pfeffer and Salancik, after reviewing the literature, also argue that there is some evidence to support the resource-dependence adaptation model in business and industry. "Mergers follow patterns of resource interdependence. Mergers made to cope with competitive interdependence are most likely when competitive uncertainty is highest — at intermediate levels of industrial concentration."[224]

In addition to external conditions, Blau and Meyer identify three internal structural factors that influence the development of organizations.[225] First, there is managerial succession. In many organizations, even bureaucratic ones, written rules may not be necessary when working relationships have been established for a long time. However, when succession occurs, the basis for these relationship disappears. The successor often has to employ bureaucratic rules and procedures — in some cases even hire additional "lieutenants" — to maintain order.

A second structural condition is the failure of simpler modes of coordination, such as through the use of contracts. Contracting was widely used in large-scale industries a century ago. Factory managers would negotiate with foremen as to the price for finished goods. The foremen would then hire workers to complete the task. But contracting had a number of problems. One was that the expertise of the foremen was limited compared to that of trained engineers. Another was that because the foremen had different ways of organizing their work and workmen, they often produced nonstandard products. Foremen also tended to be wasteful when it came to materials, tools and power, which were usually supplied by the managers. But as Weber pointed out, bureaucracy was specifically designed to overcome such problems, since expertise, precision and efficiency were its major traits.[226]

The third internal structural factor affecting the bureaucratic growth may be the quest for power in organizations. Many non-Marxist scholars contend that organizations grow and become more bureaucratized as people attempt to transform power relations, which are inherently unstable, into stable and legitimate relations of authority. Power can be legitimated through rules and regulations that substitute for the will of the boss, which often generates resentment.[227] Many Marxist scholars argue that capitalists seek growth in order to dominate a market and increase profits. Corporate managers may also seek growth in order to expand their base of power within the organization. Bureaucratic control also may have the effect of obscuring class antagonisms.[228]

Blau and Meyer also argue that the time of origin affects the bureaucratic growth of an organization. As a rule, the older the organization, the less bureaucratized. Organizations often resist change and innovation even when they would improve efficiency. However, massive reorganization efforts can stimulate the development of bureaucratic features.[229]

MASS MEDIA AND SOCIAL SYSTEMS THEORY

Within the general theoretical framework presented above, Donohue, Tichenor and Olien point out that the mass media may be characterized as an institution, or subsystem, which, among other things, processes and disseminates information that contributes to maintenance of the social system as a whole, other subsystems, or the media subsystem itself.[230] Mass media share facets of controlling, and being controlled by, other subsystems. The researchers define a social system as "a series of interrelated subsystems with primary functions including the generation, dissemination and assimilation of information to effect further control as a means to an end or as an end in itself."[231] Social control is not the only function served by the media, but all communication processes have a control function within them, either latent or manifest.

Two key assumptions underlie the notion that the mass media are agents of social control. The first is that knowledge is a basis of social power, a proposition that is well-recognized in the literature.[232] The second, less well-known assumption is that control of knowledge is central to development and maintenance of power.[233] As collectors and disseminators of knowledge, mass media play an important role in maintenance of social power.

The maintenance function, according to Donohue, Tichenor and Olien, may be fulfilled by two sets of processes: feedback-control and distribution control. Feedback control means that the media perform a feedback, or regulatory, function for other subsystems.[234] The information provided is used to make decisions or take various actions that, in turn, perform a maintenance function. The principle of feedback control is illustrated in an investigative story of a college professor who allegedly used his position and university facilities to develop a drug that made him financially wealthy. A general norm in higher education is that such behavior often creates a conflict of interest and violates basic values concerning the proper role of the university in the community. In response to the story, the university launched an investigation.[235]

Distribution control, on the other hand, can occur either independent of or jointly with feedback control and serves a maintenance function through selective dissemination and withholding of information. Censorship is the most extreme form of distribution control. A more common example is the downplaying of conflict news that occurs in small community newspapers. Numerous studies have found, in fact, that newspapers in small towns are much less likely than those in large communities to criticize local elites or institutions.[236] There are two major reasons for this. First, the amount of conflict and criticism in the small community is limited because, quite simply, the variety and number of special interest groups is limited. There are not enough individuals to create a critical mass for the development of special interest groups,[237] which in turn means less competition for limited resources and less social conflict and criticism of dominant power groups.

The second reason media in small communities tend to be less critical of local power structures is that the cultural environment does not encourage or tolerate a wide range of behaviors, opinions or values, at least openly. Social actors in such systems are expected to conform to a more narrow set of norms

How the Mass Media Really Work

and values than actors in large, complex systems. As a rule of thumb, a diversity of opinion is not encouraged in a small organizational environment. Elites often share similar interests, values, goals and world views and, traditionally, decision-making relies more heavily on consensus than debate. Consensus is valued in part because social conflict usually is perceived to be disruptive of community solidarity, and small, homogenous communities are not structurally designed to deal effectively with open conflict. Conflicts usually are handled informally, and decisions on crucial issues often are reported by local media after the fact.[238] But even when conflict or debate emerges between different groups or elites, media in small communities tend to limit reporting of such conflicts.[239]

In contrast, media in more complex, or pluralistic, communities are much more likely to publish news that is critical of elites or that is conflict-oriented.[240] Criticism and social conflict are much more common features of large, pluralistic communities because they contain a much greater variety of special interest groups competing for social, political and economic resources. Decision-making in such communities is often expected to take into account (at least to a limited extent) diverse perspectives and views, and such communities are structurally organized to deal with conflict, having mechanisms such as boards of inquiry (e.g., racial discrimination commissions, civilian police review boards), formal labor-management negotiators, formalized grievance procedures, and administrative law judges. Although stories about conflict are often viewed as threatening to the social order, such stories often play a significant role in contributing to system stability because they introduce alternative ideas or innovations that may enable organizations and institutions to change. As Donohue, Tichenor and Olien put out:

> Conflict control may include the *generation* of conflict situations as well as the direct dissipation of tension. This principle is widely recognized in the political realm; the point here is that it applies equally well to the scientific area but is expressed by different means. Media reporting of a clash between scientific opinion on supersonic transports and governmental policies regarding such technology represents a generating of conflict. From a systems perspective, such reporting is functional for maintenance of the total system in that it increases the likelihood of preserving an equilibrium state.[241]

Donohue, Olien and Tichenor argue that the notion of the mass media as a "Fourth Estate watchdog" is fundamentally a myth, "in the sense of a sentinel of the general community keeping watch over central powers of government."[242] Research (see review below) strongly shows that media depend heavily on the centers of power for the news, and such dependence lends support to dominant institutions, ideologies and value systems. At the same time, the conception of the media as lap dogs of political or economic elites is inadequate. The media often attack or criticize powerful elites, who in turn are often critical of the media. Watergate and Irangate are good examples. The most appropriate canine analogy, according to Donohue, Olien and Tichenor, is the guard dog.

> "Guard dog" is basically an authority support conception, in that it suggests a sentry not for the community as a whole, but for those particular groups who have the power and influence to create and command their own security systems. It is quite different from a "lap dog" notion, however. The press is conditioned, like a guard dog, to be suspicious of all potential intruders, and it occasionally barks loudly for reasons that individuals in the master household can neither understand nor prevent. When that happens, the immediate response is to "silence that mutt," which is on a par with "why doesn't the press stop yapping about Irangate?"[243]

The press is most likely to "bark" at those in power when they are attacked by another powerful group or when those in power violate the rules (i.e., laws and norms) of the system. The media's role is not to protect individual elites or organizations, per se, but, rather, to protect "the system." Any individual actor is expendable, but attacking or challenging basic elements of the system (e.g., laws, values, norms) is much more problematic. Mainstream media provide broad-based support for dominant institutions and values. Structural change comes slowly.

More formally, some of the major propositions in media systems theory are summarized in Table on the next page. As with all system theories, it is assumed that social actors have needs, and among them are needs for information or entertainment (see P1). Social actors are also assumed to be goal-oriented, although the pursuit of such goals (e.g., love, money, fame) often is not formally constructed (as a business sets written objectives and goals). Some needs for information or entertainment may have a psychological or biological origin, but the majority arise in a social and cultural context that is shaped to a large extent by the interests and needs of elites, historical conditions, and dominant value and normative systems (P2 and P2a). In modern capitalist societies, large-scale business and governmental bureaucratic organizations play a disproportionate role in shaping needs for information. A white-collar worker, for example, is expected to keep up on the news that might help or hinder the competitiveness of the products his or her company sells. Such a worker also is likely to follow

MAJOR PROPOSITIONS OF MEDIA SYSTEMS THEORY

1. Social actors have needs, among them are needs for information and entertainment.
2. Needs for information and entertainment arise primarily in a social context.
   a. Needs for information and entertainment are shaped largely by the interests and goals of those in power, historical conditions, and dominant value and normative systems.
   b. As a social system becomes more pluralistic, needs for information and entertainment increase and become more diverse.
   c. As a social system becomes more pluralistic, the number and variety of mass media and formalized means of communication increase (i.e., media systems become more complex).
      1. As the number and variety of mass media increase, competition increases.
      2. Competition promotes the growth of the corporate form of organization (i.e., large-scale, functionally complex media).
      3. Corporate organizations are more profitable and have a greater capacity to adapt to changing conditions.
3. Needs for information or entertainment can be satisfied by mass media consumption.
4. Mass media content generally promotes the interests of elite groups and dominant value systems.
   a. Elite groups seek to control the mass media to promote their interests and goals.
   b. Mass media depend heavily on elites for the news.
   c. Heavy dependence on elites helps to legitimize the news.
   d. Heavy dependence on elites for news produces a status-quo bias (i.e., media content promotes interests and goals of elites).
5. Although mass media content generally supports elite interests and dominant value systems, under some conditions it may also promote social change.
   a. As a social system becomes more pluralistic, mass media content contains more social conflict and is more critical of the status quo.
      1. The content of media in pluralistic systems is more critical of the status quo because those systems have a greater diversity of groups whose goals are unfulfilled by existing social and political arrangements.
      2. The content of media in pluralistic systems is more critical because media there have greater autonomy from established power groups.
   b. The greater the disagreement among elites on a particular issue, the greater the media coverage.
   c. The greater the power of a social group or movement, the greater its capacity to obtain media coverage.
6. The potential for social change increases as coverage of a conflict increases.
7. Social change that accommodates needs and interests of alternative or disenfranchised groups contributes to social order.
8. Mass media content that satisfies social actors' needs for information or entertainment contributes to social order.

the stock market to keep abreast of his or her own personal investments. A general sentiment in such a society also is that each citizen should be well-informed before voting, and that each should seek out information that helps him or her make a selection.

Although needs for information and entertainment exist in all social systems, as a system grows and becomes more pluralistic, needs increase and become more diverse (P2b), and the number and variety of mass media also increase (P2c). The emergence of the modern newspaper and other media is directly related to the growing demands for information brought on by urbanization and industrialization. Manufacturers need access to markets, and advertising was one efficient method for reaching such markets. The penny press emerged in the 1830s as the first mass media
to offer access to mass markets, and the dramatic growth of the newspaper in the 19th century is directly related to the growth of advertising. As urban populations grew, so did needs for information, and newspapers were one mechanism for meeting both of these needs.

More formally, Ball-Rokeach and DeFleur have argued that dependence on mass media, at the individual as well as organizational and subsystem levels, increases as a social system becomes more complex.[244] Several factors explain this. First, as a social system grows and becomes more complex, the amount of personal contact people and organizations have with each other decreases, which in turn means greater dependence on formalized communication to accomplish tasks. Second, increasing complexity gives rise to problems of coordination and control. Mass media are one type of formalized method of communication for reducing such problems and integrating social actors.[245]

One consequence of the growth in the number and variety of media in a social system is increasing competition (P2c1). Competition promotes the growth of the corporate form of organization (i.e., large-scale, functionally complex media), primarily because, as Marx pointed out, it stimulates the innovative process which in turn generates economies of scale (P2c2). Media systems may expand as long as demand exceeds supply. This was the case in the United States until the early 1920s, when the number of newspapers began to decline. The more a newspaper exhibited the characteristics of the corporate form of organization, the more profitable it was and the greater was its capacity to adapt to changing conditions (P2c3).

The system model also assumes that needs for information or entertainment can be satisfied (P3). In capitalistic systems, the satisfaction of such needs is usually determined by the marketplace. Mass media programming or publications that attract enough advertising, viewership and/or readership survive, while those that do not perish. In noncapitalist economies, the satisfaction of needs is determined by elite groups who control the media. These groups may or may not obtain feedback from other segments of the population. If viewers or readers are satisfied with the media content they consume, then it is also posited that such content has the effect of integrating them into the system, reducing the potential for social action that challenges dominant power groups (P8). This integrating effect may be viewed as coercive or benign, depending upon whose interests are being served.

Mass media content generally promotes the interests of elite groups and dominant value systems (P4). The legitimacy of the media, in fact, depends heavily on serving such interests. Elite and challenging groups seek to control the media to promote their own interests (P4a), but elites are much more successful partly because they confer greater status, legitimacy and rewards to media. Challenging groups also seek to use media to reach their goals, but they are often marginalized by established powers and, thus, are perceived by the media to be less credible and newsworthy.[246] As a general rule, then, the greater the power of a group or organization, the greater its ability to command the attention of the media. Dominant values and norms in a system also shape media content, which in turn reinforces them.[247]

Media also depend heavily on elites and dominant institutions (police, courts, legislature, president) for the news because they offer a predictable, daily supply of news (P4b). Media have limited capacity to independently determine the social and political agenda — that power is reserved to the elites and the institutions they run. One consequence of this dependence is increased legitimacy for the role of the mass media in society (P4c). Another, however, is a status-quo bias. Social problems and conflicts are usually framed from the perspective of the elite groups and dominant value systems. News and entertainment programming provides strong support for such values as capitalism, social order, the family, Western religion, representative democracy, and moderatism in politics.[248]

Although mass media content generally supports the status quo, under some conditions it may also promote social change (P5). Social change may be defined as the difference between current and antecedent conditions in social organization or social structure. As a system becomes more pluralistic, media content contains more social conflict and is more critical of the status quo (P5a). Such content does not guarantee change, but it is an antecedent condition. One reason content becomes more critical as a system becomes more pluralistic is that those systems have a greater diversity of groups whose goals are unfulfilled by existing social and political arrangements (P5a1). Another reason is that media in pluralistic systems have more autonomy from established power groups (P5a2). A major factor contributing to this autonomy is the decline of the owner-manager and the rise of the professional manager and technocrats. Increasing complexity associated with news production has forced owners to rely more heavily on specialists. These technocrats, in turn, have developed their own codes of ethics and professional standards which seek to legitimate their roles and give them more autonomy. The movement toward autonomy also has been enhanced by the dispersion of ownership; that is, the proportion of stock or equity that any single individual or entity owns in newspapers has declined since the turn of the century. Dispersion of ownership occurs when a media owner's holdings are divided among heirs, when the media company goes public, or when capital requirements increase substantially beyond the means of any single stockholder.

The probability that mass media may promote social change also increases when elite groups themselves disagree over basic policy issues (P5b). Although elite groups share a number of concerns and have many similar goals and values (e.g., inflation is bad, family is good), they disagree often on the best policy or approach for reaching those goals or enhancing those values.[249] This disagreement is responsible for a large proportion of the news that appears in media situated in representative democratic systems and, in turn, increases the probability of change (P6). The probability of change also is proportional to the power of the group (P5c), which explains in part why media defer to established authorities and elites (P4a-d). As a rule of thumb, the more radical the group or idea, the less media coverage it will receive. One exception is when violence breaks out, in which case media focus on restoring social order and usually cast the challenging groups as lawbreakers. Alternative groups or social movements are most successful when their needs can be accommodated without disrupting in any major way the existing distribution of power. Finally, to the extent that media content satisfies needs for information, such content can be expected to contribute to social order (P7 and P8).

It is important to point out that the theoretical perspective taken here does not mean that the content of the media is always functional for maintenance of the system as a whole, subsystems, organizations or individuals. News coverage is sometimes dysfunctional for many elite groups, particularly when those groups fight over fundamental questions of resource allocation. Empirical evidence presented below also will demonstrate that news reports sometimes are favorable toward alternative or challenging groups. Some studies also indicate that exposure to media reports may produce beliefs that run counter to the dominant values.

Nevertheless, the fact that mass media rely much more heavily on established power groups for news means that news content generally legitimizes those groups and the dominant values in the system. Under a systems model, the argument is that media content, when taken as a whole, contributes to social order — it serves the needs of various elite groups and helps them to achieve their goals, often to the disadvantage of less powerful groups. Social change can occur and the ideas of challenging groups can make their way into the general value system (e.g., the changing role of women in society). But mainstream media do not normally challenge the basic institutions and values of the system, nor do they produce major shifts of power. Instead, they play an important role in regulating and controlling change.

RESEARCH AND MEDIA SYSTEMS THEORY

Empirical research provides a great deal of support for the general media system model outlined above. Studies show that mass media are highly responsive to political and economic centers of power and promote values generally consistent with capitalist ideals and elite interests.[250] Journalists rely heavily on bureaucratic, especially governmental, institutions for the news, and they eschew alternative, unorthodox points of view.[251] One consequence of this is that social problems are usually framed from the position of those in power.[252] Agenda-setting studies show that media play an important role in transmitting the political and economic priorities of elites to the masses.[253] Challenging groups also seek to use media to reach their goals, but they are often marginalized by established powers and, thus, are perceived by the media to be less credible and newsworthy.[254] For example, the Glasgow University Media Group has documented how media blame labor unions, not management, for industrial disputes.[255] During the 1960s, police and the media often portrayed student activists as unkempt brats who needed old-fashioned discipline.[256] Political groups that are perceived as deviant by newspaper editors are generally given less favorable coverage.[257] And media coverage of protests by anarchist groups focused most heavily on their violations of social norms, rather than the substantive nature of their protests.[258] As a general rule of thumb, then, the greater the power of a group or organization, the greater its ability to command the attention of the media.

The system-maintenance function of the media also is served by the finding that journalists tend to support the dominant values and social norms in a social system, such as "responsible capitalism."[259] Evidence of bias in coverage of Latin America and other foreign countries is well-documented.[260] Reporters often identify or sympathize with their sources, expressing strong support, for example, in the goals of city hall.[261] Studies of television programs suggest that institutionalized power groups, such as the police, are usually portrayed as humanely and sympathetically, while other characters, including victims, are portrayed as stereotypes, often with negative overtones.[262] As a rule of thumb, media fail to report class conflict, ignore common working class interests and take for granted a national consensus.[263] A well-documented finding in both England and the United States is that ownership of newspapers is relatively concentrated in the hands of a few powerful corporations or individuals,[264] which is often interpreted to mean that content is becoming less diverse or more homogenous. Competition in the U.S. daily newspaper field also has declined over the last 80 years.[265] And prominent elite media companies, such as the publishers of the New York Times and Washington Post, are strongly interconnected with other power centers via memberships on boards of directors.[266]

Although journalists tend to support the dominant system of values, other research shows that they generally are more liberal than elites, as well as the general public, on a wide variety of social and political issues.[267] These findings and those from other studies suggest that, contrary to some critical theories of ideology,[268] media have the capacity at times to produce content that is critical of dominant groups and beneficial to disadvantaged groups. Polls and historical research show that conservatives are more critical than liberals of investigative reporting and that journalists often are sensitive to the concerns of minorities and consumers groups, are critical of business, and believe that private business is profiting at the expense of Third World countries.[269] One analysis of U.S. network television news coverage of Latin America also failed to produce evidence of a conservative, status-quo bias.[270] Media reports also helped to legitimize rural protest groups in Minnesota, whose goal was to block construction of a power line that would serve a large, Midwestern metropolitan area.[271] Studies often find that media coverage influences governmental policy at the national level[272] as well as the local.[273] And a recent study found that, contrary to the expectations of the researcher, media coverage of separate protest marches in Washington sponsored by gay and lesbian organizations and pro-choice groups were much more favorable than unfavorable to each of those challenging groups.[274]

Although media need a consistent, inexpensive supply of news and depend heavily on political and economic elites for the news,[275] it is also important to point out that elites depend heavily on the media to achieve their goals. It is widely agreed, for example, that a state or national politician cannot be elected today without effective media coverage. Candidates rely less and less on the political party machine and more and more on direct coverage in media to get elected. This dependence, in turn, has lessened to some extent the power of the traditional political parties.

Although ownership of newspapers is becoming more centralized (i.e., reduction in number of owners), to date there is little evidence showing that this has led to a reduction in message diversity[276] or that other media sectors, like magazines and broadcast television stations, are experiencing the same trends.[277] In fact, some studies have found that media in larger, more pluralistic communities cover a broader range of topics and contain more news.[278] A systems perspective is that current declines in newspaper circulation and national network television penetration reflect increasing differentiation of the social structure and that such differentiation nevertheless can, under some circumstances, promote increased criticism of established institutions and greater diversity in media content.[279] For example, even though research shows that small, community newspapers often omit news that is critical of established institutions and elites, media in more pluralistic communities are much more likely to publish news that is critical of elites or conflict-oriented.[280] Another study showed that veteran reporters at mainstream newspapers can write stories that challenge components of the dominant ideology.[281] Studying Canadian press coverage of disarmament, peace and security issues, another reported that commentaries, columns and op-ed pieces often challenged the dominant view of bureaucrats.[282] And a study of the press in India suggests that the news media have the potential to challenge the status quo.[283] The researcher found that such challenges may not be direct or comprehensive, but some kinds of news stories may represent a challenge indirectly by contributing, for example, to public awareness of problems with the status quo, which in turn can promote discontent and support for social change.

Research also shows that alternative media often challenge dominant ideologies and contribute to mobilizing and promoting social movements or causes. Challenging the arguments of the "routines theorists,"[284] one participant observation study found that reporters at an alternative radio station could create oppositional news using conventional routines and reportorial techniques.[285] A historical review reported that alternative media have helped to promote the American revolution, abolitionism, and equality for women, minorities, and gay rights groups.[286] And even though one study discussed earlier found that the mainstream mass media marginalize anarchist groups, the study also found that the alternative press idolized them.[287]

Although social control is one of the major functions of media, it does not explain the origins and nature of media themselves.[288] As noted earlier, a basic proposition in media systems theory is that the structure of a social system sets parameters or constraints on the number and type of media in that system, as well as media content.[289] Specifically, Tichenor, Donohue and Olien point out that homogeneous, traditional societies or communities have a limited number of mass media sources, and those sources tend to represent the interests and concerns of a homogeneous, undifferentiated audience. But, as the level of structural pluralism increases, demand for specialized sources of information and news increases, and social actors respond by increasing the number and diversity of print and electronic media. The rapid proliferation of newsletters, cable systems, highly specialized academic journals and fax machines are examples of how social actors have responded to increasing pluralism. Pluralism also is a strong predictor of the amount and percentage of news space allocated to public affairs issues[290] and to the number and variety of media in a community.[291]

Research on the ideological effects of the media indicates that the media may have dysfunctional consequences for some groups, but this is not always the case and, furthermore, media consumers are not easily manipulated. Hartmann and Husband found that English children's use of mass media leads to distorted perceptions of immigrants. More specifically, the researchers found that: (1) Children living in areas of low immigration rely more heavily on the media for their information about "coloured people" than others; (2) Media reports about immigrants contain the inference of conflict more often than other sources; and (3) Children who rely on media are more prone to think about race relations in terms of conflict, even though they are more likely to live in areas where racial conflict is absent.[292] In contrast, two other studies conducted in the United States have reached opposite conclusions. One, which was conducted during the 1960s, reported that the greater the number of mass media messages white Southerners attended to, the less likely they were to have strict segregationist attitudes.[293] Although this relationship was not particularly strong, it did hold up when controlling for education. Mass media, the researchers argued, often subvert traditional, patrimonial ways and usher in modern attitudes that promote social change. Researchers behind the *Great American Values Test* concluded that a specially designed 30-minute television program broadcast in 1979 also was able to increase anti-racist beliefs and the importance of equality itself as a basic social value.[294] The researchers also found that people who have a high dependency on television changed their values more and contributed more money to groups that promote anti-racism and equality than people with low dependence on television.

Cultivation analysis also has been interpreted as supporting the systems model.[295] This research shows that television exaggerates the amount of crime and violence in society and that such content is cognitively translated into increased support for authoritarian measures by police and the state.[296] Gerbner and his colleagues argue that television "is the central cultural arm of American society" whose primary function is "to spread and stabilize social patterns, to cultivate not change but resistance to change."[297] Some re-analysis of the original cultivation data, however, fails to support the theory,[298] and cross-cultural

How the Mass Media Really Work

research suggests that cultivation effects may depend on a variety of factors.[299] In contrast to some critical theories of media, a large body of research also indicates that media often impact public policy. Researchers at Northwestern University, for instance, found that investigative stories on police brutality "produced swift and fundamental revisions of regulations regarding police misconduct."[300] Another study found that media coverage of murder cases influences the way prosecutors handle cases.[301]

Another study suggests that television may actually promote beliefs that oppose economic inequalities.[302] The data, obtained from personal interviews with a probability sample of U.S. adults in 1986, show that people who benefit most from the system — men, whites, conservatives, and those who have high incomes, education and occupational prestige — are most likely to favor economic inequalities. However, the study found no support for the media hypotheses. In fact, the data suggest that television viewing reduces support for beliefs that promote economic inequality, even when controlling for all of the other factors. Gamson's peer group study also suggests that people often use media to challenge and criticize established authorities. He challenges both the radical view that working people are incorporated by the dominant ideology and the mainstream social science view that working people are uninterested in politics and unable to engage in well-reasoned discussions. Using data collected in peer group sessions with 188 "working people," he concludes that "(a) people are not so passive, (b) people are not so dumb, and (c) people negotiate with media messages in complicated ways that vary from issue to issue."[303]

In short, the empirical research suggests that media content provides broad-based support for the status quo, but it can, under many instances, promote conflict, criticism and social change. As Herbert Gans puts it:

> [N]ews is not so much conservative or liberal as it is reformist; indeed, the enduring values are very much like the values of the Progressive movement of the early twentieth century. The resemblance is often uncanny, as in the common advocacy of honest, meritocratic, and anti-bureaucratic government, and in the shared antipathy to political machines and demagogues, particularly of populist bent.[304]

And, comparing the mass media to legal systems, Jeffrey Alexander observes:

> In distinguishing the news media from the law, the significant point is the media's flexibility. By daily exposing and reformulating itself vis-a-vis changing values, group formations, and objective economic and political conditions, the media allows "public opinion" to be organized responsively

on a mass basis. By performing this function of information-conduit and normative-organizer, the news media provides the normative dimension of society with the greatest flexibility in dealing with social strains.[305]

SUMMARY

Modern social systems theory was built upon the ideas of Spencer, Marx, Durkheim and others. This theory is distinguished from other perspectives by its emphasis on the totality of the whole, its notion of boundary maintenance, and its idea of interdependence of the parts. The general model of social change in systems theory can be described as neo-evolutionary — as social systems grow, they become, under certain conditions, more differentiated, functionally specialized and interdependent. The mass media, like other major institutions, are a product of increasing differentiation and play an important maintenance function. The media, in turn, are controlled by other subsystems. Mass media are not a necessary condition for social organization, but they are for complex social organization.

A review of the empirical literature clearly shows that media play an important role in explaining the persistence and stability of modern capitalism. Media depend heavily on political and economic centers of power for the news. One consequence of this is that the construction of social problems usually is framed from the position of those in power, and news content generally promotes values consistent with capitalist ideals and elite interests. Mainstream media rarely, if ever, facilitate or cause radical social change. The watchdog function of the press is largely a myth. Like police and schools, media are an important agent of social control.

At the same time, however, this review shows that it would be inaccurate to argue that social actors are slaves to a dominant ideology or that media are lap dogs of the powerful. Depending in part on what they read and see in the media, ordinary citizens also can develop highly critical views of those in power and the social system in general. As a group, journalists are more liberal than elites and the public, and media content, especially in pluralistic systems, is much more critical of those elites and dominant values than content in small, homogeneous systems. Investigative reporting and news about social movements often promotes change and reform, often to the displeasure of conservatives and sometimes to the benefit of underprivileged groups. More accurately, the news media may be characterized as a guard dog, which provides broad-based support for dominant institutions and values in a social system but can criticize those in power, especially when they violate laws or norms.

The notion that mass media can criticize those in power or promote social reform has not gone unnoticed in studies of ideology. As noted earlier, nearly all contemporary theories of ideology acknowledge that news may be critical of those in power. However, virtually none of these theories has specified the conditions in which alternative or challenging ideas and groups may emerge and gain access to media. Such access or the structural changes that sometimes result from criticisms of the dominant ideology are usually viewed either as anomalies that have little impact in the system or as accommodations that contribute to greater hegemonic control. As a consequence, such theories are at a loss to explain many of the contributions that mass media have made to social and political reforms during the 19th and early 20th centuries (e.g., the emergence of minimum wage laws, social security, labor laws, anti-trust laws, welfare, progressive income tax system), as well as more recent challenges to some dominant values regarding health care reform, parenthood (e.g., the Murphy Brown television show and the single motherhood issue) and homosexuality (e.g., coverage of the social protests in Washington regarding military policies; TV movies about fired military personnel). These reforms (or reforms in progress) should not be summarily dismissed as meaningless or as mere accommodations. They should be seen as changes that have from time to time worked to the benefit of disadvantaged or challenging groups and the working classes.

Source: David Pearce Demers, *The Menace of the Corporate Newspaper: Fact or Fiction?* (Iowa State University Press, 1996).

ENDNOTES

1. Pamela J. Shoemaker, "Mass Communication by the Book: A Review of 31 Texts," *Journal of Communication,* 37(4): 109-131 (Summer 1987), p. 119.

2. Shoemaker, "Mass Communication by the Book," p. 125.

3. J. Herbert Altschull, *Agents of Power* (New York: Longman, 1984); W. Lance Bennett, *News: The Politics of Illusion,* 2nd ed. (New York: Longman, 1988); Robert Cirino, *Power to Persuade* (New York: Bantam Books, 1974); Stanley Cohen and Jock Young (eds.), *The Manufacture of News* (London: Constable, 1981); David Pearce Demers, *Menace of the Corporate Newspaper: Fact or Fiction?* (Ames: Iowa State University Press, 1996); Edward Jay Epstein, *News From Nowhere* (New York: Random House, 1973); Stuart Ewin, *Captains of Consciousness: Advertising and the Social Roots of the Consumer Culture* (New York: McGraw Hill, 1976); Mark Fishman, *Manufacturing the News* (Austin: University of Texas Press, 1980); Edward S. Herman and Noam Chomsky, *Manufacturing Consent: The Political Economy of the Mass Media* (New York: Pantheon, 1988); Doris A. Graber, *Mass Media and American Politics,* 3rd ed. (Washington, D.C.: Congressional Quarterly Press, 1989); Herbert J. Gans, *Deciding What's News* (New York: Vintage, 1979); Todd Gitlin, *The Whole World Is Watching* (Berkeley: University of California Press, 1980);David L. Paletz and Robert M. Entman, *Media Power Politics* (New York: The Free Press, 1981); Fred Powledge, *The Engineering of Restraint* (Washington, D.C.: Public Affairs Press, 1971); Leon Sigal, *Reporters and Officials* (Lexington, MA: Heath, 1973); Phillip J. Tichenor, George A. Donohue and Clarice N. Olien, *Community Conflict and the Press* (Beverly Hills, CA: Sage, 1980); and Jeremy Tunstall, *Journalists at Work* (London: The Anchor Press, 1971).

4. This section on the Titanic draws from Michael Emery, Edwin Emery and Nancy L. Roberts, *The Press and America: An Interpretive History of the Mass Media* (Boston: Allyn and Bacon, 2000); Lee W. Merideth, *1912 Facts about the Titanic* (Mason City, IA: Savas Publishing Company, 1999); Marc Shapiro, *Total Titanic* (New York: Byron Preiss Multimedia, 1998); Stephen J. Spignesi, *The Complete Titanic: From the Ship's Earliest Blueprints to the Epic Film* (Secaucus, NJ: Birch Lane Press, 1998); Jay Stevenson and Sharon Rutman, *The Complete Idiot's Guide to The Titanic* (New York: Alpha Books, 1998); and Geoff Tibballs, *The Titanic: The Extraordinary Story of the Unsinkable Ship* (Pleasantville, NY: Reader's Digest, 1997).

5. A brief biography of Carr Vattel Van Anda is available in Kristen Dollase, "Van Anda, Carr Vattel," pp. 711-712 in Joseph P. McKerns, *Biographical Dictionary of American Journalism* (New York: Greenwood Press, 1989). Also see Barnett Fine, *A Giant of the Press* (Oakland, CA: 1968).

6. For a listing of many of these works, including Web sites, see Spignesi, *The Complete Titanic,* pp. 407-421.

7. The editorial is reprinted in Spignesi, *The Complete Titanic*, p. 187-189.

8. Jim Speers, "Thrilling Story by Titanic's Surviving Wireless Man," *The New York Times* (April 19, 1912), p. 1.

9. The story is reprinted in Spignesi, *The Complete Titanic,* pp. 196-197. The quoted material is from p. 197.

10. Gordon W. Allport and Leo J. Postman, *The Psychology of Rumor* (New York: Holt, 1947).

11. Spignesi, *The Complete Titanic*, p. 186.

12. The front pages of hundreds of newspapers published at the time of the September 11 attacks are available at <www.September11news.com>.

13. Ralph D. Berenger (ed.), *Global Media Go to War: Role of News and Entertainment Media During the 2003 Iraq War* (Spokane, WA: Marquette Books, 2004).

14. Douglas Blanks Hindman and Kathy Coyle, "Audience Orientations to Local Radio Coverage of a Natural Disaster," *Journal of Radio Studies*, 6(1):8-26 (1999), p. 22.

15. Karen E. Altman, "Consuming Ideology: The Better Homes in America Campaign," *Critical Studies in Mass Communication,* 7:286-307 (1990); J. Herbert Altschull, *Agents of Power* (New York: Longman, 1984); W. Lance Bennett, *News: The Politics of Illusion,* 2nd ed. (New York: Longman, 1988); Robert Cirino, *Power to Persuade* (New York: Bantam Books, 1974); Stanley Cohen and Jock Young (eds.), *The Manufacture of News* (London: Constable, 1981); David Demers, *Global Media: Menace or Messiah?* (Cresskill, NJ: Hampton Press, 1999); Edward Jay Epstein, *News From Nowhere* (New York: Random House, 1973); Stuart Ewin, *Captains of Consciousness: Advertising and the Social Roots of the Consumer Culture* (New York: McGraw Hill, 1976); Mark Fishman, *Manufacturing the News* (Austin: University of Texas Press, 1980); Edward S. Herman and Noam Chomsky, *Manufacturing Consent: The Political Economy of the Mass Media* (New York: Pantheon, 1988); Doris A. Graber, *Mass Media and American Politics,* 3rd ed. (Washington, D.C.: Congressional Quarterly Press, 1989); Herbert J. Gans, *Deciding What's News* (New York: Vintage, 1979); Todd Gitlin, *The Whole World Is Watching* (Berkeley: University of California Press, 1980); Harvey Molotch and Marilyn Lester, "Accidental News: The Great Oil Spill as Local Occurrence and National Event," *American Journal of Sociology, 81*:235-260 (1975); Harvey Molotch and Marilyn Lester, "News as Purposive Behavior," *American Sociological Review, 81*:235-260 (1974); David L. Paletz and Robert M. Entman, *Media Power Politics* (New York: The Free Press, 1981); David L. Paletz, Peggy Reichert and Barbara McIntyre, "How the Media Support Local Government Authority," *Public Opinion Quarterly, 35*:80-92 (1971); Fred Powledge, *The Engineering of Restraint* (Washington, D.C.: Public Affairs Press, 1971); Leon Sigal, *Reporters and Officials* (Lexington, MA: Heath, 1973); Lawrence C. Soley, "Pundits in Print: 'Experts' and Their Use in Newspaper Stories," *Newspaper Research Journal, 15*(2):65-75 (1994); Phillip J. Tichenor, George A. Donohue and Clarice N. Olien, *Community Conflict and the Press* (Beverly Hills, CA: Sage, 1980); and Jeremy Tunstall, *Journalists at Work* (London: The Anchor Press, 1971).

16. David Pearce Demers, *The Menace of the Corporate Newspaper: Fact or Fiction?* (Ames: Iowa State University Press, 1996), pp. 3-4.

17. For evidence of the media's role in social change, see Donald L. Barlett and

James B. Steele, *America: What Went Wrong?* (Kansas City: Andrew and McMeel, 1992); Fred J. Cook, *The Muckrakers: Crusading Journalists Who Changed America* (Garden City, NY: Doubleday & Company, 1972); Leonard Downie, Jr., *The New Muckrakers* (New York: Mentor, 1976); Mark Neuzil and William Kovarik, *Mass Media and Environmental Conflict: America's Green Crusades* (Thousand Oaks, CA: Sage, 1996); David L. Protess, Fay Lomax Cook, Jack C. Doppelt, James S. Ettema, Margaret T. Gordon, Donna R. Leff and Peter Miller, *The Journalism of Outrage: Investigative Reporting and Agenda-Building in America* (New York: Guilford Press, 1991); Matthew Schneirov, *The Dream of a New Social Order: Popular Magazines in America: 1893-1914* (New York: Columbia University Press, 1994); Leonard Sellers, *Investigative Reporting: Methods and Barriers* (Ph.D. Diss., Stanford, 1977); and James Playsted Wood, *Magazines in the United States: Their Social and Economic Influence* (New York: The Ronald Press Company, 1949).

18. David Demers and K. Viswanath (eds.), *Mass Media, Social Control and Social Change: A Macrosocial Perspective* (Ames: Iowa State University Press, 1999).

19. L. Brent Bozell III and Brent H. Baker (eds.), *And That's The Way It Is(n't): A Reference Guide to Media Bias* (Alexandria, VA: Media Research Center, 1990), quoted material is from the book's back cover.

20. Jeff Cohen and Norman Solomon, *Through the Media Looking Glass: Decoding Bias and Blather in the News* (Monroe, ME: Common Courage Press, 1995), p. 22.

21. For details, see Steven R. Knowlton and Karen L. Freeman (eds.), *Fair & Balanced: A History of Journalistic Objectivity* (Northport, AL: Vision Press, 2005).

22. Former ABC News President James Hagerty, quoted in Edith Efron, "Do the Networks Know What They Are Doing?" pp. 133-149 in David J. Leroy and Christopher H. Sterling (eds.), *Mass News: Practices, Controversies and Alternatives* (Englewood Cliffs, NJ: Prentice-Hall, 1973), p. 134.

23. Journalists often argue that they try to be "fair" rather than "objective," the former arising in part from problems in trying to define the latter. Presumably this means that one does not have to give all sides equal weight in a story, as would be required under the ethic of objectivity. However, journalists have never satisfactorily defined fairness and how it differs from objectivity. A better explanation is that "fairness" is used to help deflect criticism when equal weight is not given to all sides in a story. For more on this topic, see, e.g., The Freedom Forum Media Studies Center, "The Fairness Factor," *Media Studies Journal*, 6(4), (Fall 1992).

24. Quoted in Persico, p. 8. Original Source: Richard H. Rovere, *Senator Joe McCarthy* (New York: Harcourt, Brace and Company, 1959), pp. 137, 166.

25. For a discussion of the mainstream bias, see Chapter 8 in David Demers, *Global Media: Menace or Messiah?* 2nd ed. (Cresskill, NJ: Hampton Press, 2001).

26. Everette E. Dennis, "The New Journalism: How It Came to Be," pp. 115-132 in Michael C. Emery and Ted Curtis Smythe (eds.), *Readings in Mass Communication: Concepts and Issues in the Mass Media,* 2nd ed. (Dubuque, Iowa: Wm. C. Brown Company Publishers, 1974).

27. Truman Capote, *In Cold Blood: A True Account of a Multiple Murder and Its Consequences* (New York: New American Library, 1965).

28. Bill Morlin, "White Separatists to be Featured at Survivalist Expo," *The* (Spokane) *Spokesman-Review* (January 31, 1997), p. B1.

29. Carol J. Williams, "Times Change for Oppressor and Oppressed," *The* (Spokane) *Spokesman-Review* (January 31, 1997), p. A1.

30. "The Bucs Stopped: Cardinals Are Spoilers in Tampa Thanks to Late-game Interception," *The Arizona Republic* (September 30, 2013), p. A1.

31. Craig Harris and Yvonne Wingett Sanchez, "Another Report Due by Year-End: Findings Could Lead to Lawsuits," *The Arizona Republic* (September 30, 2013), p. A1.

32. Having pointed out that news is not objective in any absolute sense, I now face the problem of relativism — if there is no objectivity, then is every news account of an event equivalent and is there no truth? The answer is "no," and I will pull myself out of the quagmire of relativism by building a case for what I call "relative objectivity." Basically, this is the idea that contemporary Western-style journalism incorporates more points of view than one can get from communist or totalitarian media, which of course limit expression to the groups in power.

33. Douglas A. Gentile (ed.), *Media Violence and Children: A Complete Guide for Parents and Professionals* (Westport, CT: Praeger, 2003).

34. One story was about an attempt to bribe Native Americans to turn them against the colonists and the other was about a scandal involving the French king and his daughter-in-law.

35. Herbert J. Gans, "Deciding What's News," *Columbia Journalism Review* (January/February 1979), pp. 40-45.

36. This essay was originally published in *Global Media News*. See David Demers, "When Is a Terrorist a Terrorist? Reuters Policy Exposes Parochialism in U.S. Media," *Global Media News*, 4(1):1, 11 (Winter 2002). Sources include Todd Alan Kreamer, *The Early America Review, Vol. 1*, No. 2 (Fall 1996, a copy of the article is posted at <www.earlyamerica.com/review/ fall96/index.html>); Kim Campbell, "When Is 'Terrorist' a Subjective Term?", *The Christian Science Monitor* (September 27, 2001), p. 16; Peter Wrothington, "War: Winning Is Everthing," *The Toronto Sun* (September 29, 2001), p. 26.

37. For a review of the literature on social change, see David Pearce Demers, *The Menace of the Corporate Newspaper: Fact or Fiction?* (Ames: Iowa State University Press, 1996), pp. 109-114. For a discussion of social changes that have taken place in the United States during the 20th century, see L. W. Banner, *Women in Modern America: A Brief History,* 2nd ed. (Orlando, FL: Harcourt Brace Jovanovich, 1984); R. Blauner, "The Ambiguities of Racial Change," pp. 54-64 in M. L. Andersen and P. H. Collins (eds), *Race, Class, and Gender* (Belmont, CA: Wadsworth, 1992); Celeste M. Condit, "Hegemony in a Mass-Mediated Society: Concordance about Reproductive Technologies," *Critical Studies in Mass Communication, 11*:205-230 (1994); J. R. Howard, *The Cutting Edge: Social Movements and Social Change in America* (Philadelphia: J. B. Lippincott, 1974); R. H. Lauer (ed.), *Social Movements and Social Change* (Carbondale: Southern Illinois University Press, 1976); D. McAdam, J. D. McCarthy, and N. Z. Mayer, "Social Movements," pp. 695-737 in N. J. Smelser (ed.), *Handbook of Sociology* (Newbury Park, CA: Sage, 1988). For additional evidence of the

How the Mass Media Really Work

media's role in social change see Donald L. Barlett and James B. Steele, *America: What Went Wrong?* (Kansas City: Andrew and McMeel, 1992); Leonard Downie, Jr., *The New Muckrakers* (New York: Mentor, 1976); Mark Neuzil and William Kovarik, *Mass Media and Environmental Conflict: America's Green Crusades* (Thousand Oaks, CA: Sage, 1996); David L. Protess, Fay Lomax Cook, Jack C. Doppelt, James S. Ettema, Margaret T. Gordon, Donna R. Leff and Peter Miller, *The Journalism of Outrage: Investigative Reporting and Agenda-Building in America* (New York: Guilford Press, 1991); and Leonard Sellers, *Investigative Reporting: Methods and Barriers* (Ph.D. Diss., Stanford, 1977).

38. Herbert Gans, *Popular and High Culture* (New York: Basic Books, 1999). Gans argues that elite or high culture is on the decline in American society.

39. John W. C. Johnstone, Edward J. Slawski, and William W. Bowman, *The News People: A Sociological Portrait of American Journalists and Their Work* (Urbana, IL: University of Illinois Press, 1976); David Shaw, "Public and Press — Two Viewpoints," *Los Angeles Times* (August 11, 1985); and David H. Weaver and G. Cleveland Wilhoit, *The American Journalist: A Portrait of U.S. News People and Their Work* (Bloomington, IN: Indiana University Press, 1986).

40. S. Robert Lichter and Stanley Rothman, "Media and Business Elites, " *Public Opinion Quarterly, 4*:42-6 (1981).

41. W. Q. Morales, "Revolutions, Earthquakes, and Latin America: The Networks Look at Allende's Chile and Somoza's Nicaragua," pp. 79-116 in W. C. Adams (ed.), *Television Coverage of International Affairs* (Norwood, NJ: Ablex, 1982).

42. The state supreme court eventually allowed construction of the power line, after which the media coverage of the protest groups took on a more negative tone. See Olien, Donohue and Tichenor, "Media and Stages of Social Conflict."

43. For review, see David L. Altheide, *Media Power* (Beverly Hills, CA: Sage, 1985). Also see Wayne Wanta, Mary Ann Stephenson, Judy VanSlyke Turk and Maxwell E. McCombs, "How President's State of Union Talk Influenced News Media Agendas," *Journalism Quarterly, 66*:537-41 (1989).

44. David Pritchard, "Homicide and Bargained Justice: The Agenda-Setting Effect of Crime News on Prosecutors," *Public Opinion Quarterly, 50*:143-59 (1986).

45. J. R. Ballinger, "Media Coverage of Social Protest: An Examination of Media Hegemony," paper presented to the Association for Education in Journalism and Mass Communication, Kansas City, MO. (August 1993).

46. See, e.g., Fishman, *Manufacturing the News,* and Tuchman, *Making News.*

47. M. Meyers, "Reporters and Beats: The Making of Oppositional News," *Critical Studies in Mass Communication, 9*:75-90 (1992).

48. P. Bruck, "Strategies for Peace, Strategies for News Research," *Journal of Communication, 39*(1):108-29 (1989).

49. Hemant Shah, "News and the "Self-Production of Society," *Journalism Monographs, Vol. 144* (April 1994).

50. See e.g., Epstein, *News From Nowhere*; Gitlin, *The Whole World Is Watching*; Schudson, "The Politics of Narrative Form"; and Sigel, *Reporters and Officials.*

51. N. Eliasoph, "Routines and the Making of Oppositional News," *Critical Studies in Mass Communication, 5*:313-34 (1988).

52. John Downing, "Alternative Media and the Boston Tea Party, " pp. 180-191 in John Downing, Ali Mohammadi and Annabelle Sreberny-Mohammadi (eds.), *Questioning the Media* (Newbury Park: Sage, 1990).

53. McLeod and Hertog, "The Manufacture of 'Public Opinion' by Reporters."

54. Paul Hartmann and Charles Husband, "The Mass Media and Racial Conflict," pp. 288-302 in Stanley Cohen and Jock Young (eds.), *The Manufacture of News* (London: Constable, 1981).

55. D. R. Matthews and J. W. Protho, *Negroes and the New Southern Politics* (New York: Harcourt, Brace & World, 1966), p. 344.

56. Sandra J. Ball-Rokeach, Melvin Rokeach and Joel W. Grube, *The Great American Values Test: Influencing Behavior and Belief Through Television* (New York: Free Press, 1984) and Sandra J. Ball-Rokeach, Melvin Rokeach and Joel W. Grube, "Changing and Stabilizing Political Behavior and Beliefs," pp. 280-90 in Sandra J. Ball-Rokeach and Muriel G. Cantor (eds.), *Media Audience and Social Structure* (Newbury Park, CA: Sage, 1986).

57. David L. Protess, Fay Lomax Cook, Jack C. Doppelt, James S. Ettema, Margaret T. Gordon, Donna R. Leff, and Peter Miller, *The Journalism of Outrage: Investigative Reporting and Agenda-Building in America* (New York: Guilford Press, 1991).

58. Pritchard, "Homicide and Bargained Justice."

59. David Pearce Demers, "Media Use and Beliefs About Economic Equality: An Empirical Test of the Dominant Ideology Thesis," presented to the Midwest Association for Public Opinion Research (Chicago, November 1993).

60. William A. Gamson, *Talking Politics* (Cambridge, MA: Cambridge University Press, 1992), p. 4.

61. For a discussion of social changes that have taken place in the United States during the 20th century, see L. W. Banner, *Women in Modern America: A Brief History,* 2nd ed. (Orlando, FL: Harcourt Brace Jovanovich, 1984); R. Blauner, "The Ambiguities of Racial Change," pp. 54-64 in M. L. Andersen and P. H. Collins (eds), *Race, Class, and Gender* (Belmont, CA: Wadsworth, 1992); Celeste M. Condit, "Hegemony in a Mass-Mediated Society: Concordance about Reproductive Technologies," *Critical Studies in Mass Communication, 11*:205-230 (1994); J. R. Howard, *The Cutting Edge: Social Movements and Social Change in America* (Philadelphia: J. B. Lippincott, 1974); R. H. Lauer (ed.), *Social Movements and Social Change* (Carbondale: Southern Illinois University Press, 1976); D. McAdam, J. D. McCarthy, and N. Z. Mayer, "Social Movements," pp. 695-737 in N. J. Smelser (ed.), *Handbook of Sociology* (Newbury Park, CA: Sage, 1988).

62. Jesse Jackson's remarks were made in a speech he gave July 30, 1997, at the annual meeting of the Association for Education in Journalism and Mass Communication, Chicago.

63. David L. Protess, Fay Lomax Cook, Jack C. Doppelt, James S. Ettema, Margaret T. Gordon, Donna R. Leff, and Peter Miller, *The Journalism of Outrage: Investigative Reporting and Agenda-Building in America* (New York: Guilford Press, 1991), p. 246.

64. For additional evidence of the media's role in social change see Donald L. Barlett and James B. Steele, *America: What Went Wrong?* (Kansas City: Andrew and McMeel, 1992); Leonard Downie, Jr., *The New Muckrakers* (New York: Mentor, 1976); Mark Neuzil and

How the Mass Media Really Work

William Kovarik, *Mass Media and Environmental Conflict: America's Green Crusades* (Thousand Oaks, CA: Sage, 1996); David L. Protess, Fay Lomax Cook, Jack C. Doppelt, James S. Ettema, Margaret T. Gordon, Donna R. Leff and Peter Miller, *The Journalism of Outrage: Investigative Reporting and Agenda-Building in America* (New York: Guilford Press, 1991); and Leonard Sellers, *Investigative Reporting: Methods and Barriers* (Ph.D. Diss., Stanford, 1977).

65. Herbert J. Gans, *Deciding What's News* (New York: Vintage, 1979), pp. 68-69.

66. Jeffrey Alexander, "The Mass News Media in Systemic, Historical and Comparative Perspective," pp. 17-51 in Elihu Katz and Tomás Szecskö (eds.), *Mass Media and Social Change* (Beverly Hills, CA: Sage, 1981).

67. The full name is dichlorodiphenyltrichloroethane.

68. Rachel Carson, *Silent Spring* (Greenwich, CN: Fawcett Publications, 1962).

69. Carson was not opposed to the use of chemicals to control pests. Indeed, DDT was credited for saving millions of lives around the world, because it killed malaria-carrying mosquitoes. However, she believed that too little concern had been given to the adverse environmental effects of the chemicals.

70. Sources for this brief biography of Stowe include John R. Adams, *Harriet Beecher Stowe* (New York: Twayne Publishers, 1963); Harriet Beecher Stowe, *Uncle Tom's Cabin* (New York: Macmillan Publishing Company, 1994 [1852]); and Noel Bertram Gerson, *Harriet Beecher Stowe: A Biography* (New York: Praeger Publishers, 1976).

71. John Tebbel, *A History of Book Publishing in the United States: Volume 1, The Creation of an Industry, 1630-1865* (New York: R.R. Bowker, 1972-1981).

72. Upton Sinclair, *The Jungle* (New York: The New American Library, 1960 [1905]).

73. Sources for this brief biography of Morrison include Clenora Hudson-Weems, *Africana Womanism: Reclaiming Ourselves* (New York: Bedford Publishers, 1993), and "Biography — Toni Morrison," NobelPrize.org <http://nobelprize.org/literature/laureates/1993/ morrison-bio.html>.

74. Scholastic Books, "Meet J. K. Rowling," www.scholastic.com; SingleParents; J. K. Rowling, "The Not Especially Fascinating Life So Far of J. K. Rowling," <www.cliphoto.com/potter/rolwing.htm>.

75. Ari Armstrong, Values of Harry Potter: Lessons for Muggles (Ember Publishing, 2011).

76. Carl Bernstein and Bob Woodward, *All the President's Men* (New York: Simon and Schuster, 1974).

77. Thomas Carlyle, *Heroes: Hero-Worship and the Heroic in History* (New York: Cas. Scribner and Sons, 1841), p. 164.

78. Dominic F. Manno, "The 'Fourth Estate': Who Used the Term First?" pp. 24-25 in Hiley H. Ward, *Mainstream of American Media History: A Narrative and Intellectual History* (Boston: Allyn and Bacon, 1997).

79. George A. Donohue, Clarice N. Olien and Phillip J. Tichenor, "A Guard Dog Conception of Mass Media," paper presented at the annual meeting of the Association for Education in Journalism and Mass Communication, San Antonio, Texas (August 1987), pp. 2-3.

80. Andrew A. Lipscomb (ed.), *The Writings of Thomas Jefferson*, Volume 11 (Washington, D.C.: Thomas Jefferson Memorial Association, 1904), pp. 32-34.

81. George A. Donohue, Clarice N. Olien and Phillip J. Tichenor, "A Guard Dog Conception of the Mass Media," paper presented to the Association for Education in Journalism and Mass Communication (San Antonio, Texas, August 1987), p. 10.

82. George A. Donohue, Phillip J. Tichenor and Clarice N. Olien, "Mass Media Functions, Knowledge and Social Control," *Journalism Quarterly,* 50:652-9 (1973).

83. Ironically, though, investigative journalists appear to be unaware of the morality tales in their stories, according to mass communication researchers James S. Ettema and Theodore L. Glasser. "These reporters do acknowledge that their stories do not 'speak themselves,' but they maintain that their narrative skills are employed strictly in the service of cognition. ... the selection and sequence of facts is determined by a 'logical progression,' not, of course, by any moral order." In other words, reporters see themselves as fact gatherers, not as preachers of right and wrong. James S. Ettema and Theodore L. Glasser, "Narrative Form and Moral Force: The Realization of Innocence and Guilt Through Investigative Journalism," *Journal of Communication,* 38[3]:8-26 (Summer 1988), p. 23.

84. After 1968, a majority of Americans said the war was "a mistake." Harold W. Stanley and Richard G. Niemi, *Vital Statistics on American Politics,* 4th ed. (Washington, D.C.: Congressional Quarterly Press, 1994), p. 356.

85. See Harold D. Lasswell, "The Structure and Function of Communication in Society," pp. 84-99 in Lyman Bryson (ed.), *The Communication of Ideas* (New York: Institute for Religious and Social Studies, 1948). Also see Charles C. Wright, "Functional Analysis and Mass Communication," *Public Opinion Quarterly,* 24:605-620 (1960).

86. See, e.g., Albert Bandura, *Social Learning Theory* (Englewood Cliffs, N.J.: Prentice-Hall, 1977).

87. George Gerbner, Larry Gross, Marilyn Jackson-Beeck, S. Jeffries-Fox, and Nancy Signorielli, "Cultural Indicators: Violence Profile No. 9," *Journal of Communication,* 28:176-207 (Summer 1978).

88. The following sources were used for this introduction: Fred J. Cook, *The Muckrakers: Crusading Journalists Who Changed America* (Garden City, NY: Doubleday & Company, 1972), see Chapter V; Michael Emery, Edwin Emery and Nancy L. Roberts, *The Press and America: An Interpretive History of the Mass Media,* 9th ed. (Boston: Allyn and Bacon, 2000), pp. 223-226; and Ida M. Tarbell, *The History of the Standard Oil Company* (New York: McClure, Phillips & Co. 1904). Also see Ida M. Tarbell, *All in the Day's Work: An Autobiography* (New York: Macmillan, 1939) and Kathleen Brady, *Ida Tarbell: Portrait of a Muckraker* (New York: Seaview/Putnam, 1984).

89. When Standard Oil heard it was being investigated, the company hired Mark Twain to be its public relations front-man. Twain contacted McClure and asked whether *McClure's* magazine intended to run a story. "You will have to ask Miss Tarbell," he said. McClure was a reporter's publisher. He supported numerous investigative projects and earned a reputation as one of the finest publishers in the history of magazine journalism.

90. This image of Rockefeller contrasted sharply with his role as a father. He is described as extremely devoted and loving with his children.

91. The irony is that after the break-up of Standard Oil, John D. Rockefeller became even richer. As he predicted, the company was worth a lot more broken up than it was

How the Mass Media Really Work

as one single trust. To make matters worse, the new companies also engaged in price-fixing, thwarting some of the anti-trust efforts. However, the investigation took a psychological toll on Rockefeller and his family. Rockefeller experienced such stress that all of the hair on his body fell out. When Tarbell met him, she was shocked at his appearance — he looked liked a very old man. Rockefeller's son, John D. Rockefeller Jr., also had several mental breakdowns.

92. Unlike newspapers, magazines also have had the ability to reach national audiences. The problem for newspapers was technical: How could a newspaper be published daily and distributed nationally? Until recently, this was not economically feasible (*USA Today* is an exception). But timeliness is less important for magazines, which generally publish weekly or monthly. Many magazines, in fact, depend on national or international distribution to survive.

93. For a general historical review of the turn of the century, see Harry J. Carman, Harold C. Syrett, and Bernard W. Wishy, *A History of the American People: Volume II – Since 1865* (New York: Alfred A. Knopf, 1967).

94. Matthew Josephson, *The Robber Barons: The Great American Capitalists, 1861-1901* (New York: Harcourt, Brace and Company, 1934).

95. The negative coverage of labor unions reflects the dependence that newspapers had on powerful political and economic elites of the times. Politicians and police were solidly behind the capitalists who ran the factories. The muckraking magazines offered one of the few sympathetic voices for the workers.

96. Adam Smith, *An Inquiry Into the Nature and Causes of the Wealth of Nations* (Buffalo, NY: Prometheus Books, 1991[1776]).

97. Karl Marx, *Capital: A Critique of Political Economy,* Vols. 1-3, trans. by Samuel Moore and Edward Aveling (New York: International Publishers, 1987).

98. Richard Hofstadter, *The Progressive Movement, 1900-1915* (Englewood Cliffs, NJ: Prentice-Hall, 1963).

99. See, e.g., Marco Giugni, Doug McAdam and Charles Tilly (eds.), *How Social Movements Matter* (Minneapolis: University of Minnesota Press, 1999).

100. Tebbel and Zuckerman, *The Magazine in America,* pp. 15-17.

101. William Gamson, *The Strategy of Social Protest,* 2nd ed. (Homewood, IL: Dorsey, 1990).

102. Sources for this brief biography include Gerald C. Hynes, "A Biographical Sketch of W. E. B. Du Bois," retrieved from <www. Duboislc.org>; Manning Marable, *W. E. B. Du Bois, Black Radical Democrat* (1986); David Levening Lewis, *W. E. B. Du Bois: Biography of a Race, 1868-1919* (1993).

103. *Life* and *Saturday Evening Post* were resurrected as a monthly and quarterly, respectively, in the 1970s, but *Life* was permanently shut down in 2000 and the *Post*, which is being published by a nonprofit organization, has never been able to achieve the glory it once had.

104. Sources for this section include Lisa Granatstein, "National Magazine Awards," *Mediaweek* (May 6, 2002), and various issues of *Newsweek* between Sept. 13, 2001, and October 15, 2001.

105. Interestingly, Mankiewicz appears to have gotten the idea of "Rosebud" from

Hearst's real-life mistress, Marion Davies, who told Mankiewicz that "rosebud" was the nickname Hearst had given to an intimate part of her body. For the record, though, the prop in the movie is quite different.

106. Welles worried that media mogul Ted Turner, who had purchased the rights to *Citizen Kane*, would "colorize" his black-and-white masterpiece — that is, transform the movie into full color. Welles, like many purists, see black and white film as a more abstract art form. The movie has not been colorized as of this writing.

107. "Motion Pictures: The Art of Film: Types of Motion Pictures: Fictional Genres," *Encyclopedia Britannica* (Chicago: CD Rom version, 1999 edition).

108. Roger Ebert, "Citizen Kane," *Roger Ebert's Video Companion 1998 Edition* (Kansas City, MO: Andrews McMeel Publishing, 1998), p. 147.

109. Sources for this brief biography include Joseph McBride, *Steven Spielberg: A Biography* (New York: Simon & Schuster, 1997); Philip M. Taylor, *Steven Spielberg: The Man, His Movies and Their Meaning* (London: Batsford, 1999); and Anthony Breznican, "Spielberg's Family Values," *USA Today* (June 23, 2005), p. A1.

110. For a review, see Shearon A. Lowery and Melvin L. DeFleur, *Milestones in Mass Communication Research*, 2nd ed. (New York: Longman, 1988).

111. A book of Murrow's broadcasts from London was published in 1941. Edward R. Murrow, *This is London* (New York: Simon and Schuster, 1941). Also see Joseph E. Persico, *Edward R. Murrow: An American Original* (New York: Dell, 1988), p. 173.

112. Erik Barnouw, *The Gold Web* (New York: Oxford University Press, 1968), p. 151.

113. Janet Murrow kept a diary that has been an invaluable source of information to historians about Ed. She died in 1999. Ed attended Washington State College, which is now Washington State University and houses the Edward R. Murrow School of Communication.

114. During times of war especially, mass media almost always rally behind the national interest (see, for example, Chapter 6's discussion about filmmakers supporting the U.S. government during World War II). This is the case even in countries whose journalists adhere to the so-called "ethic of objectivity" (see Media Issues Box 4.1 in Chapter 4). Media help build and maintain morale and, thus, play a social control function.

115. A more formal definition of "propaganda" is the dissemination or promotion of ideas or doctrines, often deceptive or distorted, to further a cause.

116. See Media Issues Box 1.1 in Chapter 1 and Media Issues Box 4.1 in Chapter 4 for a more in-depth discussion of the ethic of objectivity.

117. I generated this estimate from statistics on radio station formats. About 23 percent of AM radio stations and 7 percent of FM stations focus primarily on news and talk, whereas the others focus on music. See Table 7.3.

118. Sources for this story include Hadley Cantril, *The Invasion from Mars: A Study in the Psychology of Panic* (Princeton, NJ: Princeton University Press, 1940) and Shearon A. Lowery and Melvin L. DeFleur, *Milestones in Mass Communication Research*, 2nd ed. (New York: Longman, 1988), pp. 55-78. A CD of the original broadcast also has been published: War of the Worlds (Plymouth, MN: Metacom, 1994).

119. Daniel Steven Erickson, *This Land Is Your Land : A Rhetorical Analysis of Woody*

How the Mass Media Really Work

Guthrie's Music (Pullman, WA: Unpublished Master's Thesis, 2000).

120. Sources for this section include Greg Braxton, "Them's Fightin' Words," *The Los Angeles Times* (April 5, 1998), p. 4; Jeff Daniel, "Springer Fights His Way to the Top of the Trash Heap," *Everyday Magazine* (February 1, 1998), p. D3; Michael Cameron, "Springer TV Show Murder Charge," *The Sunday Telegraph* (July 30, 2002), p. 3; Paul Gallagher, "Springer Sued Over 'Murderous' Show," *The Scotsman* (July 12, 2002), p. 5.

121. Braxton, "Them's Fightin' Words," *The Los Angeles Times* (April 5, 1998), p. 4.

122. The Jerry Springer Show is seen in more than 190 U.S. markets and is a hit in 40-plus foreign countries. It was the first talk show to beat Oprah Winfrey in more than a decade.

123. Braxton, "Them's Fightin' Words," *The Los Angeles Times* (April 5, 1998), p. 4.

124. Statistics on viewing are from Nielsen Media Research-NTI (2001), Veronis, Suhler and Television Bureau of Advertising, Inc.

125. Lazarsfeld and Merton did not specifically discuss the narcotizing effects of mass media on children. However, I argue that the concept is no less applicable to children, who may whittle away their time in front of the television instead of being involved in other activities that contribute more effectively to their social and intellectual development.

126. Paul F. Lazarsfeld and Robert K. Merton, "Mass Communication, Popular Taste, and Organized Social Action," pp. 554-578 in Wilbur Schramm and Donald F. Roberts (eds.), *The Process and Effects of Mass Communication*, rev. ed. (Urbana: University of Illinois Press, 1971, originally published in 1954), p. 565.

127. Lazarsfeld and Merton, "Mass Communication, Popular Taste, and Organized Social Action," pp. 565-566.

128. Sources for this vignette include Joseph Wershba, "Edward R. Murrow and the Time of His Time," Eve's Magazine (www.evesmag.com/murrow.htm; Copyright 2000); "Senator Joseph R. McCarthy," *See It Now,* CBS News (March 9, 1954); Crosby's quote taken from Erik Barnouw, The Image Empire (New York: Oxford University Press, 1970), p. 116.

129. Cited in Leonard Berkowitz, *Aggression: Its Causes, Consequences and Control* (Philadelphia: Temple University Press, 1993).

130. David Pearl, Lorraine Bouthilet, and Joyce Lazar (eds.) *Television and Behavior: Ten Years of Scientific Progress and Implications for the Eighties*, Vols. I & II (Washington, D.C.: U.S. Government Printing Office, 1982).

131. Bruce D. Bartholow, Karen E. Dill, Kathryn B. Anderson, and James J. Lindsay, "The Proliferation of Media Violence and Its Economic Underpinnings," pp. 1-18 in Douglas A. Gentile (ed.), *Media Violence and Children: A Complete Guide for Parents and Professionals* (Westport, CT: Praeger, 2003), pp. 4-5.

132. Sources for this section on Oprah include Deborah Tannen, "The TV Host Oprah Winfrey," *Time* (January 19, 2000), available at <www.time.com/time/time100/artists>; "The Cult of Oprah," *The Irish Times* (August 5, 2000), p. 61; Richard Huff, "The Power of Oprah: From Beef to Books, Americans Experience a Formidable Force," (New York) *Daily News* (January 28, 1998).

133. Michael Morgan, Susan Leggett and James Shanahan, "Television and Family Values: Was Dan Quayle Right?" *Mass Communication & Society,* 2(1/2): 47-63 (1999), p. 47.

134. *Time* magazine online, <www.timemagazine.com>.

135. The origins of the term "cyberspace" are usually traced to William Gibson's science fiction novel, *Neuromancer* (New York: Ace Books, 1984), who used the term to refer to the imagined world created by people who communicated with each other via computers.

136. This estimate comes from Nua Internet Surveys, <http://www.nua.com>, a worldwide clearinghouse for polls and surveys on the Internet.

137. Tae-hyun Kim, "Internet Empowers Korean Social Movement," pp. 231-244 in David Demers (ed.), *Global Media News Reader* (Spokane, WA: Marquette Books, 2002), p. 241.

138. A summary of the Pew study can be found at <www.nua.ie/surveys/index.cgi?f=VS&art_id=905357358&rel=true>.

139. Howard Kurtz, "After Blogs Got Hits, CBS Got a Black Eye," *Washington Post* (September 209, 2004), p. C01

140. Stephen D. Cooper, *Watching the Watchdog: Bloggers as the Fifth Estate* (Spokane, WA: Marquette Books, 2006).

141. M. Francis Abraham, *Modern Sociological Theory* (Delhi, India: Oxford University Press, 1982).

142. Marvin E. Olsen, *The Process of Social Organization* (New York: Holt, Rinehart & Winston, 1968), p. 227.

143. Warren Breed, "Mass Communication and Sociocultural Integration," *Social Forces,* 37:109-16 (1958); Warren Breed, "Social Control in the Newsroom: A Functional Analysis," *Social Forces,* 33:326-55 (1955); Melvin L. DeFleur and Sandra Ball-Rokeach, *Theories of Mass Communication,* 5th ed. (New York: Longman, 1989); Morris Janowitz, *The Community Press in an Urban Setting* (New York: Free Press, 1952); Robert E. Park, *The Immigrant Press and Its Control* (New York: Harper, 1922); Eric W. Rothenbuhler, "Neofunctionalism for Mass Communication Theory," *Mass Communication Yearbook,* vol. 6 (Newbury Park, Calif.: Sage, 1987); Kim A. Smith, "Newspaper Coverage and Public Concern About Community Issues: A Time-Series Analysis," *Journalism Monographs,* vol. 101 (February 1987); Phillip J. Tichenor, George A. Donohue and Clarice N. Olien, *Community Conflict and the Press* (Beverly Hills, Calif.: Sage, 1980); and Charles R. Wright, *Mass Communication: A Sociological Perspective,* 3rd ed. (New York: Random House, 1986).

144. Joseph T. Klapper, *The Effects of Mass Communication* (New York: The Free Press, 1960); Sidney Kraus and Dennis Davis, *The Effect of Mass Communication on Political Behavior* (University Park, Penn.: Pennsylvania State University Press, 1976); Werner J. Severin and James W. Tankard, Jr., *Communication Theories: Origins, Methods, Uses* (New York: Hastings House, 1979); Gaye Tuchman, "Mass Media Institutions," pp. 601-26 in Neil J. Smelser (ed.), *Handbook of Sociology* (Beverly Hills, Calif.: Sage, 1988).

145. Historically, research questions on the media were framed in individualistic,

rather than systemic, terms. For example, the Payne Fund Studies examined the psychological and physiological effects of movies on children. See Shearon T. Lowery and Melvin L. DeFleur, *Milestones in Mass Communication* (New York: Longman, 1989). The research agenda also was heavily influenced by the advertising industry's need to understand and control the effects of advertising. See Todd Gitlin, "Media Sociology: The Dominant Paradigm," *Theory and Society,* 6:205-53 (1978).

146. Carl P. Burrowes, "The Functionalist Tradition and Communication Theory," paper presented to the Association for Education in Journalism and Mass Communication (Kansas City, Mo., August 1993); Gitlin, "Media Sociology: The Dominant Paradigm"; Denis McQuail, *Mass Communication Theory: An Introduction,* 3rd ed. (London: Sage, 1994), p. 78; and Tuchman, "Mass Media Institutions."

147. Abraham, *Modern Sociological Theory*; Jeffrey C. Alexander (ed.), *Neofunctionalism* (Beverly Hills, Calif.: Sage, 1985); Lewis Coser, *The Functions of Social Conflict* (New York: The Free Press, 1956); William J. Goode, "A Theory of Role Strain," *American Sociological Review,* 25:483-96 (1960); Alvin W. Gouldner, "The Norm of Reciprocity," *American Sociological Review,* 25:161-78 (1960); Olsen, *The Process of Social Organization*; Rothenbuhler, "Neofunctionalism for Mass Communication Theory"; Arthur L. Stinchcombe, *Constructing Social Theories* (Chicago: University of Chicago Press, 1968); and Jonathan H. Turner, *The Structure of Sociological Theory* (Homewood, Ill.: The Dorsey Press, 1978).

148. Walter Buckley, *Sociology and Modern Systems Theory* (Englewood Cliffs, N.J.: Prentice-Hall, 1967), Chapter 1.

149. Peter L. Berger and Thomas Luckmann, *The Social Construction of Reality* (New York: Anchor Books, 1966).

150. Buckley, *Sociology and Modern Systems Theory,* p. 9.

151. See, e.g., Abraham, *Modern Sociological Theory*, pp. 42-3.

152. Vilfredo Pareto, *The Mind and Society: A Treatise on General Sociology* (New York: Dover, 1973).

153. Abraham, *Modern Sociological Theory,* p. 39.

154. A. D. Hall and R. E. Fagen, "Definition of Systems," *General Systems,* 1:18-28 (1956).

155. Herbert Spencer, *First Principles,* vol. 1 (New York: De Witt Revolving Fund, 1958 [1862]). Also see Herbert Spencer, *Principles of Sociology* (New York: Appleton, 1897) and Emile Durkheim, *The Division of Labor in Society,* trans. by W. D. Halls (New York: The Free Press, 1984 [1893]).

156. Spencer, *First Principles,* p. 592.

157. Buckley, *Sociology and Modern Systems Theory,* p. 12.

158. Some scholars have made a distinction between the organismic metaphor, which uses the human body as the basis for comparison, and the organic metaphor, which uses the species metaphor. No distinction is made here because the similarity of the terms invites misinterpretation.

159. Olsen points out that a social system model can be used by exchange, symbolic interactionist, ecological, and power theorists as well. However, he says the perspective appears to be most compatible with a functionalist perspective.

160. Robert K. Merton, *Social Theory and Social Structure,* 3rd ed. (New York: The Free

Press, 1968 [1949]) and Talcott Parsons, *The Social System* (New York: The Free Press, 1951);

161. See, e.g., Parsons, *The Social System*, and Ralf Dahrendorf, *Class and Class Conflict in Industrial Society* (Stanford, Calif.: Stanford University Press, 1959 [1957 German version]).

162. G. A. Theodorson and A. G. Theodorson, *A Modern Dictionary of Sociology* (New York: Crowell, 1969), p. 133.

163. Parsons dismissed such criticisms, but many researchers who were attracted to functionalism did not criticize the existing power structure. See Ruth A. Wallace and Alison Wolf, *Contemporary Sociological Theory* (Englewood Cliffs, N.J.: Prentice-Hall, 1986), pp. 35-6 and 59-60. Neofunctionalism is not subject to the same shortcomings.

164. Parsons, *The Social System*, p. 46. Parsons' observations appear to be as true today as they were in his time. See, e.g., James B. Rule, *Theories of Civil Violence* (Berkeley, Calif.: University of California Press, 1988).

165. Chin-Chuan Lee, *Media Imperialism Reconsidered* (Beverly Hills, Calif.: Sage, 1980) and Alvin Y. So, *Social Change and Development: Modernization, Dependency and World-System Theories* (Newbury Park, Calif.: Sage, 1990).

166. Daniel Lerner, *The Passing of Traditional Society* (New York: Macmillan, 1958).

167. August Comte, "The Progress of Civilization Through Three States," in A. Etzioni and E. Etzioni-Halevy (eds.), *Social Change* (New York: Basic Books, 1973) and Herbert Spencer, "The Evolution of Societies," in A. Etzioni and E. Etzioni-Halevy (eds.), *Social Change* (New York: Basic Books, 1973).

168. Harold D. Lasswell, "The Structure and Function of Communication in Society," pp. 84-99 in Wilbur Schramm and Donald F. Roberts (eds.), *The Process and Effects of Mass Communication* (Urbana, Ill.: University of Illinois Press, 1971).

169. Charles R. Wright, *Mass Communication: A Sociological Perspective* (New York: Random House, 1959).

170. Paul Lazarsfeld and Robert Merton, "Mass Communication, Popular Taste and Organized Social Action," pp. 95-118 in L. Bryson (ed.), *The Communication of Ideas* (New York: Harper and Brothers, 1948).

171. Merton, *Social Theory and Social Structure*.

172. Melvin L. DeFleur, "Mass Media as Social Systems," pp. 63-83 in Wilbur Schramm and Donald F. Roberts, *The Process of Effects of Mass Communication* (Urbana, Ill.: University of Illinois Press, 1971), p. 83. Italics in original.

173. Breed, "Mass Communication and Sociocultural Integration"; Janowitz, *The Community Press in an Urban Setting*; and Charles R. Wright, "Functional Analysis and Mass Communication," *Public Opinion Quarterly,* 24:605-20 (1960).

174. Buckley, *Sociology and Modern Systems Theory,* p. 18.

175. Albion W. Small, *General Sociology* (Chicago: University of Chicago Press, 1905), pp. 619-20.

176. Small, *General Sociology,* p. ix.

177. Robert E. Park and E. W. Burgess, *Introduction to the Science of Sociology* (Chicago: The University of Chicago Press, 1921), p. 42.

178. S. F. Nadel, *The Theory of Social Structure* (New York: The Free Press, 1957), p.

128).

179. Nadel, *The Theory of Social Structure,* p. 153.

180. Park, *The Immigrant Press and Its Control.*

181. Janowitz, *The Community Press in an Urban Setting.*

182. To escape the philosophical dilemma between mechanistic and vitalist conceptualizations of life, de la Mettrie argued that "matter was in itself neither organic nor inorganic, neither living nor dead, neither sensible nor insensible. The difference between these states or properties of material things sprang, not from the intrinsic natures of their raw materials, but from the different ways in which these materials were organized." Quoted in S. Toulmin and J. Goodfield, *The Architecture of Matter* (New York: Harper & Row, 1962), p. 318.

183. Ludwig von Bertalanffy, "General System Theory," pp. 6-21 in Brent D. Rubin and John Y. Kim (eds.), *General Systems Theory and Human Communication* (Rochelle Park, N.J.: Hayden Book Company, 1975).

184. Buckley, *Sociology and Modern Systems Theory,* pp. 58-62.

185. Olsen, *The Process of Social Organization,* pp. 234-5.

186. See Marion J. Levy, Jr., *The Structure of Society* (Princeton, N.J.: Princeton University Press, 1952), pp. 76-83.

187. Buckley, *Sociology and Modern Systems Theory,* and Rubin and Kim (eds.), *General Systems Theory and Human Communication.*

188. Kenneth D. Bailey, *Sociology and the New Systems Theory* (Albany, N.Y.: State University of New York Press, 1992).

189. For review, see Stephen W. Littlejohn, *Theories of Human Communication* (Belmont, Calif.: Wadsworth, 1983). Also see Peter Monge, "The Systems Perspective as a Theoretical Basis for the Study of Human Communication," *Communication Quarterly,* 25:19-29 (1977).

190. Jonathan H. Turner, *Herbert Spencer: A Renewed Appreciation* (Beverly Hills, Calif.: Sage, 1985), p. 31.

191. Jonathan H. Turner, *The Structure of Sociological Theory* (Homewood, Ill.: The Dorsey Press, 1978), p. 105.

192. Durkheim, *The Division of Labor in Society.*

193. Turner, *The Structure of Sociological Theory,* pp. 110-1.

194. See, e.g., Lee, *Media Imperialism Reconsidered;* So, *Social Change and Development: Modernization, Dependency and World-System Theories;* and Immanuel Wallerstein, *The Modern World-System I: Capitalist Agriculture and the Origins of the European World-Economy in the Sixteenth Century* (New York: Academic Press, 1974) and *The Modern World-System II: Mercantilism and the Consolidation of the European World-Economy, 1600-1750* (New York: Academic Press, 1980).

195. Dennis H. Wrong, "The Oversocialized Conception of Man in Modern Sociology," *American Sociological Review,* 26:183-93 (April 1961).

196. See, e.g., Robert Cooley Angell, *The Integration of American Society* (New York: Russell & Russell, 1975 [1941]).

197. As van den Berghe put it: "Dysfunctions, tension and 'deviance' do exist and can persist for a long time, but they tend to resolve themselves or to be 'institutionalized'

in the long run. In other words, while perfect equilibrium or integration is never reached, it is the limit towards which social systems tend .... Change generally occurs in a gradual, adjustive fashion, and not in a sudden, revolutionary way. Changes which appear to be drastic, in fact affect mostly the social superstructure while leaving the core elements of the social and cultural structure largely unchanged." Pierre L. van den Berghe, "Dialectic and Functionalism," in R. Serge Denisoff et al. (ed.), *Theories and Paradigms in Contemporary Sociology* (Itasca: F. E. Peacock Publishers, 1974), p. 281.

198. Dahrendorf, *Class and Class Conflict in Industrial Society.*

199. He also suggests abandoning the concept of function — which may be defined as contribution that the part makes to the whole — because it takes for granted what should be part of the empirical investigation. See Turner, *The Structure of Sociological Theory,* p. 110.

200. Jeffrey C. Alexander, "The Mass News Media in Systemic, Historical and Comparative Perspective," pp. 17-51 in Elihu Katz and T. Szecsko (eds.), *Mass Media and Social Change* (Beverly Hills, Calif.: Sage, 1981), does a superb job of integrating the two in his comparative, historical, systemic analysis of the development of newspapers in the United States and Europe.

201. D. Atkinson, *Orthodox Consensus and Radical Alternation* (New York: Basic Books, 1972).

202. As noted in Chapter 3, the idea that structures may dissolve was addressed by Spencer, although Parsons and other structural functionalists gave little attention to de-differentiation and dissolution. See Edward A. Tiryakian, "On the Significance of De-Differentiation," pp. 118-34 in S. N. Eisenstadt and H. J. Helle (eds.), *Macro-Sociological Theory* (Beverly Hills, Calif.: Sage Publications, 1985).

203. Dahrendorf, *Class and Class Conflict in Industrial Society.*

204. George C. Homans, *Social Behavior: Its Elementary Forms* (New York: Harcourt Brace Jovanovich, Inc., 1974).

205. Claude Levi-Strauss, *Totemism* (Boston: Beacon Press, 1963).

206. S. N. Eisenstadt, "Macro-Societal Analysis — Background, Development and Indications," pp. 7-24 in S. N. Eisenstadt and H. J. Helle, *Macro-Sociological Theory: Perspectives on Sociological Theory* (Newbury Park, Calif.: Sage Publications, 1985), p. 19.

207. Marvin E. Olsen, *The Process of Social Organization* (New York: Holt, Rinehart and Winston, 1968).

208. Eisenstadt, "Macro-Societal Analysis."

209. Olsen, *The Process of Social Organization,* pp. 229-31.

210. The growth of functionalism during the early part of the 20th century was a reaction in part to the failure of deterministic, mechanical and positivist theories to explain human behavior.

211. See Appendix A for an essay on social action, determinism and quantitative research methods.

212. Alexander (ed.), *Neofunctionalism;* Kenneth E. Boulding, *The World as a Total System* (Beverly Hills, Calif.: Sage, 1985); Niklas Luhmann, *The Differentiation of Society* (New York: Columbia University Press, 1982); Richard Münch, "Parsonian Theory Today: In Search of a New Synthesis," pp. 116-55 in Anthony Giddens and Jonathan H. Turner

(eds.), *Social Theory Today* (Stanford, Calif.: Stanford University Press, 1987).

213. Alexander (ed.), *Neofunctionalism,* pp. 9-10.

214. Eisenstadt, "Macro-Societal Analysis."

215. Eisenstadt, "Macro-Societal Analysis," pp. 20-1.

216. The first item in this list was added by this author.

217. See, e.g., Richard P. Applebaum, *Theories of Social Change* (Chicago: Markham, 1970); Peter M. Blau and Marshall W. Meyer, *Bureaucracy in Modern Society,* 3rd ed. (New York: Random House, 1987), Chapter 6; and Howard E. Aldrich and Peter V. Marsden, "Environments and Organizations," pp. 361-92 in Neil J. Smelser (ed.), *Handbook of Sociology* (Newbury Park, Calif.: Sage, 1988).

218. Frederick Taylor, *Scientific Management* (New York: Harper & Row, 1964 [1947]).

219. A. H. Hawley, *Human Ecology: A Theory of Community Structure* (New York: Ronald Press, 1950) and Michael T. Hannan and John H. Freeman, "The Population Ecology of Organizations," *American Journal of Sociology,* 82:929-64 (1977).

220. See, e.g., John Dimmick and Eric Rothenbuhler, "The Theory of the Niche: Quantifying Competition Among Media Industries," *Journal of Communication,* 34(1):103-19 (1984).

221. Dimmick and Rothenberger, "The Theory of the Niche," p. 107.

222. Blau and Meyer, *Bureaucracy in Modern Society.*

223. Aldrich and Marsden, "Environments and Organizations," p. 365.

224. Jeffrey Pfeffer and Gerald R. Salancik, *The External Control of Organizations* (New York: Harper & Row, 1978), pp. 139-40.

225. Blau and Meyer, *Bureaucracy in Modern Society,* pp. 33-8.

226. H. H. Gerth and C. Wright Mills, *From Max Weber: Essays in Sociology* (New York: Oxford University Press, 1946), p. 214.

227. For this view, Blau and Meyer cite Jeffrey Pfeffer, *Power in Organizations* (Marshfield, Mass.: Pitman, 1981).

228. Richard Edwards, *Contested Terrain* (New York: Basic Books, 1979), p. 145.

229. Blau and Meyer, *Bureaucracy in Modern Society,* p. 38-41.

230. George A. Donohue, Phillip J. Tichenor and Clarice N. Olien, "Mass Media Functions, Knowledge and Social Control," *Journalism Quarterly,* 50:652-9 (1973). Also see Breed, "Mass Communication and Sociocultural Integration"; Janowitz, *The Community Press in an Urban Setting;* and Clarice N. Olien, Phillip J. Tichenor and George A. Donohue, "Media Coverage and Social Movements," pp. 139-63 in Charles T. Salmon (ed.), *Information Campaigns: Balancing Social Values and Social Change* (Newbury Park, Calif.: Sage Publications, 1989).

231. Donohue, Tichenor and Olien, "Mass Media Functions, Knowledge and Social Control," p. 652.

232. See, e.g., Ben H. Bagdikian, *The Information Machines: Their Impact on Men and the Media* (New York: Harper and Row, 1971); Coser, *The Functions of Social Conflict;* John K. Galbraith, *The New Industrial State,* 3rd ed. (Boston: Houghton Mifflin, 1978); and Robert E. Park, "News as a Form of Knowledge," *American Journal of Sociology,* 45:669-86 (1940).

233. Donohue, Tichenor and Olien, "Mass Media Functions, Knowledge and Social Control."

234. Donohue, Tichenor and Olien, "Mass Media Functions, Knowledge and Social

Control," p. 653.

235. The first story appeared in the (Minneapolis) *Star Tribune*, May 30, 1992. The university professor was later forced to resign and was prosecuted by federal authorities.

236. Breed, "Mass Communication and Sociocultural Integration"; Janowitz, *Community Press in an Urban Setting*, and Arthur J. Vidich and Joseph Bensman, *Small Town in Mass Society* (Princeton, N.J.: Princeton University Press, 1968), p. 31.

237. Thomas C. Wilson, "Community Population Size and Social Heterogeneity: An Empirical Test," *American Journal of Sociology*, 91:1154-69 (1986).

238. Clarice N. Olien, George A. Donohue and Phillip J. Tichenor, "The Community Editor's Power and the Reporting of Conflict," *Journalism Quarterly*, 45:243-52 (1968).

239. One exception is when conflict erupts between the local community and an outside source of power (e.g., state or federal government), in which case local media coverage tends to support local norms and interprets the conflict through the perspective of local elites.

240. George A. Donohue, Clarice N. Olien and Phillip J. Tichenor, "Reporting Conflict by Pluralism, Newspaper Type and Ownership," *Journalism Quarterly*, 62:489-99,507 (1985) and Tichenor, Donohue and Olien, *Community Conflict and the Press*.

241. Donohue, Tichenor and Olien, "Mass Media Functions, Knowledge and Social Control," pp. 653-4. Also see Coser, *The Functions of Social Conflict*, for a discussion how conflict may contribute to social stability.

242. George A. Donohue, Clarice N. Olien and Phillip J. Tichenor, "A Guard Dog Conception of the Mass Media," paper presented to the Association for Education in Journalism and Mass Communication (San Antonio, Texas, August 1987). An updated version of this paper was slated to be published in the *Journal of Communication* as this book was going to press.

243. Donohue, Olien and Tichenor, "A Guard Dog Conception of the Media," p. 10.

244. Sandra J. Ball-Rokeach, "The Origins of Individual Media System Dependency: A Sociological Framework," *Communication Research*, 12:485-510 (1985); Sandra J. Ball-Rokeach and Melvin L. DeFleur, "A Dependency Model of Mass Media Effects," *Communication Research*, 3:3-21 (1976); and DeFleur and Ball-Rokeach, *Theories of Mass Communication*.

245. David Pearce Demers, "Structural Pluralism, Intermedia Competition and Growth of the Corporate Newspaper in the United States," *Journalism Monographs*, vol. 145 (June 1994).

246. Mark Fishman, *Manufacturing the News* (Austin, Texas: University of Texas Press, 1980); Edward S. Herman, "Diversity of News: Marginalizing the Opposition," *Journal of Communication*, 35(3):135-46 (1985); Todd Gitlin, *The Whole World Is Watching: Mass Media and the New Left* (Berkeley, Calif.: University of California Press, 1980); C. N. Olien, G. A. Donohue and P. J. Tichenor, "Media and Stages of Social Conflict," *Journalism Monographs*, vol. 90 (November 1984); and David L. Paletz and Robert M. Entman, *Media Power Politics* (New York: Free Press, 1981).

247. Herbert J. Gans, *Deciding What's News* (New York: Vintage, 1979) and Jack Newfield, "Journalism: Old, New and Corporate," in Ronald Weber (ed.), *The Reporter as Artist: A Look at the New Journalism* (New York: Hastings House, 1974).

248. Gans, *Deciding What's News.*

249. Jonathan H. Turner and David Musick, *American Dilemmas: A Sociological Interpretation of Enduring Social Issues* (New York: Columbia University Press, 1985).

250. Karen E. Altman, "Consuming Ideology: The Better Homes in America Campaign," *Critical Studies in Mass Communication,* 7:286-307 (1990); W. Lance Bennett, *News: The Politics of Illusion,* 2nd ed. (New York: Longman, 1988); Stuart Ewin, *Captains of Consciousness: Advertising and the Social Roots of the Consumer Culture* (New York: McGraw Hill, 1976); Fishman, *Manufacturing the News;* Doris A. Graber, *Mass Media and American Politics,* 3rd ed. (Washington, D.C.: Congressional Quarterly Press, 1989); Gans, *Deciding What's News;* Gitlin, *The Whole World Is Watching;* Harvey Molotch and Marilyn Lester, "Accidental News: The Great Oil Spill as Local Occurrence and National Event," *American Journal of Sociology,* 81:235-60 (1975); Paletz and Entman, *Media Power Politics;* Fred Powledge, *The Engineering of Restraint* (Washington, D.C.: Public Affairs Press, 1971); Tichenor, Donohue and Olien, *Community Conflict and the Press;* and Gaye Tuchman, *Making News: A Study in the Construction of Reality* (New York: The Free Press, 1978).

251. J. Herbert Altschull, *Agents of Power* (New York: Longman, 1984); Robert Cirino, *Power to Persuade* (New York: Bantam Books, 1974); Stanley Cohen and Jock Young (eds.), *The Manufacture of News* (London: Constable, 1981); Edward Jay Epstein, *News From Nowhere* (New York: Random House, 1973); Gitlin, *The Whole World Is Watching;* Molotch and Lester, "Accidental News," Powledge, *The Engineering of Restraint;* Michael Schudson, "The Politics of Narrative Form: The Emergence of News Conventions in Print and Television," *Daedalus,* 11:97-112 (1982); Lawrence C. Soley, "Pundits in Print: 'Experts' and Their Use in Newspaper Stories," *Newspaper Research Journal,* 15(2):65-75 (1994); Tichenor, Donohue and Olien, *Community Conflict and the Press;* Tuchman, *Making News;* and Jeremy Tunstall, *Journalists at Work* (London: The Anchor Press, 1971).

252. Mayer N. McCarthy and John D. Zald, "Resource Mobilization and Social Movements: A Partial Theory," *American Journal of Sociology,* 82:1212-41 (1977) and Mayer N. McCarthy and John D. Zald (eds.), *The Dynamics of Social Movements: Resource Mobilization, Social Control and Tactics* (Cambridge, Mass.: Winthrop Publishers, 1979).

253. David Pearce Demers, Dennis Craff, Yang-Ho Choi, and Beth M. Pessin, "Issue Obtrusiveness and the Agenda-Setting Effects of National Network News," *Communication Research,* 16:793-812 (1989); Graber, *Media Power in Politics,* pp. 75-150; Gerald M. Kosicki, "Problems and Opportunities in Agenda-Setting Research," *Journal of Communication,* 43(2):100-28 (1993); Maxwell McCombs, "News Influence on Our Pictures of the World," pp. 1-16 in Jennings Bryant and Dolf Zillmann (eds.), *Media Effects: Advances in Theory and Research* (Hillsdale, N.J.: Lawrence Erlbaum Associates, 1994); and Maxwell E. McCombs and Donald L. Shaw, "The Agenda-Setting Function of the Mass Media," *Public Opinion Quarterly,* 36:176-87 (1972).

254. Fishman, *Manufacturing the News;* Herman, "Diversity of News"; Gitlin, *The Whole World Is Watching;* Olien, Donohue and Tichenor, "Media and Stages of Social

Conflict"; and Paletz and Entman, *Media Power Politics.*

255. Glasgow University Media Group, *Bad News* (London: Routledge & Kegan Paul, 1976).

256. Gitlin, *The Whole World Is Watching.*

257. Pamela Shoemaker, "Media Treatment of Deviant Political Groups," *Journalism Quarterly,* 61:66-75,82 (1984).

258. Douglas M. McLeod and James K. Hertog, "The Manufacture of "Public Opinion" by Reporters: Informal Cues for Public Perceptions of Protest Groups, " *Discourse and Society,* 3(3), 259-75 (1992).

259. Gans, *Deciding What's News*; Newfield, "Journalism: Old, New and Corporate"; Robert A. Peterson, Gerald Albaum, George Kozmetsky and Isabella C. M. Cunningham, "Attitudes of Newspaper Business Editors and General Public Toward Capitalism," *Journalism Quarterly,* 61:56-65 (1984).

260. Edward S. Herman and Noam Chomsky, *Manufacturing Consent: The Political Economy of the Mass Media* (New York: Pantheon, 1988).

261. Walter Gieber and Walter Johnson, "The City Hall Beat: A Study of Reporter and Source Roles," *Journalism Quarterly,* 38:289-97 (1961); Paletz and Entman, *Media Power Politics*; and David L. Paletz, P. Reichert and B. McIntyre, "How the Media Support Local Government Authority, *Public Opinion Quarterly,* 35:808-92 (1971).

262. G. Hurd, "The Television Presentation of the Police," in T. Bennett et al. (eds.), *Popular Television and Film* (London: BFI/Open University Press, 1981).

263. Stuart Hall, "Culture, the Media and the Ideological Effect," pp. 315-48 in James Curran, Michael Gurevitch and Janet Woollacott (eds.), *Mass Communication and Society* (London: Edward Arnold, 1977) and John Hartley, *Understanding News* (London: Methuen, 1982).

264. Bagdikian, *Media Monopoly*; Compaine, Sterling, Guback and Noble, *Who Owns the Media*; Peter Dreier and Steven Weinberg, "Interlocking Directorates," *Columbia Journalism Review* (November/December 1979), pp. 51-68; and Graham Murdock and Peter Golding, "Capitalism, Communication and Class Relations," pp. 12-43 in James Curran, Michael Gurevitch and Janet Woollacott (eds.), *Mass Communication and Society* (Beverly Hills, Calif.: Sage, 1977).

265. Demers, "Structural Pluralism, Intermedia Competition and the Growth of the Corporate Newspaper in the United States."

266. Dreier and Weinberg, "Interlocking Directorates."

267. John W. C. Johnstone, Edward J. Slawski, and William W. Bowman, *The News People: A Sociological Portrait of American Journalists and Their Work* (Urbana, Ill.: University of Illinois Press, 1976); David Shaw, "Public and Press — Two Viewpoints," *Los Angeles Times* (August 11, 1985); and David H. Weaver and G. Cleveland Wilhoit, *The American Journalist: A Portrait of U.S. News People and Their Work* (Bloomington, Ind.: Indiana University Press, 1986).

268. The Frankfort school has played an important role in shaping theories of ideology. Space prohibits a detailed examination of all of the theorists of this school, but it is important to point out that a wide range of views emerged from the school. Adorno and Horkheimer, for example, were pessimistic about the potential for emancipation —

the culture of neocapitalism is a mass culture, imposed from above, not by any indigenous culture; it promotes obedience, impedes critical judgment, and displaces dissent. Benjamin, on the other hand, was more optimistic, believing that the media had the power to raise consciousness and critical ideas. One of the best-known critiques comes from Marcuse, who argued that technology has played a major role in the survival of modern capitalism. A highly technologized culture, he asserted, generates affluence, which removes dissent; promotes development of a bureaucratic welfare state that dominates people's lives; increases leisure time that creates the illusion of freedom; stimulates automation which shifts the labor force into white-collar positions and reduces the sense of work-place repression; and blurs the distinction between consumption patterns. More than Gramsci, Marcuse emphasizes the structural controls that contribute to maintenance of capitalism and represses the development of class consciousness. See Theodore Adorno and Max Horkheimer, *Dialectic of the Enlightenment* (London: Verso, 1979) and Herbert Marcuse, *One-Dimensional Man* (Boston: Beacon Press, 1964).

269. S. Robert Lichter and Stanley Rothman, "Media and Business Elites, " *Public Opinion Quarterly,* 4:42-6 (1981).

270. W. Q. Morales, "Revolutions, Earthquakes, and Latin America: The Networks Look at Allende's Chile and Somoza's Nicaragua," pp. 79-116 in W. C. Adams (ed.), *Television Coverage of International Affairs* (Norwood, N.J.: Ablex, 1982).

271. The state supreme court eventually allowed construction of the power line, after which the media coverage of the protest groups took on a more negative tone. See Olien, Donohue and Tichenor, "Media and Stages of Social Conflict."

272. For review, see David L. Altheide, *Media Power* (Beverly Hills, Calif.: Sage, 1985). Also see Wayne Wanta, Mary Ann Stephenson, Judy VanSlyke Turk and Maxwell E. McCombs, "How President's State of Union Talk Influenced News Media Agendas," *Journalism Quarterly,* 66:537-41 (1989).

273. David Pritchard, "Homicide and Bargained Justice: The Agenda-Setting Effect of Crime News on Prosecutors," *Public Opinion Quarterly,* 50:143-59 (1986).

274. J. R. Ballinger, "Media Coverage of Social Protest: An Examination of Media Hegemony," paper presented to the Association for Education in Journalism and Mass Communication, Kansas City, Mo. (August 1993).

275. See, e.g., Fishman, *Manufacturing the News,* and Tuchman, *Making News.*

276. See, e.g., Benjamin Compaine, "The Expanding Base of Media Competition, *Journal of Communication,* 35(3):81-96 (1985) and Maxwell McCombs, "Effect of Monopoly in Cleveland on Diversity of Newspaper Content, *Journalism Quarterly,* 64:740-4,792 (1987).

277. Compaine, Sterling, Guback and Noble, *Who Owns the Media,* and D. Waterman, "A New Look at Media Chains and Groups: 1977-1989," *Journal of Broadcasting & Electronic Media,* 35:167-78 (1991).

278. W. R. Davie and J. Lee, "Television News Technology: Do More Sources Mean Less Diversity?" *Journal of Broadcasting & Electronic Media,* 37:453-64 (1993), and Donohue, Olien, and Tichenor, "Reporting Conflict by Pluralism, Newspaper Type and Ownership."

279. David Pearce Demers, "Corporate Newspaper Structure and Editorial Page

Vigor," paper presented to the International Communication Association (Albuquerque, N.M., May 1995) and David Pearce Demers, "Effects of Competition and Structural Pluralism on Centralization of Ownership in the U.S. Newspaper Industry," paper presented to the Association for Education in Journalism (Minneapolis, August 1990).

280. Donohue, Olien and Tichenor, "Reporting Conflict by Pluralism, Newspaper Type and Ownership," and Tichenor, Donohue and Olien, *Community Conflict and the Press.*

281. M. Meyers, "Reporters and Beats: The Making of Oppositional News," *Critical Studies in Mass Communication,* 9:75-90 (1992).

282. P. Bruck, "Strategies for Peace, Strategies for News Research," *Journal of Communication,* 39(1):108-29 (1989).

283. Hemant Shah, "News and the "Self-Production of Society," *Journalism Monographs,* vol. 144 (April 1994).

284. See e.g., Epstein, *News From Nowhere*; Gitlin, *The Whole World Is Watching*; Schudson, "The Politics of Narrative Form"; and Sigel, *Reporters and Officials.*

285. N. Eliasoph, "Routines and the Making of Oppositional News," *Critical Studies in Mass Communication,* 5:313-34 (1988).

286. John Downing, "Alternative Media and the Boston Tea Party, " pp. 180-91 in John Downing, Ali Mohammadi and Annabelle Sreberny-Mohammadi (eds.), *Questioning the Media* (Newbury Park: Sage, 1990).

287. McLeod and Hertog, "The Manufacture of 'Public Opinion' by Reporters."

288. Following Durkheim, a distinction is made here between the functions and causes.

289. See, e.g., Tichenor, Donohue, and Olien, *Community Conflict and the Press.*

290. G. A. Donohue, C. N. Olien, P. J. Tichenor and D. P. Demers, "Community Structure, News Judgments and Newspaper Content," paper presented at the annual meeting of the Association for Education in Journalism and Mass Communication (Minneapolis, August 1990).

291. Demers, "Structural Pluralism, Intermedia Competition, and the Growth of the Corporate Newspaper in the United States."

292. Paul Hartmann and Charles Husband, "The Mass Media and Racial Conflict," pp. 288-302 in Stanley Cohen and Jock Young (eds.), *The Manufacture of News* (London: Constable, 1981).

293. D. R. Matthews and J. W. Protho, *Negroes and the New Southern Politics* (New York: Harcourt, Brace & World, 1966), p. 344.

294. Sandra J. Ball-Rokeach, Melvin Rokeach and Joel W. Grube, *The Great American Values Test: Influencing Behavior and Belief Through Television* (New York: Free Press, 1984) and Sandra J. Ball-Rokeach, Melvin Rokeach and Joel W. Grube, "Changing and Stabilizing Political Behavior and Beliefs," pp. 280-90 in Sandra J. Ball-Rokeach and Muriel G. Cantor (eds.), *Media Audience and Social Structure* (Newbury Park, Calif.: Sage, 1986).

295. George Gerbner and Larry Gross, "Living With Television: The Violence Profile," *Journal of Communication,* 26(2):173-99 (1976) and George Gerbner, Larry Gross, Michael Morgan and Nancy Signorielli, "Growing Up With Television: The Cultivation Perspective," pp. 17-41 in Jennings Bryant and Dolf Zillman (eds.), *Media Effects: Advances in Theory and Research* (Hillsdale, N.J.: Lawrence Erlbaum Associates, 1994).

How the Mass Media Really Work

296. From the perspective of the individual, the distorted image of crime conveyed on television is generally dysfunctional; it leads to the development of the irrational beliefs, or a "mean world syndrome." However, from the perspective of those in power, such "mean world" beliefs may be very functional for supporting authoritarian actions.

297. Gerbner and Gross, "Living With Television," p. 175.

298. Paul M. Hirsch, "The 'Scary World' of the Nonviewer and Other Anomalies: A Reanalysis of Gerbner et al.'s Findings on Cultivation Analysis, Part I," *Communication Research,* 7:403-56 (1980); Paul M. Hirsch, "On Not Learning From One's Own Mistakes: A Reanalysis of Gerbner et al.'s Findings on Cultivation Analysis, Part II," *Communication Research,* 8:3-37 (1981); and M. Hughes, "The Fruits of Cultivation Analysis: A Re-Examination of Some Effects of Television Watching," *Public Opinion Quarterly,* 44:287-302 (1980).

299. Gerbner, Gross, Morgan and Signorielli, "Growing Up With Television."

300. David L. Protess, Fay Lomax Cook, Jack C. Doppelt, James S. Ettema, Margaret T. Gordon, Donna R. Leff, and Peter Miller, *The Journalism of Outrage: Investigative Reporting and Agenda-Building in America* (New York: Guilford Press, 1991).

301. Pritchard, "Homicide and Bargained Justice."

302. David Pearce Demers, "Media Use and Beliefs About Economic Equality: An Empirical Test of the Dominant Ideology Thesis," presented to the Midwest Association for Public Opinion Research (Chicago, November 1993).

303. William A. Gamson, *Talking Politics* (Cambridge, Mass.: Cambridge University Press, 1992), p. 4.

304. Gans, *Deciding What's News,* pp. 68-9.

305. Alexander, "The Mass News Media in Systemic, Historical and Comparative Perspective," p. 21.

INDEX

A

administrative law, 193
advertising manager, 36
advertising, 7, 30, 32-34, 36, 60, 77, 96, 101, 103, 111, 113, 118, 122, 137, 148, 158, 173, 176, 190, 196, 199
agenda-setting function, 199
agents of social control, 23, 92, 176, 192

B

Ball, Lucille, 149
Ball-Rokeach, Sandra, 176
Berners-Lee, Tim, 167
Berry, Chuck 142
blogs, 172-174
book, 4, 7-9, 14, 33, 39, 43, 61, 65, 69, 76-89, 103, 105-108, 115, 128, 133, 136, 138, 162-164, 168, 171, 172, 175, 176, 181, 182, 189, 193
Brinkley, David, 153
broadcast television, 125, 201
Brokaw, Tom, 154
Brown, Helen Gurley, 114, 115
Buckley, Jr., William F., 114
bureaucracy, 189-191

C

cable television, 164, 165
Cameron, James, 13
Campbell, John, 58

capitalism, 60, 61, 65, 82, 87, 93, 97, 103, 105, 107, 140, 185, 197, 199, 200, 204
carriers, 80
Carson, Rachel Louise, 75
Chomsky, Noam, 207, 208, 226
circulation manager, 36
class consciousness, 200
clients, 102
code of ethics, 22, 36
codes of ethics, 22, 198
coercion, 21, 23
communication, 2, 6, 7, 13, 20, 29, 30, 32, 34, 37, 40, 41, 47, 56, 65-67, 69, 71, 80, 91-93, 95, 101, 130, 134, 138, 148, 149, 161, 166, 167, 171, 174, 176, 180-182, 184, 190-193, 195-197, 199-202
computer, 167
convergence of technology, 168
copyright, 4, 151
corporate form of organization, 195, 196
corporate communications, 62
corporation, 132
critical theory, 92
Cronkite, Walter, 153
culture, 7, 22, 32, 35, 55, 62, 66, 85, 100, 101, 105, 124, 173, 179, 185, 188, 199, 200
cyberspace, 167

D

dailies, 43
decoding, 43
demo, 2, 22, 43, 49-52, 60, 61, 71, 88, 89, 92-95, 100, 107, 111, 112, 151, 153, 157, 169, 171, 174, 184, 197, 198

How the Mass Media Really Work

M

N

O-P

objectivity (see *ethic of objectivity*)

Olien, Clarice N., 7, 32, 91-94, 176, 191-193

organic model, 178, 181

Pareto, Vilfredo, 177

Partisan Press, 45, 73

pass-along rate, 113

penny press, 45, 59, 60, 196

Phillips, David Graham, 107

photojournalism, 111

pilot, 174

political advertising, 96

power, 7, 8, 26, 28, 32, 33, 35, 40, 41, 55, 57, 58, 60, 62, 66, 70-73, 80, 83, 89, 91-97, 101, 104, 107, 117, 123-125, 130, 132, 134-136, 138-140, 149, 153, 155, 163, 167-170, 172-179, 184, 186-195, 197-200, 202, 204, 205

Presley, Elvis, 142, 143, 158

printing press, 101, 168, 174

privacy, 58

process model, 181, 182

producer, 122, 128, 151

production, 13, 67, 102, 107, 121, 123, 127, 131, 164, 168, 179, 198, 201

programming, 30, 32, 33, 40, 55, 56, 61, 71, 131, 133, 135-141, 148, 149, 151, 155, 156, 159-161, 165, 166, 196, 197

progressive social movement, 107

propaganda, 62, 99, 135

prosocial effects, 126

psychological effects, 40

public, 4, 7, 23, 25, 28, 32, 33, 36-39, 45, 46, 52, 53, 56, 58, 59, 61, 66-69, 71, 73-78, 83, 86, 87, 92, 99, 101-103, 109, 115, 116, 134, 135, 145, 148, 151, 153, 155, 156, 163, 170, 176, 179, 181, 186, 187, 191, 196, 198-204

public domain, 4, 153

public relations, 28, 32, 77, 102

publisher, 4, 36, 58, 102, 104

Pulitzer Prize, 84, 85, 89, 108

Q-R

quantitative research methods, 176, 188

radio, 6, 11, 14, 16, 19, 24, 26, 29, 30, 61, 67, 104, 121-123, 125, 132, 134-138, 140, 144, 151, 159, 164, 168, 170, 190, 201

Rather, Dan, 154, 174

rating, 46

rationality, 189

Reasoner, Harry, 154

reporters, 7, 22, 32, 38, 44, 53, 66-68, 89, 91, 95, 98, 109, 116, 199, 201

resolution, 140

Riis, Jacob, 107

Rock 'n' Roll, 142, 144

roles, 5, 13, 22, 23, 36, 74, 77, 101, 131, 149, 165, 176, 182, 185, 198, 199

S

satellite television, 155

scientific journals, 119

screenplay, 129

screenwriter, 121

servers, 13

share, 24, 52, 77, 89, 182, 191, 193, 198

Sinclair, Upton, 83, 107, 108

Smothers Brothers, 156-158

snapper, 166

social actors, 94, 175, 176, 178, 181-184, 188, 192, 194-196, 202, 204

social change, 5, 7, 8, 35-41, 65, 67-72, 78, 80, 81, 83, 92, 94, 96-98, 129, 130, 140, 142, 148, 162, 166, 180, 184-186, 188, 189, 191, 195, 197-199, 201-204

social control, 5, 7, 8, 20, 21, 23-25, 29, 31-36, 40, 41, 56, 57, 61, 71, 81, 86, 92, 94, 101, 104, 105, 116, 125, 127, 132, 134-136, 146, 148, 149, 176, 181, 182, 187, 188, 191-193, 199, 201, 204

social distance, 173

How the Mass Media Really Work

T

U-V

W-Z

ABOUT THE AUTHORS

Taehyun Kim earned a master's degree in journalism from The Ohio State University and a Ph.D. in Interdisciplinary Studies (mass communication, sociology and political science) through the Edward R. Murrow School of Communication at Washington State University. Dr. Kim taught at the University of Louisiana at Monroe before joining the Department of Journalism at California State University, Northridge, as an assistant professor in 2008. Dr. Kim is a media sociologist. His primary research interests include the effects of corporate structure on editorial vigor, global warming disinformation campaigns, and the system maintenance function of the Korean ethnic media during the 1992 Los Angeles riots.

Dan Erickson earned a master's degree in communication through the Edward R. Murrow School of Communication at Washington State University. He is a communication instructor at Yakima Valley Community College in Washington state, where he teaches public speaking, mass media, and feature writing courses. He is an expert on the life and music of Woody Guthrie and has written three books, including *At the Crossing of Justice and Mercy* (2013). He plays guitar and sings and has written and recorded more than 100 songs in a variety of musical styles.

David Demers earned master's degrees in sociology and journalism from The Ohio State University and a Ph.D. in mass communication from the University of Minnesota. He taught at Washington State University and two other universities for more than 24 years before leaving to spend more time managing a publishing company and writing about civil liberties, including a trilogy of books titled *The Lonely Activist: An American Odyssey*. He is author or editor of more than a dozen academic books and 125 refereed and professional articles. He teaches a mass media law course through the Walter Cronkite School of Journalism and Mass Communication at Arizona State University.